THE CAPM® EXAM

How To Pass On Your First Try

Andy Crowe, PMP

Velociteach Press

Published by Velociteach Press
1201 Roberts Blvd, STE 225
Kennesaw, GA 30152

All inquiries should be addressed to:
        e-mail: info@velociteach.com

First Edition,   First printing: April, 2006
                  Second printing, July, 2006
                  Third printing, November, 2006

International Standard Book No.   ISBN-13: 978-0-9729673-2-X
                                      ISBN-10: 0-9729673-2-X

ATTENTION CORPORATIONS, UNIVERSITIES, COLLEGES, AND PROFESSIONAL ORGANIZATIONS. Quantity discounts may be available on bulk purchases of this book. For information, please contact IPG distribution at www.ipgbook.com.

Printed and bound in the USA.

To Clint, Kyle, and Anne

Also By This Author...

ALPHA PROJECT MANAGERS:

WHAT THE TOP 2% KNOW THAT EVERYONE ELSE DOES NOT

Andy Crowe

Contents

Foreword

The CAPM Exam is harder than most people first realize. Many people find that out when they first sit down to test, and the questions begin to scroll by. In order to pass the exam and earn CAPM certification, you will need to demonstrate a solid knowledge of the PMBOK Guide and the processes of project management.

That's where this book comes in. It shows you want to study, how to focus your time, and gives you hundreds of practice questions.

The Project Management Institute's processes are not arbitrary. They are derived from a compilation of generally accepted best practices, industry knowledge, and wisdom that has taken decades to evolve into its current form. Those who attempt to pass the exam without truly understanding the driving philosophy and reasons behind the material are doing themselves and the project management profession a great disservice.

This book is clearly organized and presents the material in an easily understandable format without insulting the reader's intelligence. Every process, input, tool and technique, and output is clearly explained, and the reasons underlying it are addressed.

I believe you will find this end result to be the most complete, concise, and up to date study resource for the CAPM Exam. The time you spend in this book should be well-rewarded when you sit for the exam.

I'll be celebrating with you when you pass!

Andy Crowe

About the Author

Andy Crowe speaks, writes, and researches prolifically on project management. In addition to this book, he has authored Alpha Project Managers: What The Top 2% Know that Everyone Else Does Not, and The PMP Exam: How to Pass on Your First Try. Crowe is founder and CEO of Velociteach, a company passionate about the dissemination of best practices in project management, headquartered in Kennesaw, GA. He spends much of his time writing in the Blue Ridge Mountains.

About Velociteach

Velociteach, a Kennesaw, GA company, has experienced dramatic growth since its founding in 2002, posting triple digit growth each year since its inception. This growth, combined with Velociteach's commitment to excellent training and "outrageous customer service" have made it the industry leader in project management certification preparation and Project Management training.

As a Registered Education Provider (R.E.P.) with the Project Management Institute, Velociteach offers training around the world, teaching certification and advanced project management theory and practice.

Velociteach offers a three day accelerated learning course on the CAMP Exam and also offers online training that works with this book. Full details on this and other course offerings are available online at www.velociteach.com.

Introduction

The Certified Associate in Project Management, or CAPM certification, has steadily gained in popularity since its introduction. Achieving this certification marks an important milestone in the career of those who pursue it.

Why is the CAPM important? It is easy to look no further than the career benefits that exist in many organizations for those who hold this certification. Many people must earn their CAPM before they are able to work on the most desirable projects, or in order to realize other benefits tied to their compensation.

A second reason it is important is that the CAPM helps distinguish those who are merely interested in managing projects from the ones who treat project management as a career specialty. Earning a CAPM certification demonstrates that an individual recognizes the special combination of skills that are required to manage projects and deliver products.

Finally, earning the CAPM certification demonstrates that you have a solid knowledge of the processes of project management. It shows that you understand the theory behind project management and can thus build your practice on solid ground.

In all, there are many good reasons to pursue this certification aside from the boost it is likely to give your career, but the process is not easy. This book will cut down on the difficulty factors and demystify the material. In the following chapters, you will find exactly what you need to study for the test, how to learn it, how to apply it, and why it is important. The CAPM Exam: How to Pass on Your First Try is a complete resource to help you prepare fully for the CAPM Certification Exam.

In order to get the most from your efforts, you should read the material in this book, practice the examples, and then take and re-take the sample exam, reading the explanations that accompany each question. Additionally, Chapter 13 was written to help you know when you are ready to take the exam.

All in all, you should find your preparation for CAPM Certification a highly rewarding experience. Aside from the financial and career benefits that typically accompany it, earning your CAPM Certification, recognized by nearly every industry in over 120 countries around the world, is a very worthy goal.

Conventions Used in this Book

This edition of *The CAPM Exam: How to Pass on Your First Try* is structured differently than other exam preparation materials. Some of the key features that will help you get the most from this book are listed below:

- In order to create a comprehensive reference, every process, input, tool and technique, and output is discussed.
- To help you prioritize your study, key information for the exam is designated by a key symbol next to topics of particular importance.
- The philosophy behind each knowledge area and many of the sub-topics is explained. Because several questions on the CAPM Exam require you to *apply* the information instead of simply regurgitating it, you must understand "why" the information is structured the way it is, instead of merely memorizing it.
- A large portion of the CAPM Exam relies on understanding key terms related to project management. Many test takers go wrong by relying on their own experience to interpret terminology instead of understanding PMI's definitions. PMI's use of a term or concept may be very different than that of someone who has not had exposure to PMI's philosophy. Key terms are given special attention where necessary to help readers become acquainted with PMI's usage of project management terms and concepts.
- Instead of making the book gender neutral (he/she), the masculine pronoun was generally used. The use of this convention was not intended to diminish the role of female project managers. Rather, this choice was made to improve the readability of the book.
- The 2000 PMBOK Guide used the word "project" in its text approximately 3,006 times. Not to be outdone, the 3rd Edition PMBOK Guide has ratcheted usage of "project" up to a stunning 5,004 times! Although the author admits to using the word more than was necessary in this book, he has omitted its usage in literally thousands of instances, believing that its inclusion did not make the material easier to understand, nor would its omission result in a lower exam score; however, for those of you who take offense at this (and you know who you are), the author offers this small consolation: "project, project."

The Exam

This chapter will explore the CAPM Certification Exam, what it is like, and the material it covers. There is a lot of misinformation floating around from various sources, so this chapter should help you understand what the test is, how it is structured, and an overview of the contents. Specific strategies on how to pass the exam will be discussed in Chapter 13 – How to Pass the CAPM on Your First Try.

What the Exam Tests

Before we discuss what the CAPM Certification Exam does test, let's clear up a few misconceptions about the exam.

The CAPM Certification Exam *does not* test:

- Your project management experience
- Your common sense
- Your knowledge of industry practices
- Your knowledge of how to use software tools
- What you learned in management school
- Your intelligence

The CAPM Certification Exam *does* test:

- Your knowledge of PMI's processes of project management
- Your understanding of the many terms that are used to describe the processes
- Your ability to apply those processes in a variety of situations
- Your ability to apply key formulas to scheduling, costing, estimating, and other problems

A Passing Grade

Not to scare you right away, but truth is that the CAPM is not an easy exam. Due to recent changes in the exam, this is more true today than ever before. Those who do not pass come from a broad cross-section of people, ranging from those who have approached the exam with extensive preparation, including books and training classes, to those who have barely expended any effort. By using this book, you are tilting the scales decidedly in your favor!

The exam is pass/fail, and to pass the CAPM Exam, you have to answer at least 88 questions correctly out of the 135 graded questions on the test (more on graded questions later). That translates to 65%, and if your first reaction to the 65% mark is that it does not sound very impressive, consider that today significantly fewer first-time test takers are passing the exam than in previous years when the passing percentage was higher. The exam is tough, and 61% is a great score!

Some people find it very difficult to understand why they cannot study and make a perfect score on the CAPM. It is a good thing to want to do well on the exam, but considering the breadth of material, simply passing it is a terrific accomplishment! There will be a few questions that you will be absolutely certain you got right that you actually missed. This has more to do with the way the questions are constructed and the very tricky wording than it does with the study effort you put in, your intellectual powers, or your test-taking abilities.

Your goal in taking the CAPM should be to do your absolute best and to make sure that your best effort falls within PMI's passing score limits.

The Exam Material

Your CAPM Exam will be made up of exactly 150 questions, covering a broad variety of material, but only 135 of those questions will count. The other 15 questions are considered experimental questions that PMI is evaluating for use on future exams. The good news is that these 15 questions do not count toward your grade. The bad news is that you will never know which questions count and which do not.

PMI does provide some guidelines as to how the material will be presented. The exam was significantly updated in September of 2005, and the updated material and questions are allocated as follows:

It is recommended that you join the Project Management Institute prior to signing up to take the test. At publication time, the new member fee was $129.00 ($119.00 membership + $10.00 new member activation fee). Application may be made online at www.pmi.org, or you may obtain an application from PMI by calling (610) 356-4600.

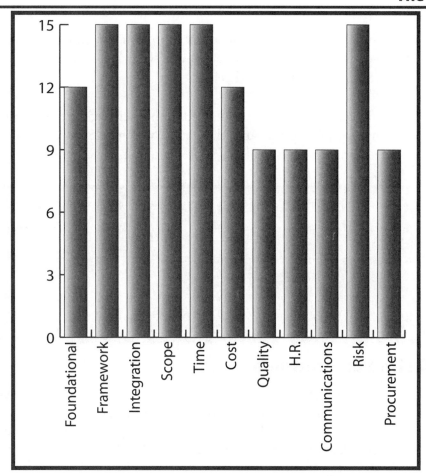

After joining PMI, you will receive a membership number that you can use to receive a $75.00 discount on the exam's non-member fee, so you instantly save money by joining. The Examination Fee will be $225.00 for a member in good standing. If you elect not to join PMI, it will cost $300.00 to apply to take the test.

In addition to the financial savings, there are many other benefits that come with joining PMI, including a subscription to PMI's publications, PM Network and PM Today; discounts on books and PMI-sponsored events; and access to a wealth of information in the field of project management.

When you get ready to apply for eligibility for CAPM Certification, you can apply online or use printed forms. If at all possible, you should apply online. Depending on the time of year, wait times have been known to stretch out for weeks when using printed forms through the mail, while online applicants usually report turnaround times within one to two weeks. The length of time can vary, depending on the volume of applications that PMI is processing. In any case, you must have your letter of eligibility from PMI to sit for the CAPM Certification Exam.

To be eligible for CAPM Certification, you will need to demonstrate that you meet certain minimum criteria. The current qualifications that PMI requires are summarized below.

Official information is contained in the Certified Associate in Project Management Credendial Handbook, which provides details on eligibility requiremens. It is available for download at www.pmi.org.

Requirements to Apply for the CAPM

- A High School diploma, Associate degree, or equivalent
- 1,500 hours of work on a project team

or

- 23 contact hours of formal project management education

The Testing Environment

The CAPM Certification Exam is administered in a formal environment. There is no talking during the exam, and you cannot bring notes, books, paper, cell phones, PDAs, or even many types of calculators into the examination room with you. The CAPM is considered a "high-stakes" or "high-security" exam and is very carefully monitored. Test takers are constantly observed by the test proctor and are under recorded video and audio surveillance. This can be distracting as well as unnerving, so it is important to be mentally prepared as you walk into the exam.

The test is delivered on a standard Windows-based PC that runs a secure, proprietary testing application. The computer setup is very straightforward, with a mouse and keyboard and a simple graphical user interface used to display the test. PMI can arrange special accommodations for those test takers who have special physical needs.

Recently, PMI has also made provision for certain test-takers who do not live near a testing center to take a paper version of the exam. While this book focuses on the computerized version of the exam, the content on both versions of the exam is identical, and your preparation should not be any different. More information on the paper-based exam may be found online at www.pmi.org.

The exam ends either when your 3-hour time limit has been reached (more on this in a moment) or when you choose to end the exam. Once the exam is over, you will know your score within a few seconds, and those results are electronically transmitted to PMI. If you passed, you are immediately a "CAPM," and you may start using that designation after your name. PMI will mail you all of the official information, including your certificate, within a few weeks. If you did not pass, you may take the exam up to three times in a calendar year. If you do not pass on your third attempt, you must wait one year to reapply.

The Time Limit

Taking a test while the clock is ticking can be unnerving. The CAPM is a long exam, but you are given a significant block of time to complete the test. From the time you begin the exam, you will have 180 minutes (3 hours) to finish. For most people, this is enough time to take the test and review the answers. The allocation works out to 72 seconds per question if no breaks are taken. While a few of the more complicated questions will certainly require more than 72 seconds, most will take much less time.

The subject of time management for the exam, along with a suggested strategy for managing your time, is covered later in Chapter 13 - How to Pass the CAPM on the First Try.

Question Format

Exam questions are given in a multiple choice format, with four possible answers, marked A, B, C, and D, and only one of those four answers is correct. Unlike in some exams, there is no penalty for guessing, so it is to your advantage to answer every question on the CAPM exam, leaving none of them blank.

Many of the CAPM questions are quite short in format; however, the CAPM Exam is famous (or infamous) for its long, winding questions that are difficult to decipher. To help you prepare, you will see different question styles represented in this book. Going through all the sample questions provided in this volume is an excellent way to prepare for the types of questions you will encounter on the actual exam.

Foundational Concepts

Difficulty	Memorization	Exam Importance
Medium	Medium	High

What is a project? How is it different from operations or a program? What is a project manager, and how do different organizational structures change the role and power of a project manager? In order to understand PMI's approach to project management, you need a solid overview to these and other topics.

While much of the rest of this book is focused on PMI's 44 processes, inputs, tools, techniques, outputs, and formulas, this chapter lays the foundation on which those knowledge areas are built.

Philosophy

PMI's philosophy of project management does not disconnect projects from the organizations that carry them out. Every project has a context and is heavily influenced by the type of organization in which the project is performed.

Another aspect to be considered in the context of the project is the roles of the different stakeholders. An effective project manager must identify the different types of project stakeholders (such as customers, the project sponsor, senior management, etc.), understand their needs, and help them all work together to create common and realistic goals that will lead to a successful project.

Importance

Because this chapter is foundational, it is highly important! There will be many questions on the CAPM Exam that test your understanding of a project manager, stakeholder, and sponsor. You must also be able to identify the different types of organizations, and to recognize a project as compared to other types of related endeavors. Spend time making certain you understand these terms and definitions.

Preparation

The volume of material here is significant, and much of the information is marked as important. Test preparation should be focused on memorization of the terms and your ability to apply them. Word for word memorization is not essential, but a solid understanding is.

Essential Terms

Begin your CAPM exam study by cementing your understanding of the following terms:

[Key Fact] Process

Processes are encountered regularly when studying for the CAPM Exam. For purposes of the test, think of a process as a package of inputs, tools, and outputs used together to do something on the project. For instance, Schedule Development is the process in which the project schedule is created. Risk Identification is the process in which the list of risks is created, etc. There are 44 unique processes you will need to understand for the exam, all of which are covered in this book.

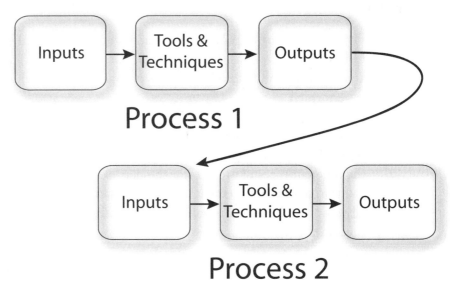

Interactions within a Process

As the preceding diagram illustrates, the outputs from one process are often used as inputs into other processes. Later in this chapter some of the most common inputs, tools, techniques, and outputs are discussed.

[Key Fact] Phases

Many organizations use project methodologies that define project phases. These phases may have names like "requirements gathering," "design," "development," "testing," and "implementation." Each phase of a project produces one or more deliverables.

One of the major problems test takers have when encountering PMI's material is to understand that all of the processes in the PMBOK may take place within each phase of the project. In other words, if your organization's methodology specifies a phase for product design, some or all of the 44 processes (described in chapters 4-13 of this book) may take place in that phase alone, only to be repeated in the subsequent project phases. Keep this fact in mind while reading the remaining chapters.

It is important to understand that PMI does not define what phases you should use on your project. That is because *the PMBOK Guide does not describe a project methodology*. Instead, *processes* are defined that will fit into your project methodology.

The example below shows how deliverables are usually associated with each phase. The deliverables are reviewed to determine whether the project should continue. This decision point is known as an exit gate or a kill point, and the decision on whether to proceed with the project is usually made by a person external to the project.

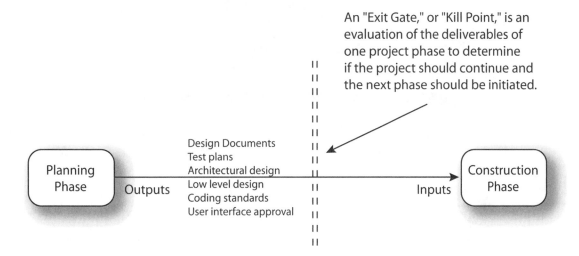

An "Exit Gate," or "Kill Point," is an evaluation of the deliverables of one project phase to determine if the project should continue and the next phase should be initiated.

Planning Phase → Outputs

Design Documents
Test plans
Architectural design
Low level design
Coding standards
User interface approval

Inputs → Construction Phase

 **Project**

A project is a temporary (finite) group of related tasks undertaken to create a unique product, service, or result. You may encounter a question on the exam that describes a situation and asks you whether that situation represents a project. If you see such a question, remember that you are looking for the following characteristics:

- A project is time-limited (it has a definite beginning and end).
- A project is unique (it has not been attempted before by this organization).
- A project is comprised of interrelated activities.
- A project is undertaken for a purpose (it will yield a specific product, service, or result).

Essential Terms

As the above diagram illustrates, companies set strategic goals for the entire organization. A company's project portfolio represents all of the project and program investments they make.

Programs represent a group of projects managed together in order to gain efficiencies on cost, time, technology, etc. For instance, by managing three related technology projects as a program, an organization might be able to save time and money by developing several common components only once and leveraging them across all of the projects that use those components.

Project management is the application of resources, time, and expertise to meet the project requirements. Project management usually applies to individual projects.

Program

A program is a larger effort than a project, because it is a group of related projects coordinated together. Programs may also include operations. Organizations often group projects into programs in order to realize some benefit that could not be achieved if those projects were not undertaken in concert.

Portfolio

A company's project portfolio represents the entire investment in projects and programs. Project portfolios should be aligned to the organization's strategic goals.

Ideally, the benefit of all project investments should be expressed in how they meet or assist the organization's strategic goals.

Progressive Elaboration

The term "progressive elaboration" simply means that you do not know all of the characteristics about a product when you begin the project. Instead, they may be revisited often and refined. For instance, you may gather some of the requirements, perform preliminary design, take the results to the stakeholders for feedback, and then return to gather more requirements. The characteristics of the product emerge over time, or "progressively."

Project Management

Project management is using skills, knowledge, and resources to satisfy project requirements.

Historical Information

Historical information is found many places on the exam, usually under the umbrella heading of organizational process assets, and it is almost always used as an input to processes wherever it is found. (Many of these terms will become more clear over the next two chapters). Historical information is found in the records that have been kept on previous projects. These records can be used to help benchmark the current project. They may show what resources were previously used and what lessons were learned. More than anything, historical information is used to help predict trends for the current project and to evaluate the project's feasibility.

Essential Terms

Because PMI advocates constant improvement and continuous learning, historical records are extremely important in project management, and they are used heavily during planning activities. They can provide useful metrics, be used to validate assumptions, and help prevent repeated mistakes.

Baseline

The term baseline is used for the project plan, time, scope, and cost. The baseline is simply the original plan plus any approved changes. Many people who take the exam do not understand that the baseline includes all approved changes, but baselines are used as tools to measure how performance deviates from the plan, so if the plan changes, the new plan becomes the baseline.

Suppose you were running a one mile race, and you considered that distance as your baseline. Your plan was to run at the healthy pace of six minutes per mile. Now suppose that the race length was changed to a three mile race. You ran the race and still finished in a respectable twenty minutes. Would you want your progress measured against the original distance or the updated one? If you did not update your baseline to three miles, your pace of twenty minutes against the original distance of one mile would not be very impressive at all. Your performance measurements would only be meaningful if you had an accurate baseline.

Remember - your project's baseline is defined as the original plan plus all approved changes. Even though the baseline changes as the plan changes, it is a good idea to keep records that show how the plan has progressed and changed over time.

Lessons Learned

Lessons learned are documents focused on variances created at the end of each process that detail what lessons were learned that should be shared with future projects. Lessons learned from past projects are an organizational process asset, which is an input into many planning processes. It is important that lessons learned put a special emphasis on variances that occurred on the project between what was planned to happen and what actually happened.

Regulation

A regulation is an official document that provides guidelines that must be followed. Compliance with a regulation is mandatory (e.g., in the United States, wheelchair ramps are required for ADA compliance). Regulations are issued by government or another official organization.

Standard

A standard is a document approved by a recognized body that provides guidelines. Compliance with a standard is not mandatory but may be helpful. For example, the size of copy paper is standardized, and it would probably be a very good idea for paper manufacturers to follow the standard, but there is not a law in most countries requiring that copy paper be made the standard size. The PMBOK Guide provides a standard for project management.

System

There are several instances of "systems" in the PMBOK Guide. A system incorporates all the formal procedures and tools put in place to manage something. The term "system" does not refer simply to computer systems, but to procedures, checks and balances, processes, forms, software, etc. For instance, the project management information system (discussed in Chapter 4 – Project Integration Management), may include a combination of high-tech and low-tech tools such as computer systems, paper forms, policies and procedures, meetings, etc.

Project Roles

Another area of study regarding the project context is that of the roles and responsibilities found on projects. You should be familiar with the following terms related to project roles:

Project Manager

The project manager is the person ultimately responsible for the outcome of the project. The project manager is:

- Formally empowered to use organizational resources
- In control of the project
- Authorized to spend the project's budget
- Authorized to make decisions for the project

Project managers are typically found in a matrix or projectized organization (more about types of organizations shortly). If they do exist in a functional organization, they will often be only part-time and will have significantly less authority than project managers in other types of organizations.

Because the project manager is in charge of the project, most of the project's problems and responsibilities belong to him. It is typically a bad idea for the project manager to escalate a problem to someone else. The responsibility to manage the project rests with the project manager, and that includes fixing problems.

 Project Coordinator

In some organizations, project managers do not exist. Instead, these organizations use the role of a project coordinator. The project coordinator is weaker than a project manager. This person may not be allowed to make budget decisions or overall project decisions, but they may have some authority to reassign resources. Project coordinators are usually found in weak matrix or functional organizations.

 Project Expeditor

The weakest of the three project management roles, an expeditor is a staff assistant who has little or no formal authority. This person reports to the executive who ultimately has responsibility for the project. The expeditor's primary responsibility lies in making sure things arrive on time and that tasks are completed on time. An expeditor is usually found in a functional organization, and this role may be only part-time in many organizations.

 Senior Management

For the exam, you can think of senior management as anyone more senior than the project manager. Senior management's role on the project is to help prioritize projects and make sure the project manager has the proper authority and access to resources. Senior management issues strategic plans and goals and makes sure that the company's projects are aligned with them. Additionally, senior management may be called upon to resolve conflicts within the organization.

 Functional Manager

The functional manager is the departmental manager in most organizational structures, such as the manager of engineering, director of marketing, or information technology manager. The functional manager usually "owns" the resources that are loaned to the project, and has human resources responsibilities for them. Additionally, he may be asked to approve the overall project plan. Functional managers can be a rich source of expertise and information available to the project manager and can make a valuable contribution to the project.

Stakeholder

Stakeholders are individuals who are involved in the project or whose interest may be positively or negatively affected as a result of the execution or completion of the project. They may exert influence over the project and its results. This definition can be very broad, and it can include a vast number of people! Often when the term "stakeholders" appears on the exam, it may be referring to the key stakeholders who are identified as the most important or influential ones on the project.

 Sponsor

The sponsor is the person paying for the project. He may be internal or external to the company. In some organizations the sponsor is called the project champion. Also, the sponsor and the customer may be the same person, although the usual distinction is that the sponsor is internal to the performing organization and the customer is external.

The sponsor may provide valuable input on the project, such as due dates and other milestones, important product features, and constraints and assumptions. If a serious conflict arises between the project manager and the customer, the sponsor may be called in to help work with the customer and resolve the dispute.

 Project Office

This term refers to a department that can support project managers with methodologies, tools, training, etc., or even ultimately control all of the organization's projects. Usually the project office serves in a supporting role, defining standards, providing best practices, and auditing projects for conformance.

Project Context

Another major area of study for the CAPM exam is the concept of a project context, or organizational environment, in which a project is carried out. A large part of the project context is determined by the organization's structure, which PMI refers to as the type of organization.

 Types of Organizations

The type of organization that undertakes a project will have an impact on the way the project is managed and even its ultimate success. There are three major types of organizations described by PMI: functional organizations, projectized organizations, and a blend of those two called matrix organizations. Furthermore, matrix organizations can be characterized as weak, strong, or balanced.

The chart that follows summarizes essential information regarding these three types of organizations. You should be very familiar with this information before taking the exam, as you may see several questions that describe a project or situation and require you to identify what type of organization is involved.

Project Context

Organizational Structures

Type	Description	Who is in Charge?	Benefits	Drawbacks
Functional	Very common organizational structure where team members work for a department, such as engineering or accounting, but may be loaned to a project from time to time. The project manager has low influence or power.	Functional (Departmental) manager	• Deeper company expertise by function. • High degree of professional specialization. • Defined career paths.	• Project manager is weak. • Projects are prioritized lower. • Resources are often not dedicated to a project.
Projectized	The organization is structured according to projects instead of functional departments. The project manager is both the manager of the project and of the people. He is highly empowered and has the highest level of control.	Project manager	• Project manager has complete authority. • Project communication is easiest since everyone is on a single team. • Loyalty is strong, to both the team and the project. • Contention for resources does not exist.	• Team members only belong to a project – not to a functional area. • Team members "work themselves out of a job" – they have nowhere to go when the project is over. • Professional growth and development can be difficult.
Matrix	A hybrid organization where individuals have both a functional manager and a project manager for projects. In a strong matrix, the project manager carries more weight. In a weak matrix, the functional manager has more authority. In a balanced matrix, the power is shared evenly between the functional and project managers.	Power shared between project manager and functional manager	• Can be the "best of both worlds." Project managers can get the deep expertise of a functional organization, while still being empowered to manage resources on the project.	• Higher overhead due to duplication of effort on some tasks. • Resources report to a functional manager and they have a "dotted line" to a project manager, sometimes causing conflict and confusion. • High possibility for contention between project managers and functional managers. • Because resources do not report to the project manager, they may be less loyal to him.

Organizational Structures

Key Fact *Project Manager's Power*

Once you are comfortable in your understanding of types of organizations and the roles that different stakeholders play in a project, you can see that the organizational context in which a project is carried out will have a great deal of influence on that project. One way that the type of organization affects the project manager in particular is in how much power he is given. The chart below illustrates the relationship between a project manager's level of empowerment and the type of organization in which he works.

The Project Manager's Power by Organization Type

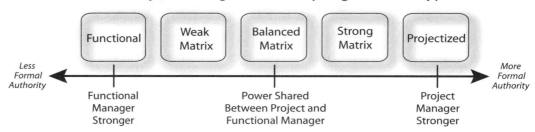

Project Manager's Management Skills

The practice of project management overlaps many other disciplines. Since most projects are performed within an organization, there are other management skills that make up the foundation of project management. These skills will probably have a significant effect on projects. The project manager should have experience in:

Leading

Motivating people and inspiring them to commit.

Communicating

Exchanging information clearly and correctly. Although communication skills are not emphasized on the exam, they are important to the project manager and critical to the success of the project.

Negotiating

Working to reach a mutual agreement. Negotiations may happen with groups or individuals inside and outside the organization.

Problem Solving

Defining the problem and dealing with the factors that contribute to or cause the problem.

Influencing

Accomplishing something without necessarily having formal power. Influencing the organization requires a keen understanding of the way the organization is structured, both formally and informally.

Management Skills

Key Fact | *Project Life Cycle*

The project life cycle is simply a representation of the phases that a project typically goes through. These phases are general, but they are representative of the common flow of activities on a project.

The six phases represented at the bottom of the graphic below describe the way in which a project typically progresses. It should be noted, however, that this depiction is very general, and different phases and phase names are used by different industries and projects.

The image also shows some other facts about the project life cycle that often appear on the CAPM exam in the form of questions. These questions typically focus on the fact that resource and cost levels rise early in the project and drop over time, or how risk and stakeholders' ability to influence the project are highest early in the project and decrease as the project progresses.

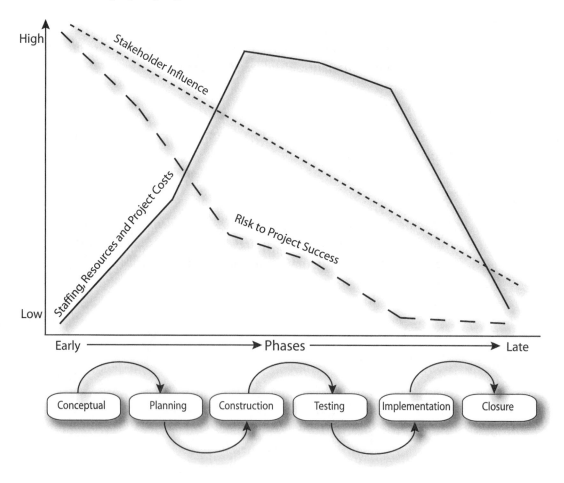

Key Fact | *The Triple Constraint*

Another fundamental topic in project management is commonly referred to as "the triple constraint." It is based on the realization that while changes do occur during a project, they do not happen in a vacuum. When the scope of a project is changed, time and cost are also affected. Of course, the same is true when changes are made to cost or time. Those changes will have some impact on the other two areas.

As many different types of changes will be requested in most projects, it is essential in project management to be mindful of the triple constraint and to help keep others aware of it. The project manager should not simply accept all changes as valid; rather, the project manager should evaluate how those changes affect the other aspects of the project.

The triple constraint, or as some know it, the iron triangle, is simply the concept that scope, time, and cost are closely interrelated. Just as you cannot affect one side of a triangle without changing one or both of the other lengths, you cannot simply change one part of the triple constraint without affecting other parts.

However common a practice it may be in some organizations to slash a budget without revisiting the scope or the schedule, the project manager should not simply accept these mandates. The triple constraint is in place whether the organization recognizes and accepts it or not.

The classic approach to the triple constraint is represented in the following diagram:

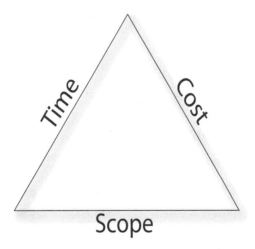

The triple constraint, also called the iron triangle

Triple Constraint

But as many topics are interrelated in project management, an expanded view of the "triple" constraint could be represented not as a triangle but as a hexagon as shown below:

Expanded view of the "triple" constraint

Common Inputs, Tools, Techniques, and Outputs

Throughout this book, several inputs, tools and techniques, and outputs of the 44 project management processes are referenced repeatedly. Since there are 592 inputs, tools and techniques, and outputs, the decision was made to discuss several of these in the following paragraphs rather than repeat them time and again throughout the book. This section should serve as a reference as you encounter these throughout the book, and spending extra time here should help improve your overall understanding of the material.

In fact, this chapter is so important that you should read it now, and then come back to reread it after you have read chapters 4–12.

Common Inputs

Key Fact

Approved Change Requests

Change requests are common on projects, and they take on many characteristics. You may receive a change request to add functionality to a computer application, to remove part of a building, or to change materials. The important thing to remember throughout this is that these are only requests until they are approved. If a change is requested, then the change is processed according to the integrated change control system. This will ensure that the change request is properly understood and considered and that the right individuals or departments are involved before approving or rejecting it.

Approved change requests are used as an input into many processes to make sure that the change gets executed and is properly managed and controlled.

 Enterprise Environmental Factors

This input can cover a lot of ground, and it appears as an input into most planning processes. In fact, it is used so frequently that you may be tempted to just skim right over it, but be careful! Enterprise environmental factors are important to your understanding of the exam material, and you should make sure you have a solid grasp of why they are used so commonly.

Consider the things that impact your project that are not part of the project itself. Just a few of these include:

- Your company's organizational structure
- Your organization's values and work ethic
- Laws and regulations where the work is being performed or where the product will be used
- The characteristics of your project's stakeholders (e.g. their expectations and willingness to accept risk)
- The overall state of the marketplace for your project

In fact, enterprise environmental factors can be anything external to your project that affects your project. That is why it is so important to consider these factors when planning your project and to explore how they will influence your project.

 Organizational Process Assets

What information, tools, documents, or knowledge does your organization possess that could help you plan for your project? Some of these might be quite obvious, such as the project plan from a previous, similar project performed by your organization, while some may be more difficult to grasp at first, such as company policy. Consider, however, that both of these assets will help you as you plan. For instance, company policy adds structure and lets you know the limits your project can safely operate within, so you do not have to waste time or resources discovering these on your own.

Common Inputs

A few examples of organizational process assets are:

- Templates for common project documents
- Examples from a previous project plan
- Organizational policies, procedures, and guidelines for any area (risk, financial, reporting, change control, etc)
- Software tools
- Databases of project information
- Historical information
- Lessons learned
- Knowledge bases

Anything that your organization owns or has developed that can help you on a current or future project may be considered an organizational process asset, and part of your job on the project is to contribute to these assets wherever possible on your project.

 Project Management Plan

The project management plan is one of the most important documents discussed in this book. It may be thought of as the culmination of all the planning processes. It is crucial that you understand what it is, where it comes from, and how it is used.

For the purpose of the exam, the definition of the project management plan is a single approved document that guides execution, monitoring and control, and closure. The use of the word single in this definition is a bit unusual, since the project management plan is actually made up of several documents; however, once these component documents become approved as the project management plan, they become fused together as one document.

Don't assume that the project management plan is always overly formal or detailed. The project management plan should be appropriate for the project. That means that it may be documented at a summary level, or it may be very detailed.

Following is a list of the components that make up the project management plan. The project management plan is covered in more detail in Chapter 4 - Integration Management under Develop Project Management Plan. Additionally, each of these components is covered in later chapters of this book.

- Project scope management plan
- Schedule management plan
    The schedule baseline
    The resource calendar
- Cost management plan
    The cost baseline
- Quality management plan
    The quality baseline
- Process improvement plan
- Staffing management plan
- Communications management plan
- Risk management plan
    The risk register
- Procurement management plan

Work Performance Information

Work performance information begins to flow as the actual work on the project is executed. Project team members, the customer, and other stakeholders will need to be informed as to the status of the deliverables, how things are performing against cost and schedule goals, how the project team is performing, and how the product stacks up against quality standards.

Although the examples above are the most common types of work performance information, any valuable information about the project that comes about as a result of performing the work would be considered work performance information.

Common Tools

Expert Judgment

The tool of expert judgment is used time and again throughout the PMBOK Guide. The tool is exactly what it sounds like, and the reason it is so common is that it can be used whenever the project team and the project manager do not have sufficient expertise. You do not need to worry about whether the experts come from inside the organization or outside, whether they are paid consultants or offer free advice. The most important things to remember for the exam are that this tool is highly favored and is very commonly found on planning processes.

Project Management Methodology

This tool of project management is important. In fact, it's very important because it underscores something that is vital to your understanding. The PMBOK Guide does not describe a methodology. The PMBOK Guide describes 44 processes used to manage a project. These processes are used by an organization's project management methodology, but they are not the methodology.

To illustrate the difference between the PMBOK Guide's 44 project management processes and a project management methodology, consider the analogy of two baseball teams. The Atlanta Braves and the New York Mets both have the same set of rules when they play, but they have very different strategies of how they will capitalize on those strengths and use those rules to their advantages. In this analogy, the rules would equate to the processes, and the strategy to methodology.

Different organizations will employ different project management methodologies, while they will all adhere to the 44 processes. And just as a team's strategy may be more nuanced and rich than the simple rules on which it is based, an organization's methodology may be a very rich and detailed implementation of the project management processes.

Project Management Information System

The Project Management Information System (PMIS) is another important tool to know for the exam. It is your system that helps you produce and keep track of the documents and deliverables. For example, a PMIS might help your organization produce the project charter by having you fill in a few fields on a computer screen. It might then create the project charter and set up a project billing code with accounting. While the PMIS usually consists primarily of software, it will often interface with manual systems.

Another important element of the PMIS is that it will contain the configuration management system, which also contains the change control system. While these will be covered in Chapter 5 - Scope Management, understanding how they fit together now will help.

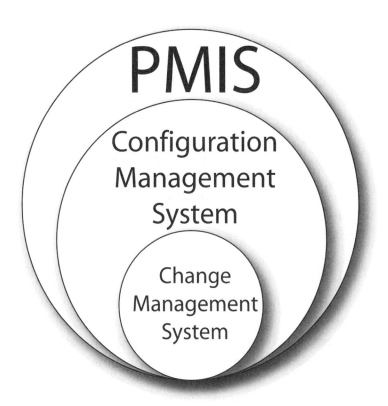

Common Outputs

 Recommended Corrective Action

Corrective action is anything done to bring future results in line with the plan. Understanding that definition of corrective action will pay big dividends on the exam. Corrective action is all about the future, and it is the actions you take to make sure that the plan and the future results line up. For instance, if the testing department has been missing their estimates by 20% ever since the project began, you might take corrective action to fix this. One way might be to go and talk with the department manager and ask her to put someone more experienced on the project. Another way might be to change the plan for future testing to allow an extra 20%. Either way, you are taking steps to make sure the plan and the results line up.

Now that you understand corrective action, be aware that a common output of processes is *recommended* corrective action. In other words, you are recommending that steps be taken. These recommendations will be evaluated to determine their impact on the rest of the plan, and will either be approved or rejected. The process where this occurs, Integrated Change Control, is covered in Chapter 4 - Project Integration Management.

Requested Changes

As work is performed, it is common for changes to be requested. These changes can take on many forms. For instance, there may be change requests to increase the scope of the project or to cut it down in size. There may be change requests to deliver the product earlier or later, to increase or decrease the budget, or to alter the quality standards.

The point to this is that these change requests are frequent as work is executed, or monitored and controlled. Like the previous example, all requested changes are brought into the process of Integrated Change Control where they will be evaluated for impact on the whole project and ultimately approved or rejected.

Updates (All Categories)

Updates as process outputs occur so often in this edition of the PMBOK as to make it very difficult for the test taker to keep it straight. For purposes of the exam, know that updates to just about every kind of plan come out of planning, executing, and monitoring and controlling processes. Most of these are common sense, and rather than take up valuable brain space explaining each individual one, the concept is addressed here and referenced throughout the book.

Project Management System

When the term "system" is encountered in this material, you should not assume that it refers to a computer system. Instead, a system is the set of rules, processes, procedures, forms, and technologies, etc., that are used to support something. In this case, the project management system is defined in the project management plan, and it is used to support the project manager's execution and monitoring and control of the project. One example component of the project management system is described below.

Work Authorization System

The work authorization system is actually part of the project management system. The work authorization system is the system used to ensure that work gets performed at the right time and in the right sequence. For example, if you had a tile specialist scheduled to come in next week and lay tile for a building project, you might want that person's manager to contact you before the specialist shows up at the job site. This conversation might be defined as part of the project's work authorization system so that the project manager retains control each time a team member takes on a new work package.

Common Outputs

 *Policy*

Although you might think of policies as a headache in your job, they are viewed favorably in project management. In fact, we think of organizational policies as an asset! The reason a policy is an organizational process asset is that it gives guidance to your actions. For instance, you may have a corporate policy that you can only hire contractors for work on internal projects. If that were the case, then having that policy could save time later in the project by preventing you from doing something your organization would frown upon.

Please note that organizational policies may not be broken, even if doing so were to save the company money. You have to follow company policy, especially where the exam is concerned.

Approved Change Requests

Approved change requests may be an output or an input, depending on which process you are performing. Approved change requests start out as recommended change requests before they are processed in Integrated Change Control. Once they are approved, they are used as inputs to various executing and controlling processes. Approved change requests can also be an output of the Manage Stakeholders process.

Approved Corrective Actions

As referenced previously, approved corrective actions start out as recommended corrective actions. They are evaluated in the Integrated Change Control process where they become an output. Approved corrective actions can also be an output of the Manage Stakeholders process. Once they are approved, they are also used as inputs to affect execution so that future results line up with the plan. Keep in mind that corrective action is taken when something in the past has not gone as planned.

Recommended Preventive Actions

Recommended preventive actions are made because a problem is anticipated. Recommendations on how to avoid the problem are made, and these recommendations are evaluated for their overall impact on the project and then approved (or rejected) in Integrated Change Control.

Common Outputs

Approved Preventive Actions

Approved preventive actions are taken to keep a problem from occurring in the first place. As was true for the previous input, approved preventive actions start out as recommended preventive actions, and they are approved in Integrated Change Control.

The PMBOK® Guide and Areas of Expertise

The PMBOK Guide is the standard document for project management. In fact, it is currently the only standard on project management accepted by the American National Standards Institute (ANSI).

Although the PMBOK Guide touches many areas, it was never intended to capture all information on project management. It is only a guide to that information. As the diagram below illustrates, there are many areas of expertise that fall at least partially outside of the PMBOK Guide.

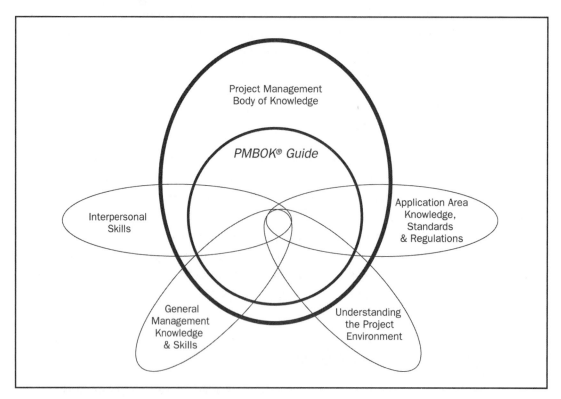

Figure 1-2. Areas of Expertise Needed by the Project Management Team

A Guide to the Project Management Body of Knowledge-Third Edition (PMBOK® Guide). ©2004 Project Management Institute, Inc. All Rights Reserved.

Diagram originally from the PMBOK Guide, used with written permission from the Project Management Institute.

Process Framework

Difficulty	Memorization	Exam Importance
Low	High	High

The process framework is the structure on which all of PMI's process material is built. The PMI processes are organized into nine knowledge areas and based on five foundational process groups:

1. Initiating
2. Planning
3. Executing
4. Monitoring and Controlling
5. Closing

Each of the 44 PMI processes performed as part of a project may be categorized into one of these process groups. Additionally, every question on the exam will tie back to one of these five areas or to professional responsibility, discussed in Chapter 13 - Professional Responsibility.

This chapter describes what processes, knowledge areas, and process groups are, explains how they are structured, and provides an overview of the project management framework.

Importance

This chapter is essential to your understanding of how this material is organized and structured. Do not be discouraged if you find the material in this chapter somewhat confusing at first. The more you read and study from this book, the better you will understand these terms and how they are applied.

Preparation

There is significant memorization that accompanies this chapter. Terms must be learned, and more importantly the overall organization of the material needs to be understood. This chapter contains only a little that will actually show up on the exam, but it has to be mastered before chapters 4 – 12 can be fully comprehended.

Essential Terms

The essential information here begins with some key terms that you will need to understand. It is not necessary to memorize all the definitions, but make sure that you do understand them. They are foundational to this book and highly important for the exam.

Processes

The term "process" is one of the most important and frequently used terms you will encounter when studying for the CAPM. Processes are composed of three elements: inputs, tools and techniques, and outputs.

The different inputs, tools and techniques, and outputs are combined to form processes, which are performed for a specific purpose. For instance, Schedule Development is a process, and as its name implies, it is performed to develop the project schedule. Risk Identification is another process, with different inputs, tools, techniques, and outputs, where (you guessed it) you identify the risks which could affect the project. There are 44 unique processes identified and described in the Guide to the PMBOK, and you will need to be familiar with all of them.

Inputs

The inputs are the starting points for the processes. Just as food is a basic building block for the production of energy in living creatures, there are specific and unique inputs into each project management process that are used as building blocks for that process. You might think of inputs as your raw materials.

Tools and Techniques

Tools and techniques are the actions or methods that are used to transform inputs into outputs. Tools can be many things, such as software, which can be used as a tool to help plan the project and analyze the schedule. Techniques are methods, such as flowcharting, which help us to frame, approach, and solve the problem. PMI combines tools and techniques since they are both used to solve problems and create outputs.

Outputs

Every process contains at least one output. The outputs are the ends of our efforts. The output may be a document, a product, a service, or a result. Usually the outputs from one process are used as inputs to other processes or as part of a broader deliverable, such as the project plan.

Knowledge Areas

The knowledge areas in this material have been organized into nine groups. Each of the 44 project management processes defined in the PMBOK Guide fit into one of these nine knowledge areas. They are:

1. Integration Management
2. Scope Management
3. Time Management
4. Cost Management
5. Quality Management
6. Human Resource Management
7. Communications Management
8. Risk Management
9. Procurement Management

Like the PMBOK Guide, this book also has a chapter for each of the knowledge areas as listed above.

Process Groups

The project management processes defined and described in the PMBOK Guide are not only presented according to the nine different knowledge areas; they are also arranged according to process groups. The same 44 processes that are included in the nine knowledge areas are organized into the five process groups.

The five process groups are:

1. Initiating
2. Planning
3. Executing
4. Monitoring and Controlling
5. Closing

Every PMI-defined process that takes place on the project fits into one of those groups.

Process Groups

Organization

As hinted at in the previous paragraphs, each process has two homes. It fits into a process group *and* a knowledge area. As the chapters in this book are aligned to knowledge areas, you will be able to see how processes are associated with different knowledge areas.

Understanding the Flow

Do not fall into the trap of thinking that the first step is to do the processes in initiation, the second step is to do the processes in planning, and so on. Although projects may flow very roughly that way, you need to understand that the scope of a project is "progressively elaborated," which means that some processes are performed iteratively. Some planning must take place, then some executing, then some controlling processes. Further planning may be performed, further executing, and so on. The five process groups are by no means completely linear.

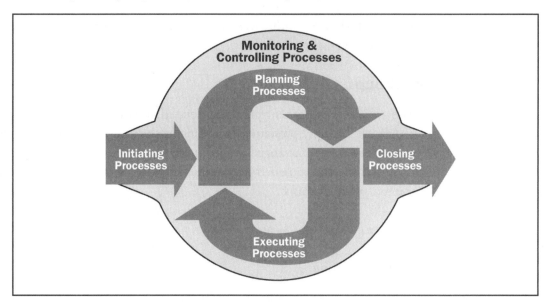

Figure 3-2. Project Management Process Groups Mapped to the Plan-Do-Check-Act Cycle

A Guide to the Project Management Body of Knowledge-Third Edition (PMBOK® Guide). ©2004 Project Management Institute, Inc. All Rights Reserved.

Used with written permission from the Project Management Institute
Illustration of the way in which process groups interrelate

Perhaps one of the biggest misconceptions people have of this material is believing that these process groups are the same thing as project phases. Understand that all 44 processes could be performed one or more times in each project phase.

Process Groups

Process Group 1 - Initiating

Integration	Scope	Time	Cost	Quality	HR	Communication	Risk	Procurement
✓								

The Initiating Process Group is one of the simpler groups in that it is made up of only two processes: Develop Project Charter and Develop Preliminary Project Scope Statement. These two processes are described in further detail in Chapter 4 – Project Integration Management. This is the process group that gets the project officially authorized and underway.

Initiating

- Develop Project Charter
- Develop Preliminary Project Scope Statement

The way in which a project is initiated, or begun, can make a tremendous difference in the success of subsequent processes and activities.

Although many processes may not be performed in a strict order, the initiating process should be performed first or at least very early on. In initiation, the project is formally begun, the project manager is named, and the preliminary scope statement is produced.

If a project is not initiated properly, the end results could range from a lessened authority for the project manager to unclear goals or uncertainty as to why the project was being performed. Conversely, a project that is initiated properly would have the business need clearly defined and would include a clear direction for the scope as well as information on why this project was chosen over other possibilities.

Initiation may be performed more than once during a single project. If the project is being performed in phases, each phase could require its own separate initiation, depending on the company's methodology, funding, and other influencing factors. There is a reason why this might be advantageous. On a longer or riskier project, requiring initiation to take place on each phase could help to ensure that the project maintains its focus and that the business reasons it was undertaken are still valid.

Initiating Processes

Process Group 2 - Planning

Integration	Scope	Time	Cost	Quality	HR	Communication	Risk	Procurement
✓	✓	✓	✓	✓	✓	✓	✓	✓

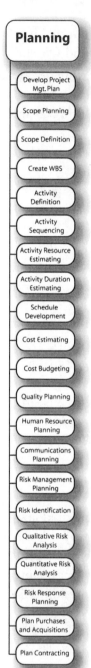

Planning

- Develop Project Mgt. Plan
- Scope Planning
- Scope Definition
- Create WBS
- Activity Definition
- Activity Sequencing
- Activity Resource Estimating
- Activity Duration Estimating
- Schedule Development
- Cost Estimating
- Cost Budgeting
- Quality Planning
- Human Resource Planning
- Communications Planning
- Risk Management Planning
- Risk Identification
- Qualitative Risk Analysis
- Quantitative Risk Analysis
- Risk Response Planning
- Plan Purchases and Acquisitions
- Plan Contracting

Planning is the largest process group because it has the most processes, but do not make the leap that it also involves the most work. Although this is not a hard and fast rule, most projects will perform the most work and use the most project resources during the executing processes.

Project planning is extremely important, both in real life and on the CAPM Exam. The processes from planning touch every one of the knowledge areas! You should be familiar with the 21 processes that make up project planning as shown in the graphic on the left of this page.

The order in which the planning processes are performed is primarily determined by how the outputs of those planning processes are used. The outputs of one process are often used as inputs into a subsequent planning process. This dictates a general order in which they must take place. For instance, the project scope statement (created during Scope Definition) is used as an input to feed the work breakdown structure (created during the Create WBS process). The work breakdown structure is then used as an input to create the activity list (created during Activity Definition). You may, for example, encounter a question similar to the one below:

What is the correct sequence for the following activities?

A. Create project scope statement. Create work breakdown structure. Create activity list.

B. Create project scope statement. Create activity list. Create work breakdown structure.

C. Create work breakdown structure. Create project scope statement. Create activity list.

D. Create activity list. Create project scope structure. Create work breakdown structure.

In this example, the correct sequence is represented by choice 'A'. This question requires an understanding of concepts introduced throughout this chapter, such as how scope items (the work breakdown structure) are created first, time-related planning processes (the activity durations) are performed second, and cost planning processes (the budget baseline) are performed third.

Planning Processes

Process Group 3 - Executing

Integration	Scope	Time	Cost	Quality	HR	Communication	Risk	Procurement
✓				✓	✓	✓		✓

As alluded to earlier, executing processes typically involve the most work. You do not need to memorize a list of executing processes like the one for planning, but you should know that the executing process group is where the work actually gets carried out. In this group of processes, parts are built, planes are assembled, code is created, documents are distributed, and houses are constructed. Other elements are also included here, such as procurement and team development. These all happen as part of the executing processes.

Some of the processes in the executing process group are intuitive, such as Direct and Manage Project Execution. Others, such as Perform Quality Assurance and Information Distribution often catch test takers by surprise because they had a different preconception of what was involved.

As Chapter 1 disclosed, there are currently 54 questions on the exam covering these seven processes, so it is important to learn them well. The key to understanding the executing processes is that you are carrying out the plan.

Executing Processes

Process Group 4 - Monitoring and Controlling

Integration	Scope	Time	Cost	Quality	HR	Communication	Risk	Procurement
✓	✓	✓	✓	✓	✓	✓	✓	✓

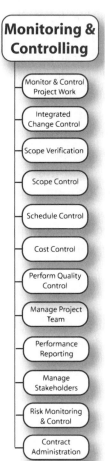

Monitoring & Controlling

- Monitor & Control Project Work
- Integrated Change Control
- Scope Verification
- Scope Control
- Schedule Control
- Cost Control
- Perform Quality Control
- Manage Project Team
- Performance Reporting
- Manage Stakeholders
- Risk Monitoring & Control
- Contract Administration

Monitoring and controlling processes are some of the more interesting processes. These processes touch each of the nine knowledge areas. Activities that relate to monitoring and controlling simply ensure that the plan is working. If it is not, adjustments should be made to correct future results. In monitoring and controlling processes, things are measured, inspected, reviewed, compared, monitored, verified, and reported. If you see one of those key words on a question, there is a good chance it is related to a monitoring and controlling process.

Planning processes are easy enough to grasp for most people. Executing processes are simply carrying out the plan, and monitoring and controlling processes are taking the results from the executing processes and comparing them against the plan. If there is a difference between the plan and the results, corrective action is taken, either to change the plan or to change the way in which it is being executed (or both) in order to ensure that the work results line up with the plan.

Monitoring and controlling processes present another rich area for exam questions. There will be 42 questions on the CAPM Exam, covering the twelve processes in this group.

Keep in mind that monitoring and controlling processes look backward over previous work results and the plan, but corrective actions, which often result from these processes, are forward-looking. In other words, monitoring and controlling is about influencing future results and not so much about fixing past mistakes. It is very important that you understand the previous statement for the exam. That concept is reinforced throughout the next several chapters.

Controlling Processes

Process Group 5 - Closing

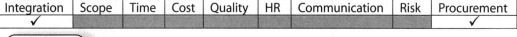

Integration	Scope	Time	Cost	Quality	HR	Communication	Risk	Procurement
✓								✓

The closing group is comprised of two very important processes. They are Close Project (covered in Chapter 4 – Integration Management) and Contract Closure (covered in Chapter 12 – Procurement Management). These two processes are sometimes difficult for people to master because in their work experience, once the customer signs off and accepts the product, the project is over.

The project does not end with customer acceptance. After the product has been verified against the scope and delivered to the customer's satisfaction, the contract must be closed out (Contract Closure), and the project records must be updated, the team must be released, and the project archives and lessons learned need to be updated (Close Project).

These processes need to be considered as part of the project, since the files, lessons learned, and archives will be used to help plan future projects.

Although there are only two processes in the closing process group, the questions about them make up 9% of the exam (18 questions), so you would do well to build a thorough understanding of what they are, how they work, and how they relate to the other processes.

If you find that you need more help in understanding the content of this chapter, read through it a couple of times before you go on. You can also read through chapter 3 of the Guide to the PMBOK after you have read this chapter. It will be much easier to comprehend now that you have an understanding of its underlying structure.

Closing Processes

Project Management Processes for the 3rd Edition PMBOK® Guide

Knowledge Area \ Process Group	Initiating	Planning	Executing	Monitoring & Controlling	Closing
Integration	• Develop Project Charter • Develop Prelim Scope Statement	• Develop Project Mgt. Plan	• Direct and Manage Project Execution	• Monitor & Control Project Work • Integrated Change Control	• Close Project
Scope		• Scope Planning • Scope Definition • Create WBS		• Scope Verification • Scope Control	
Time		• Activity Definition • Activity Sequencing • Activity Resource Est. • Activity Duration Est. • Schedule Dev.		• Schedule Control	
Cost		• Cost Estimating • Cost Budgeting		• Cost Control	
Quality		• Quality Planning	• Perform Quality Assurance	• Perform Quality Control	
Human Resource		• Human Resource Planning	• Acquire Project Team • Develop Project Team	• Manage Project Team	
Communications		• Communications Planning	• Information Distribution	• Performance Reporting • Manage Stakeholders	
Risk		• Risk Mgt. Planning • Risk Identification • Qualitative Risk Anal. • Quantitative Risk Anal. • Risk Response Plan.		• Risk Monitoring & Control	
Procurement		• Plan Purchases & Acquisitions • Plan Contracting	• Request Seller Responses • Select Sellers	• Contract Admin.	• Contract Closure

Integration Management

Difficulty	Memorization	Exam Importance	Corresponding PMBOK Chapter
High	Medium	High	Chapter 4

4

When you look at a project, do you see the forest or the trees? In other words, do you look at the big picture, focusing on the deliverables, or the smaller and more numerous tasks that must be performed in order to complete the project?

When it comes to the processes of project management, most of the PMBOK Guide is made up of trees; however, project Integration Management is the whole forest. It focuses on the larger, macro things that must be performed in order for the project to work. Whereas much of the PMBOK Guide is organized into smaller processes that produce a plan or update a document, the processes of integration are larger and more substantial.

Integration Management is the practice of making certain that every part of the project is coordinated. In Integration Management the project is started, the project manager assembles the project plan, executes the plan, and verifies the results of the work, and then the project is closed. At the same time, the project manager must prioritize different objectives that are competing for time and resources and also keep the team focused on completing the work.

Integration Management focuses on seven processes and how they fit together and interact with each other.

Philosophy

Integration Management takes a high-level view of the project from start to finish. The reason that the word "integration"

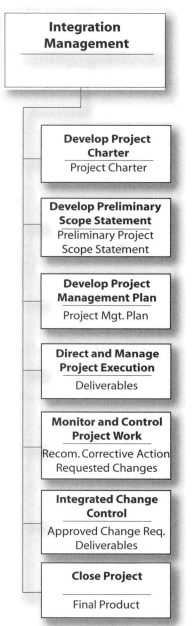

The processes of Project Integration Management with their *primary* outputs

Integration Management

Develop Project Charter
Project Charter

Develop Preliminary Scope Statement
Preliminary Project Scope Statement

Develop Project Management Plan
Project Mgt. Plan

Direct and Manage Project Execution
Deliverables

Monitor and Control Project Work
Recom. Corrective Action
Requested Changes

Integrated Change Control
Approved Change Req.
Deliverables

Close Project
Final Product

is used is that changes made in any one area of the project must be integrated into the rest of the project. For instance, the human body's various systems are tightly integrated. What you eat and drink can affect how you sleep, and how much sleep you get can affect your ability to function in other areas. When viewing your physical health, it is wise to look across your diet, exercise, sleep, stress, etc., since changes or improvements in one area will probably trickle into others.

Integration Management is similar. Changes are not made in a vacuum, and while that is true for most of the processes in this book, it is especially true among the processes of Integration Management.

The philosophy behind Integration Management is twofold:

1. During the executing processes of the project, decision-making can be a chaotic and messy event, and the team should be buffered from as much of this clamor as possible. This is in contrast to the planning processes where you want the team to be more involved. You do not want to call a team meeting during execution every time a problem arises. Instead, the project manager should make decisions and keep the team focused on executing the work packages.

2. The processes that make up project management are not discrete. That is, they do not always proceed from start to finish and then move on to the next process. It would be wonderful if the scope were defined and finished and then went to execution without ever needing to be revisited; however, that is not the way these things typically go, and the PMBOK Guide recognizes that.

Importance

The importance of this section is high! You should expect several questions on the exam that relate directly to this chapter.

Preparation

The difficulty factor on this material is considered high, primarily because there is so much information to understand. In previous versions of the exam, Integration Management was not overly difficult, but much of the material that was in other knowledge areas has now been moved into Integration Management. While the material may not present as much technical difficulty as other areas such as time, quality, or cost, it may be new to many project managers and thus present a challenge. This chapter will guide you on where to spend most of your time and how to focus your study effort.

Develop Project Charter

What it is:

The charter is the document that officially starts the project, and this is the process that creates it.

Why it is important:

The charter is one of the most important documents on a project because it is essential for creating the project. If you don't have a charter, you don't have an official project. As you will see later in this section, the lack of a charter can cause problems for the project manager that may not manifest themselves until much later.

When it is performed:

This process is one of the first ones performed. It is common for some pre-planning to take place on a project before it becomes official, but it will not be a real project until the charter is issued.

How it works:

Inputs

Contract

Not all projects are performed under contract, so this input may or may not be relevant. When a project is performed under contract for another organization, it is common for the contract to be signed prior to the project beginning. As we are ready to start the project and create the charter, the contract provides an essential input.

Project Statement of Work

The statement of work (SOW) is a written description of the project's product, service, or result. This will be supplied by the customer; however, if the customer is your own organization, the project's sponsor should supply this.

If the project is for an external customer, the SOW will typically be attached to the procurement documents and the contract.

The essential elements of the SOW are that it includes what is to be done, the business reason for doing it, and how the project supports the organization's strategy.

Enterprise Environmental Factors — See Chapter 2, Common Inputs

Organizational Process Assets — See Chapter 2, Common Inputs

Tools

Project Selection Methods

Companies select projects using a variety of methods. The most common methods seek to quantify the monetary benefits and expected costs that will result from a project and compare them to other potential projects to select the ones which are most feasible and desirable. Such methods are called "benefit measurement methods" in the PMBOK Guide.

Other methods apply calculus to solve for maximizations using constrained optimization. Constrained optimization methods are mathematical and use a variety of programming methods. If you see the terms linear programming, or non-linear programming, on the exam, you'll know they refer to a type of constrained optimization method and that the question is referring to techniques of project selection. You do not need to know how to calculate values for constrained optimization or linear programming for the exam, but you do need to know that they are project selection methods.

Following are additional terms in the fields of economics, finance, managerial accounting, and cost accounting that are sometimes used as tools for project selection. These are not listed in the PMBOK, but they may show up on the exam. It is not necessary to memorize these definitions word for word; however, it is important to understand what they are and how they are used.

Benefit Cost Ratio (BCR)

The BCR is the ratio of benefits to costs. For example, if you expect a construction project to cost $1,000,000, and you expect to be able to sell that completed building for $1,500,000, then your BCR is 1,500,000 ÷ 1,000,000 = 1.5 to 1.

In other words, you get $1.50 of benefit for every $1.00 of cost. A ratio of greater than 1 indicates that the benefits are greater than the costs.

Economic Value Add (EVA)

When you look at the value of a project, it is sometimes easy to lose sight of the big picture of adding value to shareholders. Economic Value Add, also called EVA, looks at how much value a project has truly created for its shareholders. It does more than simply look at the net profits. It also looks at the opportunity costs. By taking all of the capital costs into account, EVA can effectively show how much wealth was created (or lost) over a period of time. It takes into account the fact that there are opportunity costs to every financial expenditure, and that if a project does not make more money than those opportunity costs, it has not truly added economic value to the organization.

To calculate EVA, start with the after-tax profits of the project. Then subtract out the capital invested in that project multiplied by how much that capital cost.

For example, company XYZ invested $175,000 in a project, and that project returned a net profit of $10,000 in the first year of operation. Accountants would probably celebrate the net profit, but what does the EVA tell us about shareholder value? First, we need to determine the real cost of that capital. In this case, we will conservatively estimate 6%, since the organization could have put that same $175,000 in the bank and earned a 6% return. When we calculate EVA, we apply the following formula:

After tax profit – (capital expenditures * cost of capital), or $10,000 – ($175,000 * .06) = -$500. Even though the project returned an accounting net profit, it would have been better for XYZ to bank their money instead. In other words, XYZ actually lost $500 as far as EVA is concerned, since they would have earned $10,500 in interest if they had invested in the bank instead of the project.

Internal Rate of Return (IRR)

IRR, or "Internal Rate of Return," is a finance term used to express a project's returns as an interest rate. In other words, if this project were an interest rate, what would it be? Calculation of the IRR is no longer required on the exam, but you should understand that just like the interest rate on a savings account, bigger is better when looking at IRR.

Net Present Value (NPV)

See Present Value definition below for an explanation of Net Present Value (NPV) and Present Value (PV).

Develop Project Charter

Develop Project Charter

Opportunity Cost

Based on the theory that a dollar can only be invested at one place at a time, opportunity cost asks "What is the cost of the other opportunities we missed by investing our money in this project?" For project selection purposes, the smaller the opportunity cost, the better, because it is not desirable to miss out on a great opportunity!

Payback Period

The payback period is how long it will take to recoup an investment in a project. If someone owed you $100, you would prefer that they pay it to you immediately rather than paying you $25 per month for 4 months. As you want to recoup your investment as quickly as possible, a shorter payback period is better than a longer one.

Present Value (PV) and Net Present Value (NPV)

PV is based on the "time value of money" economic theory that a dollar today is worth more than a dollar tomorrow. If a project is expected to produce 3 annual payments of $100,000, then the present value (how much those payments are worth right now) is going to be less than $300,000. The reason for this is that you will not get your entire $300,000 until the 3rd year, but if you took $300,000 cash and put it in the bank right now, you would end up with more than $300,000 in 3 years.

PV is a way to take time out of the equation and evaluate how much a project is worth right now. It is important to understand that with PV, bigger is better.

Net Present Value (NPV) is the same as Present Value except that you also factor in your costs. For example, you have constructed a building with a PV of $500,000, but it cost you $350,000. In this case, your NPV would be $500,000 - $350,000 = $150,000.

Note that you are no longer required to calculate Present Value or Net Present Value for the exam. All you need to remember is that a bigger PV or NPV makes a project more attractive, and that NPV calculations have already factored in the cost of the project.

Return On Investment (ROI)

Return On Investment is a percentage that shows what return you make by investing in something. Suppose, for example, that a company invests in a project that costs $200,000. The benefits of doing the project save the company $230,000 in the first year alone. In this case, the ROI would be calculated as the (benefit − cost) ÷ cost, or $30,000 ÷ $200,000 = 15%. Note that you no longer need to perform this calculation on the exam, but you do need to understand that for ROI, bigger is better.

Return on Invested Capital (ROIC)

The measure of ROIC looks at how an organization uses the money invested in a project, and it is expressed as a percentage. It asks "for every dollar of cash I invest in a project, how much should I expect (or did I earn) in return?" This invested money could be cash on hand or cash that was borrowed. For the purposes of project management, the calculation is fairly simple. Use the formula:

ROIC = Net Income (after tax) from Project / Total Capital Invested in the project

For example, Fictional Enterprises invested $250,000 in a project that generated $60,000 top line revenue in its first year, with $20,000 in operational costs and a tax liability of $8,750. To calculate the ROIC, first calculate the after tax profits by subtracting the costs from the revenue. This is $60,000 – $20,000 - $8,750 = $31,250. Now apply the ROIC formula as follows: ROIC = $31,250 / $250,000 = 12.5%

This means that Fictional's project is returning 12.5% annually on the cash it invested to perform the project.

Project Management Methodology — See Chapter 2, Common Tools

Project Management Information System — See Chapter 2, Common Tools

Expert Judgment — See Chapter 2, Common Tools

Outputs

Project Charter

Once an organization has selected a project or a contract is signed to perform a project, the project charter must be created. Following are the key facts you need to remember about the project charter.

The Project Charter

- It is created during the Develop Project Charter process.
- It is created based on a business need, a customer request, or market force within the economy or society, and it should explain why the project is being undertaken.
- It is signed by the performing organization's senior management.
- It names the project manager and gives him the authority to direct the project.
- It should include the high-level project requirements.
- It should include a high-level milestone view of the project schedule. Note that you won't be able to develop the detailed schedule until much later.
- It is a high-level document that does not include project details; the specifics of project activities will be developed during the planning processes, which are carried out after Develop Project Charter is complete.
- It includes a summary-level preliminary project budget.
- It should include a milestone-level schedule.

Develop Preliminary Project Scope Statement

What it is:

> It would be wonderful if every project manager were handed a complete definition of the project's scope as soon as the project began, but often one of the most challenging aspects of project management is to develop the project's scope. This process takes a first pass at defining the scope with the understanding that it will be revised in the future.

Why it is important:

> This process gets the project pointed in the right direction by defining the initial view of the scope. The preliminary project scope statement will give definition to several other processes and will later be revised to become the completed project scope statement.

When it is performed:

> The preliminary project scope statement is created very early in the project since it sets the initial direction that will govern many of the other activities.

How it works:

Inputs

> *Project Charter — See Develop Project Charter - Outputs*
>
> *Project Statement of Work — See Develop Project Charter - Inputs*
>
> *Enterprise Environmental Factors — See Chapter 2, Common Inputs*
>
> *Organizational Process Assets — See Chapter 2, Common Inputs*

Tools

> *Project Management Methodology — See Chapter 2, Common Tools*
>
> *Project Management Information System — See Chapter 2, Common Tools*
>
> *Expert Judgment — See Chapter 2, Common Tools*

Develop Preliminary Scope

Outputs

Preliminary Project Scope Statement

As you can tell by the name of this output, the project's preliminary project scope statement is a document that is meant to be revised. It is not the final word on the project's scope. Instead, it gives direction and information to subsequent processes.

The preliminary project scope statement will explain the project's basic scope, what constraints and assumptions exist, how the project's deliverables will be accepted by the customer, what schedule milestones exist, and even a high-level work breakdown structure (discussed further in the next chapter). Also, the preliminary scope statement should include high-level preliminary cost estimates. It is developed based on information supplied by the person initiating the project (usually the sponsor or the customer).

It is important to understand that none of this information is intended to be the final word. These estimates, the definitions of scope, the work breakdown structure, and even the acceptance criteria can and probably will be revised later in the project. This preliminary project scope statement is intended to set an initial direction for the project.

Develop Preliminary Scope

Develop Project Management Plan

What it is:

When many people think of a project plan, they mistakenly think only of a Gantt chart or a schedule. Many project managers who have carried this misconception into the CAPM Exam have been chewed up and spit out by the test! As you will see in this section, the project management plan is a very important document that guides the project's execution and control, and it is much more than a schedule chart.

Why it is important:

This one should be easy. The project plan guides your work on the project. It specifies the who, what, when, where, and how. This document is used repeatedly throughout this book, so a solid understanding of it will pay dividends throughout your study.

When it is performed:

When the process of Develop Project Management Plan is performed is an interesting point, since the project management plan is not developed all at once. This plan is progressively elaborated, meaning that it is developed, refined, revisited, and updated.

How it works:

Inputs

Preliminary Project Scope Statement — See Develop Preliminary Project Scope Statement - Outputs

Project Management Processes

This input refers to the forty-four processes of project management described in the PMBOK Guide and this book. These processes are used as a framework and a guide as the project management plan is developed.

Enterprise Environmental Factors — See Chapter 2, Common Inputs

Organizational Process Assets — See Chapter 2, Common Inputs

Tools

Project Management Methodology

The reason this tool is important is that you need to realize that the PMBOK Guide does not describe a methodology. It describes the processes that take place, but it does not tell you how you should carry out these processes. An organization should provide the project manager with a project management methodology. Typically, the more experience an organization has performing projects, the more mature their methodology will be.

A methodology may be comprehensive, covering every detail of how a project is performed, or general and high-level, covering only the major project planning deliverables.

Project Management Information System — See Chapter 2, Common Tools

Expert Judgment — See Chapter 2, Common Tools

Outputs

Project Management Plan

The project management plan is the sole output of this process, and it is one of the most important outputs from any process.

To understand the project management plan, let's consider its definition. The 3rd Edition PMBOK Guide defines the project plan as "A formal, approved document that defines how the project is managed, executed, and controlled. It may be summary or detailed and may be composed of one or more subsidiary management plans and other planning documents."

The keys to understanding this are broken out below:

1. The project management plan is formal. For the exam, it is important to think of the project management plan as a formal, written piece of communication.

2. The project management plan is a single document. It is not fifteen separate plans. Once those separate documents are approved as the project plan, they become fused into a single document.

3. The project management plan is approved. In other words, there is a point in time at which it officially becomes the project plan. Who approves it is going to differ based on the organizational structure and other factors, but typically it would be:

- The project manager
- The project sponsor
- The functional managers who are providing resources for the project

It is also important to understand that we do not typically think of the customer or senior management as approving the project plan. The customer will sign a contract, but will often leave the inner workings to the performing organization (ideally, anyway). The organization's senior management usually cannot get down to the level of reviewing every component document and approving the project plan and especially not for each and every project.

4. The project management plan defines how the project is managed, executed, and controlled. This means that the document provides the guidance on how the bulk of the project will be conducted.

5. The project management plan may be summary or detailed. Even though this wording is in the definition, for the exam you will do much better to think of the project management plan as always being detailed!

The project management plan is made up of several components, which you may think of as chapters in the overall plan. More formal and mission-critical projects will have longer and more formal components. On actual projects, not every project management plan will contain every one of the components listed below, but you should be familiar with the components illustrated below before taking the exam.

Components of the Project Management Plan

| Project scope management plan | Schedule management plan | Cost management plan | Quality management plan | Process improvement plan | Staffing management plan | Communication management plan | Risk management plan | Procurement management plan | Contract management plan | Milestone list | Resource Calendar | Schedule baseline | Cost baseline | Quality baseline | Risk register |

Another important thing to note about the project management plan is that most of its components are developed in other processes. For instance, the project scope management plan is developed in Scope Planning. There are, however, two very notable exceptions. The schedule management plan and the cost management plan are not created elsewhere. Rather, they are created right here in Develop Project Plan.

The reason why this is true ties all the way back to the project charter. If you recall, when a project is initiated, the charter includes a summary budget and a summary (milestone) schedule. Since you already have these things at the time you begin Develop Project Plan, you can go ahead and develop the schedule management plan and cost management plan instead of waiting. Later, when you perform Cost Estimating and Schedule Development, you will revise these components of the project plan with more detail to reflect your deeper understanding of the project.

Component of the Project Plan	Process Where Created
Scope Management Plan	Scope Planning
Schedule Management Plan	Develop Project Plan (revised in Schedule Development)
Cost Management Plan	Develop Project Plan (revised in Cost Estimating and Cost Budgeting)
Quality Management Plan	Quality Planning
Process Improvement Plan	Quality Planning
Staffing Management Plan	Human Resource Planning
Communications Management Plan	Communications Planning
Risk Management Plan	Risk Planning
Procurement Management Plan	Plan Purchases and Acquisitions
Milestone List	Begun in Develop Project Charter and revised in Schedule Development
Resource Calendar	Activity Resource Estimating
Schedule Baseline	Schedule Development
Cost Baseline	Cost Budgeting
Quality Baseline	Quality Planning
Risk Register	Risk Identification

Develop Project Plan

Direct and Manage Project Execution

What it is:

When reading the PMBOK Guide, it is easy to walk away with the impression that the project manager must spend most of his or her time planning. Thankfully, however, that is not the case. Most of a project's time, cost, and resources are expended right here in the Direct and Manage Project Execution process. This is where things get done!

In Direct and Manage Project Execution, the team is executing the work packages and creating the project deliverables.

Why it is important:

The Direct and Manage Project Execution process is where roads get built, software applications get written, buildings are constructed, and widgets roll off the assembly line.

When it is performed:

This process is difficult to put a time frame on, and it is important that you understand why that is true. People mistakenly think about project management as occurring linearly. That is, you plan, you execute, you monitor and control, and then you close, in that order. That is wrong. On a real project, you may do some planning, some execution, and then monitor and control, only to return to more planning, more execution, and more monitoring and controlling. In reality, you may repeat this cycle numerous times.

Therefore, when looking at the process of Direct and Manage Project Execution, you should not think of it as a single occurrence, but understand that it occurs any time you are following the project management plan to create project deliverables.

How it works:

Inputs

Project Management Plan

Remember that the project management plan guides the management, execution, and monitoring and controlling of the project. In this process, we are primarily concerned with the execution of the project plan, therefore it is the essential input into this process. See the preceding process, Project Plan Development, for more details on the project management plan.

Approved Corrective Actions — See Chapter 2, Common Outputs

Approved Preventive Actions — See Chapter 2, Common Outputs

Approved Change Requests — See Chapter 2, Common Outputs

Approved Defect Repair

At some point, mistakes need to be fixed, and that is what this input is about; however, it is a bit confusing the way it is named. It is not the approved defect repair itself you are using as an input, but the approved request. Since this process focuses on the deliverables and results, the request is brought in so that the defect can be fixed.

Validated Defect Repair

This is simply an informational input to let you know that identified defects have been repaired and that those repairs have been inspected.

Administrative Closure Procedure

Before the work actually begins, the procedures by which the deliverables will be accepted and the project will be closed is documented. These procedures are brought into the Direct and Manage Project Execution process so that the work can be performed with the end goal of closing the project in mind.

Tools

Project Management Methodology — See Chapter 2, Common Tools

Project Management Information System — See Chapter 2, Common Tools

Outputs

Deliverables

This is arguably the most important output in the entire book! A deliverable is any product, service, or result that must be completed in order to finish the project. Some projects also must develop capabilities in order to finish a project, and these may be deliverables as well. For instance, a project may need to develop a new manufacturing technique before it can create a product. In that case, the capability that the team develops could be considered a deliverable.

Requested Changes — See Chapter 2, Common Outputs

Implemented Change Requests

As approved change requests are brought into this process, the implemented changes flow out.

Implemented Corrective Actions

Corrective actions are anything done to bring future results in line with the plan. It may mean either changes to the plan or changes in execution, but since this process focuses on performing the work, the assumption would be that you are making some process adjustment in the way you are performing the work.

Implemented Preventive Actions

Similar to the previous two inputs, this is the fulfillment of a request. Preventive actions are those actions taken to avoid a problem altogether. In this process, you are implementing preventive actions to the way the work is being performed.

Implemented Defect Repair

As requests for defect repair flow into this process, the fixed defects flow out.

Work Performance Information

If the deliverables are the most important output of this process, this one is the second most important. It isn't only the deliverables that flow out of this process, but also the information on the status of these deliverables. This information is used by several other processes that report on how far along a deliverable is and how it is tracking against the plan.

There could be quite a lot of work performance information of interest on the project. For instance, this process may provide information used by other processes on how the state of the deliverable lines up with the planned schedule, which milestones are being met, or how the actual costs are tracking against the estimated costs. It may also report on quality standards, such as the number of defects per thousand that are occurring.

Any information related to the deliverables being produced here could be considered work performance information.

Monitor and Control Project Work

What it is:

The process of Monitor and Control Project Work takes a look at all of the work that is being performed on a project and makes sure that the deliverables themselves and the way in which the deliverables are being produced are in line with the plan.

Why it is important:

All monitoring and controlling processes fulfill a sort of oversight role on the project. They compare the work results to the plan and make whatever adjustments are necessary to ensure that they match and that any necessary changes in the work or the plan are identified and made.

They also monitor all project information to ensure that risks are being identified and managed properly and to make sure that performance is on track.

When it is performed:

Monitor and Control Project Work is closely tied to the previous process (Direct and Manage Project Execution), and it takes place as long as there is work on the project to be done.

How it works:

Inputs

Project Management Plan — See Chapter 2, Common Inputs

Work Performance Information — See Chapter 2, Common Inputs

Rejected Change Requests

Any change requests that were processed and rejected should be brought into this process along with any supporting documentation.

Tools

Project Management Methodology — See Chapter 2, Common Tools

Project Management Information System — See Chapter 2, Common Tools

Earned Value Technique

Earned value is discussed in detail in this book in Chapter 7 - Cost Management; however, you should understand here that earned value tries to measure how much value you have earned on the project as it progresses. For instance, just because a project has used up 50% of its allotted time and budget does not mean that the work is 50% completed.

The earned value technique listed here is used to measure the work completed and feed that information back into other processes.

Expert Judgment — See Chapter 2, Common Tools

Outputs

Recommended Corrective Actions — See Chapter 2, Common Outputs

Recommended Preventive Actions — See Chapter 2, Common Outputs

Requested Changes — See Chapter 2, Common Outputs

Forecasts

One of the tools listed in this process was the earned value technique. By using earned value, the project team can forecast project results. One example of this is the estimate at completion (EAC), which is a forecast of the likely total project costs based on past performance. Another example is the estimate to completion (ETC), which estimates how much more will need to be expended based on project performance thus far.

Both of the aforementioned tools are covered in detail in this book in Chapter 7 - Cost Management, and both of them may be used here in the Monitor and Control Project Work process.

Recommended Defect Repair

Defects that require repair are marked with the status of recommended. These defects will be repaired in the previously mentioned process, Direct and Manage Project Execution.

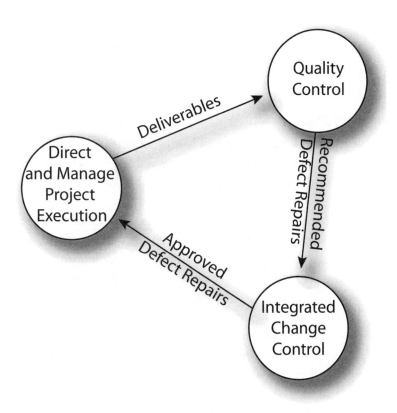

One way in which Direct and Manage Project Execution, Quality Control, and Integrated Change Control are interrelated

Monitor/Control Work

Integrated Change Control

What it is:

Some processes are more important than others for the exam, and this would qualify as one of the most important.

Every change to the project, whether requested or not, needs to be processed through Integrated Change Control. It is in this process where you assess the change's impact on the project.

Why it is important:

Integrated Change Control brings together (i.e. integrates) all of the other monitoring and controlling processes. When a change occurs in one area, it is evaluated for its impact across the entire project.

For example, suppose you came in to work one morning and found that a new legal requirement meant that the quality of your project's product needed to be improved. Would you only look at the quality processes on the project? No. After understanding the impact of this change, you would likely need to evaluate the impact on the scope of the project, the activity duration estimates, the overall schedule, the budget estimates, the project risks, contract and supplier issues, etc. In other words, you would need to integrate this change throughout every area of the project.

Integrated Change Control is unique in that the project's deliverables are both an input and an output to it, which should give you some idea of how changes flow through this process.

One way in which Integrated Change Control differs from the previous process, Monitor and Control Project Work, is that Integrated Change Control is primarily focused on managing change to the project's scope, while Monitor and Control Project Work is primarily focused on managing the way that scope is executed. For example, consider a new construction project for a hospital. If a change request were submitted that added a new wing to the hospital building, then that change request would be evaluated through Integrated Change Control to understand its impact on the whole project. If, however, the project team members were performing slower than planned, that would be factored into Monitor and Control Project Work, and corrective action would be taken to ensure that the plan and the execution lined up. Even though both are controlling processes, each has a very different focus.

When it is performed:

Like the processes Direct and Manage Project Execution and Monitor and Control Project Work, Integrated Change Control takes place as long as there is work on the project to be performed.

How it works:

Inputs

Project Management Plan — See Chapter 2, Common Inputs

Requested Changes — See Chapter 2, Common Outputs

Work Performance Information — See Chapter 2, Common Inputs

Recommended Preventive Actions — See Chapter 2, Common Inputs

Recommended Corrective Action — See Chapter 2, Common Outputs

Recommended Defect Repair — See Chapter 4, Monitor and Control Project Work

Deliverables — See Chapter 4, Direct and Manage Project Execution

Tools

Project Management Methodology — See Chapter 2, Common Tools

Project Management Information System — See Chapter 2, Common Tools

Expert Judgment — See Chapter 2, Common Tools

Change Control Board (Not listed as a tool in the PMBOK Guide)

The change control board is a formally constituted committee responsible for reviewing changes. The level of authority of a change control board varies among projects and organizations; however, it would have its level of authority spelled out in the project management plan.

Outputs

Approved Change Requests

All formally requested changes must be approved or rejected. The approved change requests are channeled back into Direct and Manage Project Execution.

Rejected Change Requests

> A requested change may be rejected for any number of reasons. The rejected change, along with any explanations and documentation, should be returned to the requestor.

Project Management Plan Updates — See Chapter 2, Common Outputs

Project Scope Statement Updates — See Chapter 2, Common Outputs

Approved Corrective Actions

> Once recommended corrective actions have been properly considered and approved in this process, they become a formal output.

Approved Preventive Actions

> Once recommended preventive actions have been properly considered and approved in this process, they become a formal output.

Approved Defect Repair

> Mistakes must be fixed, and once these recommended defect repair requests have been considered, they change in status from recommended to approved.

Validated Defect Repair

> After a defect has been repaired, it is brought back into this process to be reconsidered and validated. That is why deliverables are both an input and an output for this process.

Deliverables — See Direct and Manage Project Execution - Outputs

Close Project

What it is:

One of the key attributes of a project is that it is temporary. This means that every project eventually comes to an end, and that is exactly where this process comes into play.

Close Project is all about shutting the project down properly. This includes creating the necessary documentation and archives, capturing the lessons learned, ensuring that the contract is properly closed, and updating all organizational process assets.

Why it is important:

Projects that skip this step often are left open, limping along for months without official closure. Taking the time to do this step, and do to it properly, will ensure that the project is closed as neatly and as permanently as possible.

When it is performed:

By looking at the name of this process, you can probably deduce that this process is performed at the very end of the project. That is not to say that you wouldn't do some of it before the project ends, but it cannot be completed until the project is finished.

How it works:

Inputs

Project Management Plan — See Chapter 2, Common Inputs

Contract Documentation

This input is discussed further in Chapter 12 – Procurement Management. In summary, it is all documentation that needs to be preserved relevant to the contract. Anything that might be of future interest regarding the contract should be documented and archived as part of this process.

Enterprise Environmental Factors — See Chapter 2, Common Inputs

Organizational Process Assets — See Chapter 2, Common Inputs

Work Performance Information — See Chapter 2, Common Inputs

Deliverables — See Direct and Manage Project Execution - Outputs

Tools

Project Management Methodology — See Chapter 2, Common Tools

Project Management Information System — See Chapter 2, Common Tools

Expert Judgment — See Chapter 2, Common Tools

Outputs

Administrative Closure Procedure

Many organizations have very specific procedures that are required in order to formally close a project. This could include filling out forms, getting the customer's signature, gathering necessary project documents, meeting to document variances and the associated lessons learned, and creating the project archives.

Contract Closure Procedure

This is a formal step to confirm that any contract between the performing organization and the customer is complete. This includes completion of the terms and conditions and all necessary payments and delivery of promised items. Closing contracts is discussed further in Chapter 12 – Procurement Management.

Final Product, Service, or Result

This is the sum of all project deliverables. Acceptance by the customer(s) and project sponsor is implied in this output.

Organizational Process Assets Updates

In the course of a project, information will be gleaned, tools will be purchased or built, knowledge and experience will be gained, and documents (some of which may be reused one day) will be created. All of this should be updated as an organizational process asset and delivered to the appropriate group or individual(s) responsible for maintaining them. Often this will be the project management office.

Integration Management Questions

1. Producing a project plan may BEST be described as:

    A.   Creating a network logic diagram that identifies the critical path.
    B.   Using a software tool to track schedule, cost, and resources.
    C.   Creating a document that guides project plan execution.
    D.   Creating a plan that contains the entire product scope.

2. The project management plan updates are an output of:

    A.   Integrated Change Control.
    B.   Develop Project Plan.
    C.   Direct and Manage Project Execution.
    D.   Monitor and Control Project Work.

3. You are meeting with a new project manager who has taken over a project that is in the middle of executing. The previous project manager has left the company and the new project manager is upset that change requests are streaming in from numerous sources including his boss, the customer, and various stakeholders. The project manager is not even aware of how to process all of these incoming change requests. Where would you refer him?

    A.   Project scope statement.
    B.   Project management plan.
    C.   The previous project manager.
    D.   Project charter.

4. The preliminary project scope statement is:

    A.   Developed before the project charter, and after the project management plan.
    B.   Developed after the charter, and before the project management plan.
    C.   Developed before the contract, and after the project management plan.
    D.   Developed before the contract, and before the project management plan.

5. The work authorization system is used:

   A. So that people know when they will be performing the work.
   B. So that senior management may provide input by authorizing work requests.
   C. To ensure that only people authorized on the project are allowed to do the work.
   D. To ensure work gets performed at the right time in the right order.

6. A defect in the product was brought to the project manager's attention, and now the project team is engaged in repairing it. Which project management process would be the most applicable to this?

   A. Integrated Change Control.
   B. Monitor and Control Project Work.
   C. Direct and Manage Project Execution.
   D. Administrative Closure.

7. If you are creating a single document to guide project execution, monitoring and control, and closure, you are creating:

   A. The execution plan.
   B. The project plan.
   C. The integration plan.
   D. The project framework.

8. The change control system should be created as part of which process group?

   A. Initiation.
   B. Planning.
   C. Executing.
   D. Monitoring and controlling.

9. Which of the following statements is NOT true regarding the project charter?

   A. The project charter justifies why the project is being undertaken.
   B. The project charter assigns the project manager.
   C. The project charter specifies any high-level schedule milestones.
   D. The project charter specifies what type of contract will be used.

10. Which of the following represents the project manager's responsibility in regard to change on a project:

A. Influence the factors that cause project change.
B. Ensure all changes are communicated to the change control board.
C. Deny change wherever possible.
D. Prioritize change below execution.

11. The project plan is made up of:

A. The other planning outputs.
B. The other planning outputs, tools, and techniques.
C. The aggregate outputs of all software tools.
D. Scope verification.

12. When changes are approved and made to the project, they should be:

A. Tracked against the project baseline.
B. Incorporated into the project baseline.
C. Included as an addendum to the project plan.
D. Approved by someone other than the project manager.

13. Work performance information is used for all of the following reasons EXCEPT:

A. It provides information on resource utilization.
B. It provides information on which activities have started.
C. It shows what costs have been incurred.
D. It is used to help identify defects.

14. You are a project manager, and your team is executing the work packages to produce a medical records archive and retrieval system. Two of the project's customers have just asked for changes that each says should be the number one priority. What would be the BEST thing to do?

A. Have the project team meet with the customers to decide which would be easiest and prioritize that one first.
B. Assign someone from the team to prioritize the changes.
C. Prioritize the changes without involving the team.
D. Deny both changes since you are in project execution.

15.   The program manager is asking why your project is scheduled to take sixteen months. He claims that previous projects in the organization were able to be completed in less than half of that time. What would be the BEST thing to do?

     A.   Look for historical information on the previous projects to understand them better.

     B.   Refer the program manager to the schedule management plan.

     C.   Refer the program manager to the project plan.

     D.   Explain to the program manager that estimates should always err on the side of being too large.

Answers to Integration Management Questions

1.   C. The project plan is a single, approved plan that drives execution, monitoring and control, and closure. Note that the definition in answer 'C' was not perfect, but it was the best choice. 'A' is incorrect since it is only a part of planning. 'B' is incorrect because that will not make up the entire project plan. 'D' is incorrect since scope may or may not be a part of the project plan, but it does not make up all of it.

2.   A. This question would be nearly a pure guess unless you understand the purpose of each of the processes listed. Before you will be able to pass the CAPM exam, you will need a solid understanding of each of the 44 processes. Updates to the project plan are an output of the Integrated Change Control process. In general, updates come out of monitoring and controlling processes, which should have narrowed it down to 'A' and 'D'. From there, you should have considered the purpose of each of those two processes. Integrated Change Control changes the project (as in this case). Monitor and Control Project Execution focuses more on controlling the way in which the project is executed.

3.   B. The project plan would contain the methods for processing changes to the project.

4.   B. Questions like this will be on the exam, and in order to answer it, you have to understand the rough order in which the deliverables are produced and processes are conducted. In this case, the typical order among the items listed is contract, charter, preliminary scope statement, and project management plan. If you analyze the inputs and outputs used by the integration processes, you will gain a better understanding of this order.

5.   D. The work authorization system is covered in Chapter 2 – Foundational Terms and Concepts. The purpose of the work authorization system is to make sure work gets performed in the right sequence and at the right time. 'A' would be referring to the schedule. 'B' is incorrect since senior management should not be involved at that level. That is the job of the functional manager. 'C' is not the purpose of the work authorization system.

6.   C. Direct and Manage Project Execution is the only process in the list where defects are repaired. Approved defect repairs are an input, and implemented defect repairs are an output.

7.   B. This is the definition of the project plan.

8.   B. The change control systems are created during planning processes.

9.   D. The project charter does not specify anything about contracts. A contract with your customer would have been an input into the Develop Project Charter process, and any contracts you may use during procurement won't be identified until later in the project. 'A' is incorrect because the project charter does specify why the project is being undertaken and often even includes a business case. 'B' is incorrect because the project charter is the place where the project manager is named. 'C' is incorrect because the project charter specifies any known schedule milestones and a summary level budget.

10.   A. The project manager must be proactive and influence the factors that cause change. This is one of the key tenets of monitoring and controlling processes in general and Integrated Change Control in particular.

11.   A. The project plan consists of many things, but the only one from this list that matches is the outputs from the other planning processes, such as risk, cost, time, quality, etc. 'B' is incorrect because the other tools and techniques do not form part of the project plan.

12.   B. Did this one fool you? Approved changes that are made to the project get factored back into the baseline. Many people incorrectly choose 'A', but the purpose of the baseline is NOT to measure approved change, but to measure deviation.

13.   D. The work performance information is all about how the work is being performed, but it is not used in identifying defects. 'A' is incorrect because it does provide detail on what resources have been used and when. 'B' is incorrect because it provides information on which activities have been started and what their status is. 'C' is incorrect because it provides information on what costs were authorized and what costs have been incurred.

14. C. Prioritizing the changes is the job of the project manager. 'A' is wrong because you do not want to distract the team at this point – they should be doing the work. 'B' is wrong because it is the project manager's responsibility to help prioritize competing demands. 'D' is incorrect, because changes cannot automatically be denied simply because you are in execution.

15. A. Historical information (an organizational process asset) was covered in Chapter 2 – Foundational Terms and Concepts, and it may provide an excellent justification for why your project is taking sixteen months, or perhaps it will show you how someone else accomplished the same type of work in less time. Either way, it provides a great benchmark for you to factor in to your project. 'B' is incorrect since the schedule management plan only tells how the schedule will be managed. 'C' is incorrect because the project plan will not tell the program manager why the project is taking longer than he expects. 'D' is wrong because estimates should be accurate with a reserve added on top as needed.

Integration Mgt Answers

Scope Management

Difficulty	Memorization	Exam Importance
Low	Medium	High

5

A solid grasp of project scope management is foundational to your understanding of the material on the CAPM exam. While none of the topics in this book are particularly easy, scope management presents fewer difficulties than most other areas of the test. Most people find scope management to be more intuitive than other areas, since it has no complex formulas to memorize and no particularly difficult theories. Instead, scope management is a presentation of processes to plan, define, and control the scope of the project.

Philosophy

The philosophy behind PMI's presentation of scope management can be condensed down to these two statements: The project manager should always be in control of the scope through rigid management of the requirements, details, and processes, and scope changes should be handled in a structured, procedural, and controlled manner.

It is important to begin with the end in mind when it comes to scope management so that each requirement is documented with the acceptance criteria included. Good scope management focuses on making sure that the scope is well defined and clearly communicated and that the project is carefully managed to limit unnecessary changes. The work is closely

The processes of Project Scope Management with their *primary* outputs

Scope Management

Scope Planning
Project Scope Mgt Plan

Scope Definition
Project Scope Statement

Create WBS
WBS

Scope Verification
Accepted Deliverables

Scope Control
Requested Changes
Recom. Corrective Action

monitored to ensure that when change does happen on the project, it is evaluated, captured, and documented. Project managers should also work proactively to identify and influence the factors that cause change.

The overall goals of scope management are to define the need, to set stakeholder expectations, to deliver to the expectations, to manage changes, and to minimize surprises and gain acceptance of the product.

Importance

The topic of scope is very important on the CAPM exam. When PMI refers to the project "scope," they are referring to the work needed to successfully complete the project and only that work. Many companies have a culture in which they try to exceed customer expectations by delivering more than was agreed upon; this practice, often referred to as "gold plating," increases risk and uncertainty and may inject a host of potential problems into the project.

Preparation

While this section requires less actual memorization than some other knowledge areas, many of the test questions can be very tricky, requiring a solid and thorough understanding of the theories and practices of scope management.

Scope Management Processes

As a starting point, you should understand that the knowledge area of scope management consists of the following elements:

- Creating a plan for how scope and changes to the scope will be managed
- Defining and documenting the deliverables that are a part of the project (the scope)
- Creating the work breakdown structure (WBS)
- Checking the work being done against the scope to ensure that is complete and correct
- Ensuring that all of what is "in scope" and only what is "in scope" is completed and that changes are properly managed

Scope Mgt Processes

There are five processes in the scope management knowledge area. These are Scope Planning, Scope Definition, Create WBS, Scope Verification, and Scope Control. Below are the break-outs that show to which process group each item belongs:

Process Group	Scope Management Process
Initiating	(none)
Planning	Scope Planning, Scope Definition, Create WBS
Executing	(none)
Monitoring & Controlling	Scope Verification, Scope Control
Closing	(none)

In the knowledge area of scope management, it is also essential that you know the main outputs that are produced during each process. The different tasks that are performed in each process are summarized in the chart below.

Process	Key Outputs
Scope Planning	Project Scope Management Plan
Scope Definition	Project Scope Statement
Create WBS	Work Breakdown Structure
Scope Verification	Accepted Deliverables
Scope Control	Requested Changes to the Scope Recommended Corrective Action

Scope Planning

What it is:

The process of Scope Planning is all about developing the project scope management plan. This plan, discussed in greater detail below, is your guidebook to the other four scope processes.

Keep in mind that the scope of the product is not actually planned here, as the name of this process might mislead you to believe. Instead, you are planning how you will conduct the scope gathering, definition, monitoring and control, and verification for the entire project.

How much time and energy is invested in Scope Planning will vary from project to project, depending on the needs.

Why it is important:

This process lays the groundwork for all of the project scope activities, and the resulting plan sets the stage for how formal or informal the project scope activities will ultimately be. By deciding this in advance and documenting it in the project scope management plan, the team can understand how the scope will be organized, planned, and managed.

In actual practice, the resulting project scope management plan is typically short and borrows heavily from templates and previous examples within the performing organization.

When it is performed:

This process typically takes place quite early in the project, and certainly before any detailed scope or requirements definition takes place. Notice that it is somewhat cyclical, with the project management plan feeding into this process, and the output of this process (the project scope management plan) feeding the project management plan. If this seems confusing to you, bear in mind that projects are not a linear set of activities. In other words, the project management plan and the project scope management plan can be developed together, over multiple iterations.

Before you perform this process, you should perform the following:

1. Develop Project Charter
2. Develop Preliminary Project Scope Statement
3. Develop Project Management Plan

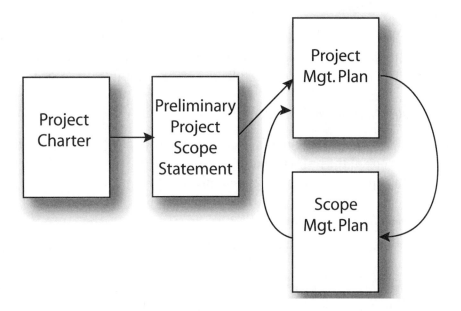

How it works:

Inputs

Enterprise Environmental Factors

Enterprise environmental factors were covered in Chapter 2 - Foundational Terms and Concepts. Think of them as a context for your project. Factors such as your organization's culture, the chain of authority, how decisions are made, and whether your organization is a projectized, matrix, or functional organization will all influence how the scope is planned and managed.

The concept here is that you should be conscious of these factors in advance, evaluating how they will influence the activities you will perform as well as your ability to perform them.

Organizational Process Assets

Once thought of as only historical information, organizational process assets make up much more. In addition to historical information gathered from previous projects, the project manager should also factor in any organizational policies and procedures that might influence how the scope is gathered and managed. A project scope management plan from a previous project would be an example of an asset, as would an organizational policy that stated that on-line meetings should be favored over physically co-locating stakeholders for all internal projects.

Project Charter

The charter is an input into this process because it describes the needs the project was undertaken to address. Factoring in these needs will help the team determine how carefully the scope needs to be managed.

Preliminary Scope Statement

The preliminary project scope statement simply gives an overview of the scope of the project, and this scope overview will be essential in creating the project scope management plan.

Project Management Plan

There is a bit of circular logic with this input, since the project scope management plan makes up a part of the project management plan, and the project management plan is used as an input into the process that creates the project scope management plan; however, don't despair! It is unlikely that you will have a complete project management plan at the point in time when you perform this process, but the elements you do have should be helpful.

Tools

Expert Judgment

As used here, the tool of expert judgment simply refers to involving someone who may have expertise on similar projects or someone who has created a project scope management plan in the past.

Templates, Forms, Standards

Any templates or previous examples of scope documents or forms would be highly useful in developing the project scope management plan.

Outputs

Key Fact

The Project Scope Management Plan

The project scope management plan defines what activities the team will perform in order to gather the project requirements, create the work breakdown structure, document the scope, place the scope under control, manage changes to the scope, and verify that all of the work and only the work was performed. It is important to note that all of the aforementioned activities are not actually performed as part of this process. Instead, we are concerned with creating the plan for how they will be performed.

Once the project scope management plan is created, it becomes part of the overall project management plan.

Scope Planning

Scope Definition

What it is:

At some point, every project must gain a detailed understanding of the requirements to be executed, verified, and delivered. The scope of the project must be understood and documented in detail, and key stakeholders must be consulted so that their needs are understood and their expectations properly managed.

Why it is important:

The scope of the project is what ultimately drives the execution of the project, and Scope Definition is the process where the project's requirements are gathered and documented. The importance of this process is directly related to how important the requirements are. A large, mission-critical project will perform this process very thoroughly, while a smaller project, or one that is highly similar to a project that has been performed previously, will probably be less formal and detailed. Likewise, a project that has extremely high material costs (e.g. an offshore drilling platform) will likely spend more time and effort on Scope Definition than a project with less risk of error.

When it is performed:

This process may be performed when the Scope Planning process has been completed. Because the project scope management plan defines how this process is performed, Scope Planning should be performed before the process of Scope Definition.

Since projects are generally progressively elaborated, this process and the requirements may be revisited many times throughout the life of the project; however, it is generally begun very early in the project lifecycle.

How it works:

Scope Definition takes the preliminary project scope statement, created earlier in the project, and refines it by performing additional analysis, factoring in any approved changes, and adding additional detail. Whereas the preliminary project scope statement was high-level and general, this process produces the actual project scope statement, which has substantially more information about the project scope and requirements.

Inputs

Organizational Process Assets — See Chapter 2, Common Inputs

Project Charter

The project charter is the organization document formally creating the project and outlining its goals. Since this process will be creating a detailed view of the scope, the project charter is needed. If the project charter does not exist, then the project manager should still capture the project's overall goals, a brief description of the scope, and the known constraints and assumptions before performing Scope Definition.

Preliminary Project Scope Statement

The preliminary project scope statement was created earlier in the project. It will be used as the primary input to this process so that the detailed project scope statement can be developed.

Project Scope Management Plan

The project scope management plan is important here because it details how the scope will be gathered and documented for this project.

Approved Change Requests

The project scope can (and usually does) change as soon as the project begins. Approved change requests should be brought into Scope Definition, whether or not this is the first time you are performing it on this project. Once an approved scope change becomes documented in the detailed scope statement and the WBS, it becomes part of the updated scope baseline.

Tools

Product Analysis

Product analysis is a detailed analysis of the project's product, service, or result, with the intent of improving the project team's understanding of the product and helping to capture that understanding in the form of requirements. The tools that may be used in product analysis will vary from industry to industry and organization to organization.

Alternatives Identification

The goal of alternatives identification is to make sure that the team is properly considering all options as they relate to the project's scope. Techniques to generate creative thought are used most often for this.

Expert Judgment

This tool involves having experts work with the project team to develop portions of the detailed scope statement. These are typically experts on the technical matters that need to be documented.

Stakeholder Analysis

Stakeholders have expectations about the project (most often focused on the product itself). These needs must be analyzed, understood, and translated into measurable, objective, and documented requirements. If they are not, then the project stands a high risk of failing product acceptance.

Outputs

Project Scope Statement

The project scope statement is the document used to level-set among the project's stakeholders. It typically has considerably more detail than the preliminary project scope statement created earlier in the project. The project scope statement contains many details pertaining to the project and product scope, including: the goals of the project, the product description, the requirements for the project, the constraints and assumptions, and the identified risks related to the scope. The objective criteria for accepting the product should also be included in the project scope statement. Finally, a cost estimate should be included with the project scope statement. This cost estimate may be order of magnitude, conceptual, preliminary, definitive, or control, depending on how much is known at the point in time the estimate is created or revised. (More discussion of these types of estimates can be found in Chapter 7 - Cost Management.)

Although the preliminary project scope statement and the more refined project scope statement have more in common than not, there are some key differences between them. The table below highlights some of the differences.

Differences between Preliminary Project Scope Statement and Project Scope Statement		
	Preliminary Project Scope Statement	**Project Scope Statement**
Process where created	Create Preliminary Project Scope Statement	Scope Definition
Knowledge area where created	Integration	Scope
When it is used	Very early in the project, and only for a relatively brief time	Throughout the project
Purpose	Provides a starting point related to the scope. Sets the direction for the project and gives rough definition to the scope.	Defines the scope in detail. Contains everything that is in the scope of the project.

Requested Changes

Because of the amount of analysis performed in this process, it is common for requested changes to the project plan to be created. These should be processed through Integrated Change Control.

Project Scope Management Plan Updates

The project scope management plan details how the scope will be gathered and documented and how changes to the scope will be managed. As the process of Scope Definition is performed, it is common for changes and updates to be made to this plan to reflect items specific to this project and this organization.

Scope Definition

Create WBS

What it is:

Once the scope of the project has been defined and the requirements have been documented, it is necessary to create the work breakdown structure (WBS) for this project.

Why it is important:

The work breakdown structure, or WBS, is one of the most important topics for the exam. The reason for its importance is tied to how it is used. After its creation, the WBS becomes a hub of information for the project. Time and cost estimates are mapped back to it, work is measured against it, and deliverables are ultimately compared to it.

When it is performed:

Create WBS is typically performed early in the project, after the scope and requirements have been gathered, but before the bulk of the work is executed.

How it works:

Inputs

Organizational Process Assets — See Chapter 2, Common Inputs

Project Scope Statement

The project scope statement describes the scope of the project in detail. It will be used in this process as a primary starting point from which to create the WBS.

Project Scope Management Plan

The project scope management plan describes how the scope of the project will be gathered and documented. Since the WBS is a critical component of that documentation, the project scope management plan is brought into this process as a key input. It will give the team guidance as to which approach will be used to create the WBS and how it should be evaluated when it is completed.

Approved Change Requests

Approved change requests should be brought into this process, whether or not this is the first time you are performing it on this project. Once an approved scope change becomes documented in the detailed scope statement and the WBS, it becomes part of the updated scope baseline.

Tools

Work Breakdown Structure Templates

WBS templates may be examples from previous projects, partially-filled-out versions of a WBS from your project office, or even commercially available templates that may be used as a starting point. Regardless of the source or the state of completion, templates can be very helpful for this process.

Decomposition

Decomposition is one of the tools used in Scope Definition to create the WBS. Decomposition involves breaking down the project deliverables into progressively smaller components. In a WBS, the top layer is very general (perhaps as general as the deliverable or product name, or some even go so far as to make the top node the overall program), and each subsequent layer is more and more specific. The key to reading the WBS is to understand that every level is the detailed explanation of the level above it.

Decomposition may be thought of as similar to the arcade game Asteroids™ from years ago. Large pieces are progressively broken down into smaller and smaller pieces.

So, how do you know when you have decomposed your WBS far enough? As you have probably realized, the nodes can be decomposed to ridiculously low levels, wasting time and actually making the project difficult to understand and change. There are many things to consider when deciding how far to decompose work, but two of the best questions to ask are:

1. Are your work packages small enough to be estimated for time and cost?
2. Are the project manager and the project team satisfied that the current level of detail provides enough information to proceed with subsequent project activities?

If you can answer "yes" to those two questions, your work packages are probably decomposed far enough.

Outputs

Project Scope Statement Updates

As you decompose the deliverable-based nodes of the work breakdown structure, it often improves your understanding of the scope itself. Updates to the project scope statement are a normal by-product of this process.

Work Breakdown Structure

The writers of the current edition of the PMBOK Guide currently advocate that the work breakdown structure always be based on the project deliverables rather than the tasks needed to create those deliverables and that it be built from the top down.

The WBS is primarily constructed using two techniques:

1. Decomposition is the practice of breaking down deliverables (product features, characteristics, or attributes) into progressively smaller pieces. This process continues until the deliverables are small enough to be considered work packages. A node may be considered a work package when it meets the following criteria:

   - The work package can not be easily decomposed any further
   - The work package is small enough to be estimated for time (effort)
   - The work package is small enough to be estimated for cost
   - The work package may be assigned to a single person

   If the node is being subcontracted outside of the performing organization, that node, regardless of size, may be considered a work package, and the subcontracting organization builds a "sub-WBS" from that node.

2. The other tool is work breakdown structure templates. A WBS template can be an example from a previous project, or a boilerplate example distributed by the project office. The important point is that it provides you with an accelerated starting point and reference when creating your breakdown of the current project's work.

The resulting WBS is a graphical, hierarchical chart, logically organized from top to bottom. Each node on the WBS has a unique number used to locate and identify it.

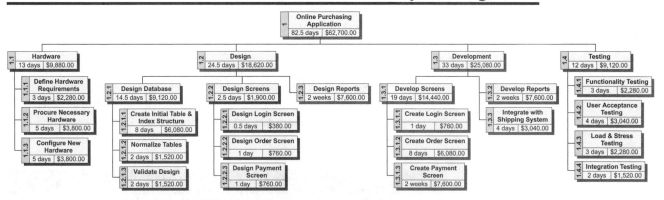

Sample WBS with time and cost estimates applied

Key Fact

Elements of a Good Work Breakdown Structure (WBS):

- It must be detailed down to a low level. The lowest level consists of work packages that define every deliverable on the project.

- It is graphical, arranged like a pyramid, where each sub-level rolls up to the level above it.

- It numbers each element, and the numbering system should allow anyone who reads the WBS to find individual elements quickly and easily.

- It should provide sufficient detail to drive the subsequent phases of planning.

- It may often be borrowed from other projects in the organization as a starting point. These starting points are known as templates.

- It is thorough and complete. If an item is not in the WBS, it does not get delivered with the project.

- It is central to the project.

- The project team, and not just the project manager, creates the WBS. Developing the WBS can also be a means of team-building.

- It is an integration tool, allowing you to see where the individual pieces of work fit into the project as a whole.

- It helps define responsibilities for the team.

- It is a communication tool.

Key Fact

WBS Dictionary

The WBS Dictionary is a document that details the contents of the WBS. Just as a language dictionary defines words, a WBS dictionary provides detailed information about the nodes on a WBS.

Because the WBS is graphical, there is a practical limit to how much information can be included in each node. The WBS dictionary solves this problem by capturing additional attributes about each work package in a different document that does not have the graphical constraints that the WBS does.

For each node in the WBS, the WBS dictionary might include the number of the node, the name of the node, the written requirements for the node, to whom it is assigned, and time, cost, and account information.

Project: Online Ordering Application	
Work Package ID: 1.1.3	
Work Package Name: Configure New Hardware	
Work Package Description: All new hardware should be configured, including any hardware settings and preparation such as formatting of storage. The correct operating system should be loaded and the appropriate patches should be applied. Any security settings, including virus scanning software, should be applied. The hardware should be added to the company domain and should be compliant with all company policy regarding hardware and security.	
Assigned to: Lee Abbott	**Department:** I.T.
Date Assigned: 2/24/05	**Date Due:** 2/20/06
Estimated Cost: $3,800.00	**Accounting Code:** HMIT-0229

Project Scope Management Plan Updates

The project scope management plan is the plan that specifies how the scope will be created, delivered, verified, and how changes will be made. As the work breakdown structure is created and the team's understanding of the work is improved, it is common for this plan to be updated.

Scope Baseline

A baseline (whether for scope, schedule, cost, or quality) is the original plan plus all approved changes. In this instance, the scope baseline represents the combination of the project scope statement, the WBS, and the WBS dictionary. When the scope baseline is created, it is placed under control, meaning that changes to the scope are made according to the scope management plan.

Requested Changes

The scope of a project is usually progressively elaborated, meaning that the team's understanding of the work to be performed progresses in iterations. Because of this, it is normal to have change requests generated as the team's understanding of the work improves. These requested changes may relate to areas of the project other than the scope, such as schedule, cost, or the contract.

Scope Verification

| Key Fact |

What it is:

Scope Verification is easily confused with other processes. Many people fall into the trap of thinking that Scope Verification means verifying that the scope is documented accurately; however, this is not correct. Scope Verification is the process of verifying that the product, service, or result of the project matches the documented scope.

In general, controlling processes compare the plan with the results to see where they differ and take the appropriate action. This fits Scope Verification very well, since the product is compared with the scope to ensure they match.

Scope Verification has quite a few similarities to the process of Quality Control, in that they both inspect the product against the scope; however, there are some key differences between them.

- Scope Verification is often performed after Quality Control, although it is not unusual for them to be performed at the same time.
- Scope Verification is primarily concerned with completeness, while Quality Control is primarily concerned with correctness.
- Scope Verification is concerned with the acceptance of the product by the project manager, the sponsor, the customer, and others, while Quality Control is concerned with adherence to the quality specification.

One more important note about Scope Verification is that if the project is canceled before completion, Scope Verification should be performed to document where the product was in relation to the scope at the point when the project ended.

Why it is important:

If the process of Scope Verification is successful, the product is accepted by the project manager, the customer, the sponsor, and sometimes by the functional managers and key stakeholders. This acceptance is a significant milestone in the life of the project.

When it is performed:

This process would be performed after at least some of the product components have been delivered, although it may be performed several times throughout the life of the project. As mentioned above, Scope Verification is typically performed at the same time as Quality Control or immediately following Quality Control.

How it works:

Inputs

Project Scope Statement

The project scope statement contains a detailed description of the project scope and deliverables, and it is this document that will be used to judge the results. The project scope statement will be used to ensure that the created product matches the scope completely.

WBS Dictionary

The WBS dictionary contains information on each work package in the work breakdown structure, such as to whom it was assigned, when it is due, where it will be performed, how much it should cost, etc. The WBS dictionary is often used in the process of Scope Verification to go through point-by-point and confirm that each work package was properly completed.

Project Scope Management Plan

The project scope management plan is an input into Scope Verification because it specifies how Scope Verification will be performed. It details who should be involved in this process and how it should be conducted.

Deliverables

Scope Verification is all about comparing the deliverables with the documented scope. This comparison may be performed several times during the life of the project.

Tools

Inspection

Inspection is the only tool employed in this process. It involves a point-by-point review of the scope and the associated deliverable. For instance, a pre-occupancy walkthrough by a building inspector would be an example of the tool of inspection. User-acceptance testing of a software product could be another example where the tool of inspection was used to make sure the deliverables matched the documented scope.

Outputs

Accepted Deliverables

Acceptance of the deliverables is the primary output of the process of Scope Verification. This process is typically performed by the project manager, the sponsor, the customer, and the functional managers.

Requested Changes

Change requests are a normal result of any inspection. When the deliverables are inspected in-depth and compared with the documented scope, change requests will often result.

Recommended Corrective Action

It is important to note that corrective action is not about fixing past mistakes. Instead, it is about asking, "What would we change to prevent this difference from happening again?" Corrective action is anything done to bring future results in line with the plan. It compares the plan with the results or deliverables and evaluates differences. Corrective action could be about changing the plan or changing the way in which the work was performed. The recommended corrective actions are a resulting output of Scope Verification.

Scope Control

What it is:

Scope Control is a process that lives up to its name. This process is about maintaining control of the project by preventing scope change requests from overwhelming the project, and also about making certain that scope change requests are properly handled.

One of the more challenging concepts behind Scope Control can be that of resolving disputes. Although many disputes over project scope or product requirements are not simple, keep in mind that the customer's interests should always be weighed heavily. That does not mean that the customer is always right! Instead, it means that the customer is one of the most important stakeholders. All other things being equal, disputes should be resolved in favor of the customer.

Why it is important:

Anyone who has managed a project where scope change was a problem knows the importance of Scope Control. This process makes certain all change requests are processed, and also that any of the underlying causes of scope change requests are understood and managed. It is important not only to manage scope change requests, but to prevent unnecessary ones.

When it is performed:

Scope Control is an ongoing process that begins as soon as the scope baseline is created. Until that point, the scope is not considered stable or complete enough to control; however, once the scope baseline is created, each scope change request must be carefully controlled and managed. Additionally, any time the work results are known to differ from the documented scope, this process should be performed, whether or not the scope change was requested in advance.

How it works:

Inputs

Project Scope Statement — See Chapter 5, Scope Definition, Outputs

Work Breakdown Structure — See Create WBS - Outputs

WBS Dictionary — See Create WBS - Outputs

As a general note regarding the three preceding inputs, you should understand that the project scope statement, work breakdown structure, and WBS dictionary all make up the scope baseline, and the process of Scope Control is all about controlling, managing, and influencing changes to this baseline.

Project Scope Management Plan

The project scope management plan, among other things, defines the scope change control system which specifies how changes and change requests to the scope will be managed. The project scope management plan gives us a road map for managing this process.

Performance Reports

The project's performance reports, an output of the Performance Reporting process discussed in Chapter 10 - Communications Management, give information on how the project is progressing, including components of the project that have been delivered.

Approved Change Requests

Approved changes to be made to the project scope statement, the WBS, or the WBS dictionary should be brought into this process as part of the overall effort to manage and control changes. Once the change is approved, it becomes part of the scope baseline.

Work Performance Information

This input is very similar in nature to the performance reports. It provides information on all aspects of the work completed as they relate to the project plan.

Tools

Change Control System

The scope change control system is the set of forms, tools, people, and procedures used to control changes to the scope baseline. The system, as it is defined here, is focused on the scope; however, it is also part of a larger change control system that controls changes across all aspects of the project.

Variance Analysis

Variance analysis can be used to measure differences between what was defined in the scope baseline and what was created. Variance analysis can be particularly useful in the process of Scope Control as a way to investigate and understand the root causes behind these differences.

Replanning

When changes are made to the project's scope baseline, additional planning must be performed in order to evaluate these changes in light of the cost, schedule, risk, quality, customer satisfaction, and other potential areas of the project management plan.

Configuration Management System

The configuration management system is the overall system used to receive change requests, review them, track them, and ultimately approve or reject them. The configuration management system may be thought of as the umbrella under which the other change control systems fit (i.e. Integrated Change Control system, scope change control system, schedule change control system, cost change control system, contract change control system).

One key to understanding the configuration management system is that it is focused on the physical characteristics of the product and not the overall project scope.

Outputs

Project Scope Statement Updates

To a large degree, the process of Scope Control is about managing change to the scope baseline, and as changes are made, updates are added to the project scope statement so that it maintains a current and accurate picture of the scope.

Work Breakdown Structure Updates

As scope changes are made to the scope baseline, these must be factored into updates to the WBS. If the change represents a new piece of scope, the work must be decomposed in the WBS down to work package level.

WBS Dictionary Updates

Any changes to the scope baseline that affect the work breakdown structure should also be updated in the WBS dictionary so that each work package description is current and accurate.

Key Fact

Scope Baseline Update

The scope baseline is comprised of the project scope statement, the work breakdown structure, and the WBS dictionary. Once the baseline is created, it may only be changed in a controlled manner. Any time a project scope change is approved, a corresponding update to the scope baseline must be made.

Requested Changes

As the project scope is controlled, change requests to the scope or to other areas of the project normally result. These change requests are funneled into the Integrated Change Control system, discussed previously in Chapter 4.

Recommended Corrective Action

As discussed earlier, corrective action is not about fixing past mistakes. Corrective action is anything done to bring future results in line with the plan. It compares the plan with the results or deliverables and evaluates differences. Again, corrective action is about asking, "What would we change to prevent this difference from happening again?" Corrective action could be about changing the plan or changing the way in which the work was performed. The recommended corrective actions are a resulting output of this process.

Organizational Process Assets Updates

Any time corrective action is implemented, changes may need to be made to the organizational process assets. The reason behind this is that the change or corrective action may have demonstrated that the organizational process assets you used (e.g. a previous project scope management plan or an organizational policy) were not wholly adequate for this project and need to be updated for future projects.

Project Management Plan Updates

The project management plan must be kept up to date throughout the life of the project. Any change in scope should be reflected in the project management plan, along with any other resulting changes in cost, schedule, risk, quality, contract, etc.

Scope Management Questions

1. Your project team is executing the work packages of your project when a serious disagreement regarding the interpretation of the scope is brought to your attention by two of your most trusted team members. How should this dispute be resolved?

   A. The project team should decide on the resolution.

   B. The dispute should be resolved in favor of the customer.

   C. The dispute should be resolved in favor of senior management.

   D. The project manager should consult the project charter for guidance.

2. Which of the following statements is FALSE regarding a work breakdown structure?

   A. Activities should be arranged in the sequence they will be performed.

   B. Every item should have a unique identifier.

   C. The work breakdown structure represents 100% of the work that will be done on the project.

   D. Each level of a work breakdown structure provides progressively smaller representations.

3. Mark has taken over a project that is beginning the construction phase of the product; however, he discovers that no work breakdown structure has been created. What choice represents the BEST course of action?

   A. He should refuse to manage the project.

   B. He should stop construction until the work breakdown structure has been created.

   C. He should consult the WBS dictionary to determine whether sufficient detail exists to properly manage construction.

   D. He should document this to senior management and provide added oversight on the construction phase.

4. The project has completed execution, and now it is time for the product of the project to be accepted. Who formally accepts the product?

   A. The project team and the customer.

   B. The quality assurance team, senior management, and the project manager.

   C. The sponsor, key stakeholders, and the customer.

   D. The project manager, senior management, and the change control board.

5. Creating the project scope statement is part of which process?

   A. Project Scope Management.

   B. Scope Planning.

   C. Scope Definition.

   D. Scope Verification.

6. The project scope statement should contain:

   A. The work packages for the project.

   B. A high level description of the scope.

   C. The level of effort associated with each scope element.

   D. A detailed description of the scope.

7. The most important part of Scope Verification is:

   A. Gaining formal acceptance of the project deliverables from the customer.

   B. Checking the scope of the project against stakeholder expectations.

   C. Verifying that the project came in on time and on budget.

   D. Verifying that the product met the quality specifications.

8. The organizational process assets would include all of the following except:

    A.   Historical information.

    B.   Organizational policies.

    C.   Lessons learned from previous projects.

    D.   The project management information system.

9. Which of the following is NOT part of the scope management plan?

    A.   The senior management statement of fitness for use.

    B.   The scope change control system.

    C.   A description of how the WBS will be created.

    D.   A description of how acceptance will be handled.

10. You have taken over as project manager for a data warehouse project that is completing the design phase; however, change requests are still pouring in from many sources, including your boss. Which of the following would have been MOST helpful in this situation:

    A.   A project sponsor who is involved in the project.

    B.   A well-defined scope management plan.

    C.   A change control board.

    D.   A change evaluation system.

11. What is the function of the project sponsor?

    A.   To help manage senior management expectations.

    B.   To be the primary interface with the customer.

    C.   To fund the project and formally accept the product.

    D.   To help exert control over the functional managers.

12.   The project manager and the customer on a project are meeting together to review the product of the project against the documented scope. Which tool would be MOST appropriate to use during this meeting?

    A.   Verification analysis.

    B.   Inspection.

    C.   Gap analysis.

    D.   Feature review.

13.   You have just assumed responsibility for a project that is in progress. While researching the project archives, you discover that the WBS dictionary was never created. Which of the following problems would LEAST likely be attributable to this?

    A.   Confusion about the meaning of specific work packages.

    B.   Confusion about who is responsible for a specific work package.

    C.   Confusion about which account to bill against for a specific work package.

    D.   Confusion about how to change a specific work package.

14.   A team member makes a change to a software project without letting anyone else know. She assures you that it did not affect the schedule, and it significantly enhances the product. What should the project manager do FIRST?

    A.   Find out if the customer authorized this change.

    B.   Submit the change to the change control board.

    C.   Review the change to understand how it affects scope, cost, time, quality, risk, and customer satisfaction.

    D.   Make sure the change is reflected in the scope management plan.

15. The product you have delivered has been reviewed carefully against the scope and is now being brought to the customer for formal acceptance. Which process is the project in?

    A.   Scope Verification.

    B.   Scope Auditing.

    C.   Scope Closure.

    D.   Scope Control.

Answers to Scope Management Questions

1. B. In general, disagreements should be resolved in favor of the customer. In this case, the customer is the best choice of the four presented. 'A' is not a good choice because it is your job to keep the team focused on doing the work and out of meetings where they are arguing about the scope. Besides, the team brought you this problem, so their ability to resolve it is already in question. 'C' is incorrect because all things being equal, project disputes should be resolved in favor of the customer and not in favor of senior management. Since you don't have enough information to steer you toward senior management, resolving it in favor of the customer was the right choice here. 'D' is incorrect because the project charter is a very general and high-level document. As it is issued before either the scope statement or the work breakdown structure is created, it would be of little use in resolving an issue of scope dispute that occurred during execution.

2. A. You don't tackle activity sequencing as part of the work breakdown structure. That part comes later. The WBS has no particular sequence to it, not to mention that it is not decomposed to activity level. 'B' is incorrect since every WBS element does have a unique identifier. 'C' is incorrect since the WBS is the definitive source for all of the work to be done. Remember – if it isn't in the WBS, it isn't part of the project. Choice 'D' is incorrect because the WBS is arranged as a pyramid with the top being the most general, and the bottom being the most specific. The lowest level of the WBS would also be the smallest representation of work.

3. B. In this situation, you cannot simply skip the WBS, as you may be tempted to do. Mark should take time to create the WBS, which is usually not a lengthy process. 'A' may sound good, but in reality a project manager needs to be ready to work to solve most problems. You might refuse to manage a project if there is an ethical dilemma or a conflict of interest, but not in other circumstances. 'C' is incorrect since the WBS dictionary cannot be created properly unless the WBS was created first. If there is a WBS dictionary and no WBS, that would be a big red flag. 'D' is incorrect since merely documenting that there is a serious problem is not a solution. Additionally, providing more oversight would not solve the problem here. The real problem is that the WBS has not been created, and that will trickle down to more serious problems in the future of the project.

4.   C. The project manager verifies the product with the key stakeholders, the sponsor, and the customer.

5.   C. The project scope statement is created as part of two processes. The first is "Create Preliminary Scope Statement," which is part of integration management, and the second is Scope Definition, where the preliminary scope statement is elaborated into the project scope statement. 'C' is the only one of those processes of the four choices provided.

6.   D. The project scope statement needs to include a detailed description of the scope. Choice 'A' is incorrect as the WBS is created later as part of the Create WBS process. 'B' is tricky, but it is incorrect. The preliminary scope statement contains a high level description of the scope, but the project scope statement is detailed. 'C' is incorrect, because the level of effort is estimated after the scope has been defined.

7.   A. It is important to understand the processes and their inputs and outputs! Whereas all of these choices may be important, the only one that is listed as a part of Scope Verification is to get customer acceptance of the product. The other activities may be done during the project, but they aren't part of the Scope Verification process. 'D' is close, but that is formally part of the Quality Control process.

8.   D. Organizational process assets include historical information, organizational policies (since those policies may help or constrain your activities), and lessons learned from previous projects. The PMIS (project management information system) is a group of tools used together as a system, but it is not considered part of organizational process assets.

9.   A is the only choice that is not part of the scope management plan. It is a made up term. 'B', 'C', and 'D' all belong.

10.   B. This one is tricky. If you missed it, don't feel bad, but it is important to know that questions like this are on the exam. The reason 'B' is correct is that the scope management plan contains a plan for how changes will be handled. If too many changes are pouring in, it is likely that the scope management plan was not well defined. 'A' is incorrect because it is not the sponsor's role to control change. He or she is paying you to handle that. 'C' is incorrect because if the change control board exists on your project, it only evaluates changes. The board is almost always reactive, not proactive. 'D' is incorrect since the change evaluation system is a made up term not found in PMI's processes.

Scope Mgt Answers

11.   C. It is the sponsor's job to pay for the project and to accept the product. Choice 'A' is really the project manager's job. 'B' is the project manager's job as well. It is not a clearly defined job for the sponsor. 'D' is not a function of the sponsor. If more control were needed over the functional managers, that would be the role of senior management.

12.   B. The project manager and customer are involved in the Scope Verification process, and the tool used here is inspection. The product is inspected to see if it matches the documented scope. 'A', 'C', and 'D' are not documented as part of the processes.

13.   D is the best choice here. The WBS dictionary contains attributes about each work package such as an explanation of the work package (which invalidates choice 'A'), who is assigned responsibility for the work package (which invalidates choice 'B'), and a cost account code (which invalidates choice 'C'). If a work package were changed, that would most likely alter the scope baseline, and information on how to go about this would be found in the scope management plan and not the WBS dictionary.

14.   C. Notice the use of the word 'FIRST'. 'A' is wrong because the customer should never bypass the project manager to authorize changes directly. It is the project manager's job to authorize changes on the project. 'B' is incorrect since all changes might not go to the change control board. Even if a change control board exists on the project, the project manager doesn't automatically just send everything their way. The project manager should deal with it first. 'D' is incorrect because the scope management plan is not even the place this would be reflected. The scope baseline would need to be updated, but only after the change had been properly evaluated.

15.   A. The customer accepts the scope of the product in Scope Verification.

Chapter 5

Time Management

6

From the indicators at the top of the page, you can tell that you may find this chapter to be slightly more difficult than the previous chapter on scope management. In order to help you prepare for this topic, this book has clearly broken down the practices and outlined the techniques and formulas you need to know in order to ace the questions on the exam. By the time you are through with this chapter, you may well have a higher level of confidence here than on any other section of the test.

Spending extra time in this chapter will yield direct dividends on the exam! Make sure that you learn both the processes and the techniques so that you may approach these questions with absolute confidence.

Philosophy

Project Time Management is concerned primarily with resources, activities, scheduling and schedule management. PMI's philosophy here, as elsewhere, is that the project manager should be in control of the schedule, and not vice versa. The schedule is built from the ground up, derived from the scope baseline and other information, and rigorously managed throughout the life of the project.

There are six processes related to time management that you should understand. They are:

1. Activity Definition (list the project activities)

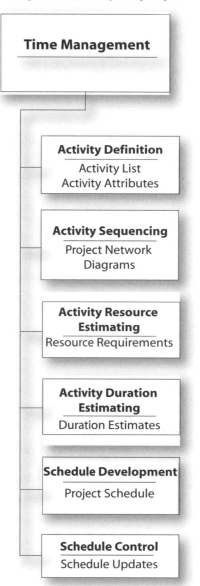

The processes of Project Time Management with their *primary* outputs

Time Management

Activity Definition
Activity List
Activity Attributes

Activity Sequencing
Project Network Diagrams

Activity Resource Estimating
Resource Requirements

Activity Duration Estimating
Duration Estimates

Schedule Development
Project Schedule

Schedule Control
Schedule Updates

2. Activity Sequencing (order the activities and create the project network diagram)
3. Activity Resource Estimating (estimating the resources needed to complete each activity)
4. Activity Duration Estimating (determine time estimates for each activity)
5. Schedule Development (create the schedule)
6. Schedule Control (monitor schedule performance)

You will see from reading this chapter that the driving philosophy behind time management is mathematical; it is primarily cold, hard analysis. The project manager does not merely accept whatever schedule goals are handed down or suggested. Instead, he builds the schedule based on the work to be done and then seeks to make it conform to other calendar requirements, constraints, and strategic goals.

Additionally, while most of the topics within the PMBOK Guide are related, the topics of scope, time, and cost (and to a slightly lesser degree, quality and risk) are particularly tightly linked. Changes made to one area will almost certainly have impacts elsewhere.

As in other areas, PMI prefers that project managers begin from the bottom up. The WBS, which was covered in the previous chapter, is a key input to time management processes. Using this comprehensive list of deliverables, you now define the work that must be done in order to produce these deliverables. Like the items in the WBS, the individual activities are then sequenced, and the resource and duration estimates are applied to these activities.

This approach has many similarities to the practices in scope management. Most similar is that your analysis and outputs are comprehensive and complete.

Importance

Time management is of high importance, both in the application of PMI's processes and on the exam. You should expect to see several questions on the exam where you will need to apply formulas, calculate the critical path, and determine the effect of a change to the schedule.

The difficulties that many people encounter here fall into three categories:

1. Modern project managers typically rely on software to perform schedule and time calculations. While this is not a bad thing, being a CAPM requires that you understand the theories and practices for time management that underlie the software.

2. Some people are intimidated by the mathematical and logical aspects of this section. Although the math is relatively simple, it does require memorization of a few key formulas.

3. Some project managers do not understand the diagramming techniques and processes. A reliance on intuition will not get you very far on these questions. You either know how to calculate them or you do not. It is far better to spend time learning the techniques than to try to fumble your way through them on the exam.

Preparation

There are six processes in the time management knowledge area. These are Activity Definition, Activity Sequencing, Activity Resource Estimating, Activity Duration Estimating, Schedule Development, and Schedule Control. Below are the break-outs that show to which process group each item belongs:

Process Group	Time Management Process
Initiating	(none)
Planning	Activity Definition, Activity Sequencing, Activity Resource Estimating, Activity Duration Estimating, Schedule Development
Executing	(none)
Monitoring & Controlling	Schedule Control
Closing	(none)

In the knowledge area of time management, it is also essential that you know the main outputs that are produced during each process. The different key outputs that are created in each process are summarized in the chart below.

Process	Key Output(s)
Activity Definition	Activity list, Milestone list
Activity Sequencing	Project schedule network diagrams
Activity Resource Estimating	Activity resource requirements, Resource breakdown structure
Activity Duration Estimating	Activity duration estimates
Schedule Development	Project schedule, Schedule baseline
Schedule Control	Performance measurements, Recommended corrective actions

Activity Definition

What it is:

Once the scope baseline has been created, it is used to decompose the work into activity detail. The main result of this planning process is the activity list. This list represents all of the schedule activities that need to take place for the project to be completed. This is primarily accomplished by taking the WBS and decomposing the work packages even further until they represent schedule activities. The difference between work packages in a WBS and an activity list is that the activity list is more granular and is decomposed into individual schedule activities. Work packages will often contain bundles of related activities that may involve multiple groups of people. It is these activities that comprise the activity list. The activity list is used as the basis for the next three planning processes, Activity Sequencing, Activity Duration Estimating, and Activity Resource Estimating.

If the project is being performed under procurement, this planning process will most likely be performed by the subcontracting organization, with the results being provided to the organization that is responsible for the management of the overall project.

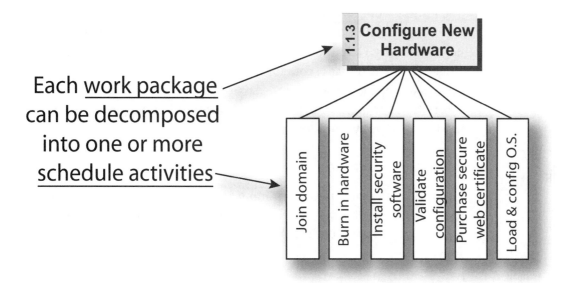

Each <u>work package</u> can be decomposed into one or more <u>schedule activities</u>

Why it is important:

Earlier in project scope management, we focused on what work needed to be performed on the project. Now, in time management, we need to focus on how and when it is accomplished. The activity list will be an essential input into building the schedule, so it is important that it be both complete and correct.

When it is performed:

The process of Activity Definition is often performed as soon as the scope has been baselined. In other words, it is common to create the activity list after the project scope statement, the work breakdown structure, and the WBS dictionary have been created and are in a stable form; however, it is also acceptable to create the activity list at the same time as the work breakdown structure and the WBS dictionary.

How it works:

Inputs

Enterprise Environmental Factors — See Chapter 2, Common Inputs

Organizational Process Assets — See Chapter 2, Common Inputs

Project Scope Statement

The project scope statement is part of the scope baseline. It contains a thorough description of the project's deliverables which will be used here in Activity Definition. Another important feature of the project scope statement is that it contains the constraints and assumptions. As the scope is being translated into activities in this process, anything that constrains your decision making, or any assumptions you are making, should be carefully considered.

Work Breakdown Structure

The WBS is the most important input into this process, since its work packages will be decomposed further down to activity level. Each work package at the bottom of the WBS will be decomposed into one or more activities.

WBS Dictionary — See Chapter 5, Create WBS

Project Management Plan — See Chapter 4, Develop Project Mgt. Plan

Tools

Decomposition

If you understood decomposition as it was used in the Create WBS process, you should have no problems understanding it here. Each work package at the bottom of the WBS is simply decomposed into smaller pieces, known as schedule activities. The project manager should solicit heavy involvement from the project team or the functional managers in this process.

Templates

Similar to the Create WBS process, templates for Activity Definition provide a starting point for the project manager. These templates may exist as examples from previous similar projects, or they may be commercially available activity list examples or even basic skeletal templates provided by the organization's project office.

Regardless of the format or the source of these templates, they provide the project team with a starting point rather than forcing them to build the activity list from scratch.

Rolling Wave Planning

The concept of rolling wave planning is a form of progressive elaboration that models project planning the way we see things in the real world.

Suppose, for example, that you are standing at the edge of a field. You may be able to see some things in great detail, even counting individual blades of grass at your feet. The further off you look, however, the less detail you will be able to perceive. Distant objects, such as a mountain range miles away, would appear general and hazy.

Rolling wave planning mirrors this construct by assuming that things in the near future should be relatively clear, while project activities in the future may not be as detailed or as easily understood. Armed with that perspective, a project manager may choose to carefully decompose certain work packages, with anticipated execution in the near term, in great detail, while delaying analysis on work packages that will not be accomplished until later in the project.

This type of planning must be revisited throughout the project, much as waves continually pound the shore.

Activity Definition

Activity Definition

Rolling wave planning is used more frequently on projects like the creation of an I.T. system, and less often on construction projects within the construction industry where unknowns may cost millions of dollars.

Expert Judgment

Expert judgment in decomposing activities may come from numerous sources, including team members, consultants, and functional managers. One of the best sources for expertise in decomposing a work package into an activity may be the person who will ultimately be responsible for executing the work package or the schedule activity, although that may not be known at this point.

Planning Component

There are times when the project team cannot decompose the work breakdown structure down to a low level because they do not have enough information. When this situation occurs, a node on the WBS will not be decomposed down to work package level.

So if no work package exists, how will the project team decompose activities? The answer is that the team does not create an activity list from these nodes. Instead, they create a planning component, which is simply a sort of summary activity that will be revisited once its parent WBS node has been defined in sufficient detail.

A control account is one type of planning component. This control account is represented as a node on the work breakdown structure. Control accounts are typically placed on nodes on the work breakdown structure where no actual work packages have been defined yet. Higher level planning is performed against the control accounts and is a way for the team to continue planning when one or more components of the project are not clear at a point in time.

Outputs

Activity List

All of the schedule activities that need to be performed in order to complete the project are compiled into the activity list. Each activity in the list should map back to one and only one work package (a work package, however, typically has more than one activity belonging to it). The activities should include enough information to transition them to the project team so that the work may be performed.

The activity list's usefulness is tied to its completeness and accuracy. It is important to identify and document each activity that must be performed in order to complete the project.

It is important to note that a line exists between the work breakdown structure and the activity list. Although the activity list is an extension of the work breakdown structure, it is not a part of the work breakdown structure. The activities are used to create the project schedule.

The activity list by itself is generally limited only to an identifier, such as an activity name or a unique numeric identifier, and a description.

Activity Attributes

As planning progresses, there will be a need to store additional information about activities. For example, the person responsible for this activity, the parts that need to be procured before this activity may be started, and the location the work will be performed could be highly important.

Activity attributes may be stored with the activity list or in a separate document and are typically added after the initial activity list has been created.

Note that any time you see the activity list, you will also see the activity attributes. The activity attributes may be thought of as an expansion of the activity list.

Key Fact

Milestone List

The key project milestones are produced as a part of this plan. These milestones may be related to imposed dates such as a contractual obligation, or projected dates based on historical information.

This list of milestones will become essential in building the schedule.

Requested Changes

As with many other key planning processes, as the process of Activity Definition is performed, change requests are a normal output. These change requests will relate to previous planning outputs that are used in this process, such as the scope baseline.

Activity Sequencing

What it is:

The Activity Sequencing process is primarily concerned with taking the activity list defined earlier and arranging the activities in the order they must be performed.

This process is all about understanding and diagramming the relationships that schedule activities have with each other.

Schedule activities logically sequenced

Why it is important:

Project schedule network diagrams have traditionally been an important part of the CAPM Exam. A network logic diagram is a picture in which each activity is drawn in the order it must be performed, and the amount of time each activity takes is represented with numbers. Activity Sequencing is the planning process in which network diagrams are produced.

Network diagramming is the preferred method for representing activities, their dependencies, and sequences.

Two examples of network logic diagramming techniques, the precedence diagramming method and the arrow diagramming method, are discussed later in this chapter.

When it is performed:

Because of the flow of inputs and outputs between other processes, the process of Activity Sequencing must be performed after Activity Definition and before Schedule Development.

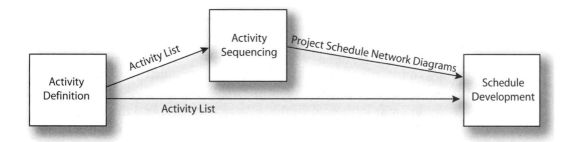

Activity Definition must be performed before Activity Sequencing or Schedule Development.

How it works:

Inputs

Project Scope Statement

The description of the project's scope will often give you information about the project that will influence the order in which certain activities are performed. For instance, if a computer system contained hardware and software, it might be necessary to procure and configure the hardware before constructing the software.

This may seem like common sense, but the project scope statement is used to ensure that nothing is missed.

Activity List

The activity list is the most important input into Activity Sequencing. It is in this process that the schedule activities from the activity list will be arranged, or sequenced, into a diagram that represents the order in which they must be performed.

Activity Attributes

The activity attributes, produced in Activity Definition, are brought into this process since they contain additional information about each activity that may influence how it is sequenced.

Milestone List

Milestones are events that must be considered in the life of the project.

There is an interesting relationship between milestones and the process of Activity Sequencing. Milestones are often imposed from outside the project (e.g. the project sponsor indicates an overall deliverable date), and activities typically come from within the project (e.g. the decomposition of work packages). Because of this, activities will often need to be arranged in a specific way in order to meet key milestones. For instance, if the customer specified a milestone of a pre-construction walkthrough at a certain point in time, then the activity of cleaning up the worksite may need to be sequenced in earlier than would otherwise be necessary.

Approved Change Requests

Any approved change requests may affect Activity Sequencing and must be factored in for planning.

Tools

Precedence Diagramming Method (PDM)

The precedence diagramming method creates a graphical representation of the schedule activities in the order in which they must be performed on the project.

Activities are represented by the nodes (rectangles), with arrows representing the dependencies that exist between the activities.

The project network diagram illustrated below uses the activity on node convention to represent the activities. In this case, the nodes are shown as rectangles, and the activities are represented inside the node, usually by letters of the alphabet. Units of duration are shown above the nodes.

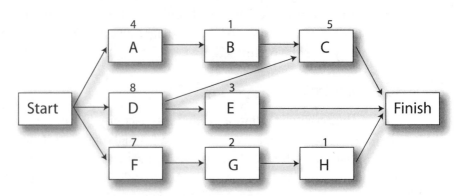

Key Fact

Arrow Diagramming Method (ADM)

The arrow diagramming method is another way of graphically representing the activities and their dependencies on a project. The arrow diagramming method, however, differs from the precedence diagramming method described earlier. When using the arrow diagramming method, the activities are not on the nodes. Instead, the activities are represented on the arrows, with the nodes being connecting points. The nodes for activity on arrow are typically represented as circles, which helps to visually differentiate them from the activity on node diagrams.

The diagrams that result from the arrow diagramming method are known as "activity on arrow" diagrams. The illustration below represents a project network diagram for activity on arrow.

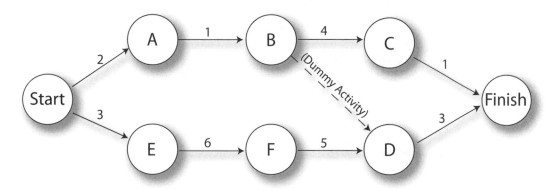

Note that a key difference between the Arrow Diagramming Method and the Precedence Diagramming Method is the ability of Activity on Arrow diagrams to show an activity with a duration of 0, such as the one depicted above in activity B-D. These activities, shown with a dashed line, are called "dummy activities." Dummy activities force the creation of new paths through the network. In the example above, activity D-Finish cannot begin until activity A-B (as well as activity F-D) is complete. Activity on arrow diagrams can contain these dummy activities with a duration of 0, while activity on node diagrams cannot.

Schedule Network Templates

Templates may be anything from an example on a previous project to a standard format issued by the project management office. Templates may contain a section from a previous project. This segment is known as a subnetwork or a fragment network.

Subnetworks or fragment networks may be particularly helpful when projects are highly similar. For instance, the activities and the sequences involved in building and testing an airplane may be highly similar from one project to another within the same organization. Using subnetworks or fragment networks prevents having to "reinvent the wheel" each time the process of Activity Sequencing is performed.

Key Fact

Dependency Determination

Dependencies are those things that influence which activities must be performed first. For example, a road must be graded before it can be paved. If grading and paving the road were two activities on the project, then we would say that the start of the activity of paving the road is dependent upon the finish of the activity of grading the road, thus these two activities have a finish-to-start relationship.

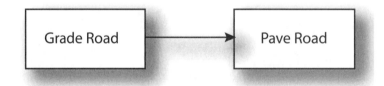

There are three kinds of dependencies that may exist among activities.

Mandatory Dependencies

A mandatory dependency is one that cannot be broken. Given the example where paving the road is dependent upon grading it, the dependency is unavoidable, or mandatory. Mandatory dependencies are traditionally known as hard logic, since a mandatory dependency is considered unmovable and always true.

Discretionary Dependencies

Discretionary dependencies, unlike the preceding example, are not always true. These would often be the result of best practices, and may vary organization to organization and even project to project. For instance, the project of managing the remodeling of a house may have a discretionary dependency between painting the walls and carpeting the floors, where painting must be completed before carpeting could be installed. There is no absolute rule that says the carpet could not be installed before the painting begins.

Discretionary dependencies are also known as soft logic or preferred logic and are typically based on historical information, expert judgment, and best practices.

External Dependencies

External dependencies are those dependencies that must be considered but are outside of the project's control and scope. For instance, if an automobile is being developed to use alternative technology, there may be an external dependency on a supplier providing a battery that meets certain specifications before the project can meet its schedule. Because these are dependencies, they must be identified and documented as part of this process.

Apply Leads and Lags

A lead is simply one activity getting a jump start on another. Consider, for instance, a software project that has a dependency between finishing the development of a section of code and beginning the quality inspection. Since the development has to finish before the testing begins, we would say that a mandatory finish-to-start dependency exists between the two activities.

An example of a lead would be if the individual performing the quality inspection gets an unfinished beta copy of the software in order to get a head start. Note that leads do not do away with the finish to start relationship that exists. Instead, it simply "cheats" that relationship.

Leads, and the rationale behind them, must be clearly explained and documented.

Think of a lag as a waiting period that exists between two activities. A lag is a situation where a waiting period must occur between one activity and another dependent activity. An example of a lag would be if one activity was to order a computer server and another activity was to configure the server, then a lag might exist between the time the server is ordered and the time it arrives and can be configured. During this lag, there is no work being performed by the organization against this activity; no resources are being expended. They are simply waiting.

Outputs

Project Schedule Network Diagrams

The name of this output may be slightly misleading. Although it is used later in creating the schedule, the schedule network diagram is not the schedule. In other words, no start or finish dates are assigned to the activities yet. They are simply arranged in the order they need to be performed on the project.

A project schedule network diagram may include a full representation of every activity in the project, or it may include summary nodes. In the event that a summary node is used, enough documentation should be included so that the basic flow of activities may be understood.

Hammock Diagrams

A hammock diagram is a way of representing a project network diagram with the schedule activities summarized in summary activities (called hammock activities). Its name comes from the way the schedule activities hang off of the hammock activities.

Graphical Evaluative Review Technique (GERT)

As addressed earlier in this chapter, project network diagrams are typically create using either the Precedence Diagramming Method (PDM) or the Arrow Diagramming Method (ADM); however, there is a third method that is sometimes used for technical schedule representations. This method is known as the Graphical Evaluative Review Technique, or GERT. The resulting GERT diagrams are much like the Activity on Node diagrams created by PDM, except for one key difference. GERT diagrams can show branches and loops, whereas other representations cannot. For instance, if you know that you may need to repeat a process several times, GERT can represent that fact, or if you want to represent an if/then condition in your schedule, GERT has the ability to show that. GERT has fallen in popularity with practioneers and software tools in recent years but is still widely used in some industries.

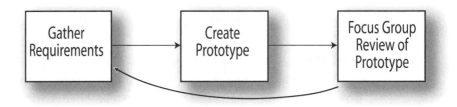

An fragment of a GERT diagram

Activity List Updates

As activities are arranged and their relationships understood, changes to the activity list are a normal by-product.

Activity Attributes Updates

As updates to the activity list are made, corresponding updates to the activity attributes must be made as well.

Requested Changes

As the activities, their relationships, and their dependencies are understood in greater detail, change requests to the project are a normal by-product.

Activity Resource Estimating

What it is:

How long an activity takes is usually a function of determining the size of the activity, the number of resources that will be applied to it, and the resource availability. This process is all about analyzing the project activity to determine the resource requirements.

Why it is important:

Understanding the number of resources required to complete an activity and determining how long they will be used for that activity is an important step in project planning and an essential ingredient to the schedule, which will be developed later.

When it is performed:

Because the process of Activity Resource Estimating uses the activity list and activity attributes, it must be performed after Activity Definition. Additionally, since the output of this process is used to build the project schedule, this process must be performed before Schedule Development. This process often goes hand in hand with Cost Estimating, since cost and time are closely linked.

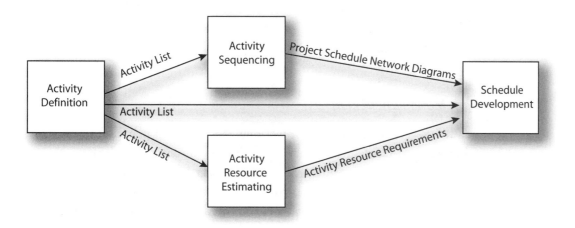

How it works:

Inputs

Enterprise Environmental Factors

Every project environment is different, and these different factors will influence how long an activity will take. For instance, an activity could require access to an aircraft manufacturer's flight simulation systems, or a project that had some manufacturing as an activity might require access to the organization's facilities in order to perform this activity.

Organizational Process Assets — See Chapter 2, Common Inputs

Key Fact

Activity List

The activity list is the most important input into this process. Each activity in the list will be evaluated and the resources will be estimated for it.

Activity Attributes

In your mind, the activity attributes should be virtually indistinguishable from the activity list. The two always go together. In this case, the activity attributes give expanded information on each activity in the activity list.

Key Fact

Resource Availability

Resources may include both physical resource and human resources, and their availability needs to be factored into the process of Activity Resource Estimating. For instance, a piece of heavy machinery may currently be available only during the months of April and May, which must be considered.

Project Management Plan

While several pieces of the project management plan may be helpful here, it is the schedule management plan, a component of the project management plan, created in Develop Project Management Plan, which is particularly helpful. The schedule management plan specifies how the schedule will be developed and managed and how changes to the schedule will be managed.

Tools

Expert Judgment

There is no substitute for asking for expert opinion on how to estimate resource needs for an activity. Asking someone who has performed this type of activity previously, a functional manager, or even the resource who will be performing the work can bring insight into the resource needs for the activities.

Alternatives Analysis

The old saying goes that "there is more than one way to skin a cat," implying that just because one way has been identified, alternatives may still be helpful. This could include outsourcing an activity, purchasing a software component off the shelf rather than building one, or using a totally different approach to complete the activity.

Published Estimating Data

Some industries have extensive data available through published, recognized sources that can help in estimating. For instance, if you take a car to a body shop for repair, they often have books provided by the insurance industry with almost every conceivable repair listed, along with how long the repair should take for an experienced person to complete.

This type of data can help give insight into the Activity Resource Estimating process.

Project Management Software

Software is a means, not the end. It can help the project manager store and organize information, experiment with alternatives, and rapidly perform the routine calculations.

Bottom-Up Estimating

It may be that you encounter an activity that cannot be estimated, either because it has not been broken down enough, or because it is simply too complex. In this case, it is appropriate to break down the activity further into progressively smaller pieces of work until these pieces may be estimated for their resource requirements.

Once these estimations have been performed, the pieces may be summed up from the bottom back to activity level.

Outputs

Activity Resource Requirements

The resources required for each schedule activity are the primary output of Activity Resource Estimating. These resources include the kind of resource and the number of these resources. The activity resource requirements need to specify, for instance, if two senior programmers are required for four months or if three junior programmers are required for five months.

Each activity resource requirement should be documented with sufficient detail to explain the decision making process used to arrive at these estimates.

Activity Attribute Updates

As the resources are analyzed for each activity, updates to the activity attributes are a normal by-product.

Resource Breakdown Structure

The resource breakdown structure, or RBS, is similar in many ways to the WBS. It is graphical and hierarchical, logically arranged from top to bottom, and it arranges the resources by category and type.

Resource Calendar (Updates)

The resource calendar, which is first produced in Develop Project Management Plan, is focused on resource utilization. It shows when the resources will be used and when they will be available for use elsewhere. For instance, if a mobile construction crane were going to be used in the first and fourth weeks of June, that would be reflected as an update on the resource calendar so that functional managers or other projects in the organization might be able to utilize it during the second and third weeks of June.

The resource calendar applies to both human and physical resources, and it applies to all resources to be used throughout the life of the project. It is first developed as part of the project management plan, but it is revised here when more details are known about the resources.

Requested Changes

As progressively detailed planning is performed, change requests to the project's scope or schedule are normal outputs of Activity Resource Estimating.

Activity Duration Estimating

What it is:

This process is exactly what it sounds like. Each activity in the activity list is analyzed to estimate how long it will take.

There is an important difference between duration and level of effort, and this process focuses on determining duration.

The duration of an activity is a function of many factors, including who will be doing the work, when they are available, how many resources will be assigned to this activity, and the amount of work contained in the activity.

Why it is important:

These activity duration estimates will become a primary input into creating the schedule when the overall project timeline has been created.

When it is performed:

Activity Duration Estimating is performed after the activity resource requirements have been gathered and before the schedule is developed.

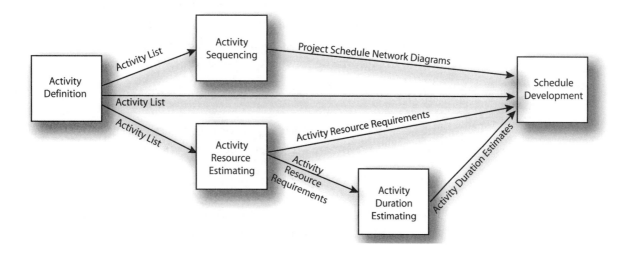

A diagram showing the order of Time Management's planning processes

Activity Duration Estimating *(sidebar)*

How it works:

Inputs

Enterprise Environmental Factors

Factors such as what records an organization requires, safety standards, and regulations can all affect how long an activity takes. For instance, it may take far longer to perform an activity in a nuclear power plant than it does in a conventional power plant due to enterprise environmental factors, and these must be considered in order to accurately estimate the duration of activities.

Organizational Process Assets

Organizational process assets could take the form of a rich database of historical information that shows the estimated and actual durations for activities for a previous project, while another organization may have specific calendar requirements when shifts or resources are available. Anything that gives structure or guidance to your Activity Duration Estimating would be considered an organizational process asset.

Project Scope Statement

The project scope statement, created earlier in Scope Definition, has the constraints and assumptions for the project that can affect this process. For instance, a constraint that a particular component of a house had to be built at a different facility and transported to the construction site would influence the activity's duration. Likewise, an assumption that a particular component of a software product could be completed by a subcontracting firm faster than it could be built internally would be helpful in performing for Activity Duration Estimating.

Activity List

The activity list is a primary input for this process. Every activity in the list should be estimated to determine its duration.

Activity Attributes

The activity attributes always accompany the activity list. These attributes provide additional information about each activity in the list.

Activity Resource Requirements

Since the duration is a function of the amount of work associated with this activity and the resources assigned to perform that work, the activity resource requirements need to be brought into this process.

Resource Calendar

This is the resource calendar that was updated in the Activity Resource Estimating process. This calendar shows physical and human resource usage across the entire project.

Project Management Plan

The project management plan is the single unified plan that details how the project will be executed, monitored, and controlled. For the process of Activity Duration Estimating, there are two components of particular interest. They are the risk register and the activity cost estimates.

The risk register provides details on the identified risks. At this point it is appropriate to review it for risks that might affect the duration of an activity. For instance, if weather is identified as a risk on a construction project, it may be appropriate to update the activity durations to reflect the risk.

If the activity cost estimates have been created at this point, then they may provide some guidance to the process of Activity Duration Estimating.

Tools

Expert Judgment

Anyone who has managed a project will attest that the duration of an activity can be notoriously hard to estimate in advance. The expert providing the judgment should follow some basis, such as historical information, whether documented or experiential.

Analogous Estimating

Analogous estimating, also known as top-down estimating, is where an activity from a project previously performed within the organization is used to help estimate another activity's duration.

Typically, the previous actual time spent on the similar activity is used as the estimate for another similar activity. The technique is combined with expert judgment to determine if the two activities are truly alike.

Parametric Estimating

If one team can install 100 feet of fence in one day, then it would take 10 teams to install 1,000 feet of fence in one day. This kind of linear extrapolation is an example of parametric estimating.

Parametric estimating can work well for activities that are either linear or easily scaled. It is not as effective for activities that have not been performed before or those for which little or no historical information has been gathered.

Three-Point Estimates

Three-point estimates, also called PERT estimates, use three data points for the duration instead of simply one. These are pessimistic, most likely (also known as realistic) and optimistic estimates.

As an example of how this is used, suppose a developer estimates that it will most likely take 9 days to write a module of code; however, he also supplies an optimistic estimate of 7 days and a pessimistic estimate of 17 days.

The project manager then applies a formula, usually in the form of a weighted average to these estimates to distill them down to a single estimate. The traditional formula for this is:

$$\frac{\text{Pessimistic} + 4X \text{ Realistic} + \text{Optimistic}}{6}$$

where P is pessimistic, O is optimistic, and R is the most likely, or realistic estimate.

In the example above, the numbers would be substituted as $(17 + 4*9 + 7) / 6 = 10$ days. This number is used as the activity duration estimate for this schedule activity.

Another important formula to memorize for the exam is used to calculate the standard deviation for an estimate.

$$\sigma = \frac{\text{Pessimistic} - \text{Optimistic}}{6}$$

The value for standard deviation tells us how diverse our estimates are. If an activity has a pessimistic and an optimistic estimate that are very far apart, the standard deviation (σ) will be very high, indicating a high degree of uncertainty and consequently a high degree of risk for this estimate. Note that this is not a real standard deviation; however, it is a widely used substitute formula in estimating activity durations.

Given these formulas, let us consider the following estimates for activities A, B, and C.

Activity	Optimistic	Pessimistic	Realistic
A	22	35	25
B	60	77	70
C	12	40	20

Now, using the formulas above, we will calculate the three point estimate for each of these activities.

Activity	Optimistic	Pessimistic	Realistic	3 Point Estimate
A	22	35	25	26.17
B	60	77	70	69.5
C	12	40	20	22

Reserve Analysis

Reserve time, also called contingency, is extra time added to a schedule activity duration estimate.

Reserve time estimates are revisited throughout the life of the project, being revised up or down as more information on schedule risk becomes available.

Outputs

Activity Duration Estimates

All of the preceding inputs and tools for this process are used together to produce one main output: the activity duration estimates.

The activity duration estimates contain an estimated duration for each activity in the activity list. Ideally these estimates represent a range such as the optimistic, pessimistic, realistic one represented in the three point estimate technique discussed earlier in this process.

Activity Attribute Updates

As each activity is being estimated at a low level, updates to the activity attributes are a normal by-product of this process.

Activity Duration Estimating

Schedule Development

What it is:

The process of Schedule Development is one of the largest of the 44 PMBOK Guide processes, containing a whopping 27 combined inputs, tools, and outputs.

As anyone who has managed a complex project will attest, developing the schedule can be one of the most daunting parts of the project.

Why it is important:

The schedule is one of the most visible and important parts of the project plan. In fact, many inexperienced project managers often mistakenly refer to the schedule as the project plan or use the two terms interchangeably.

As you could guess by the name, this process is the one where the project's schedule is developed.

When it is performed:

The process of Schedule Development is typically performed after the processes of Activity Resource Estimating, Activity Duration Estimating, and Activity Sequencing have been performed and before Cost Budgeting is performed.

How it works:

Inputs

Organizational Process Assets

As is true with other processes, assets come in many forms. For this process, organizational process assets include anything the performing organization owns that would help with this process. Items such as an overall resource calendar or examples from previous projects would be particularly helpful in performing Schedule Development.

Project Scope Statement

The project scope statement, created earlier in the Scope Definition process, is the document that defines the scope of the project. It is particularly helpful here in Schedule Development because it also contains constraints and assumptions for the project.

Since most constraints and assumptions ultimately relate to cost and time, they need to be factored into this process.

Activity List

The activity list is the list of all activities that need to be scheduled and performed on the project. It is a bit redundant here as an input, since project schedule network diagrams (see later in the list of inputs to this process) implicitly contain the activity list.

Activity Attributes

The activity attributes always accompany the activity list. They provide expanded information on each activity in the list, and these details may be important when scheduling the activity.

Project Schedule Network Diagrams

The project schedule network diagrams were created earlier in Activity Sequencing, and they now become a primary input into Schedule Development. The project schedule network diagrams show the order in which activities must be completed, while the schedule assigns dates to each of these activities.

Activity Resource Requirements

The activity resource requirements were developed previously in Activity Resource Estimating. They show which physical and human resources will be required for each activity.

Resource Calendars

The resource calendars show resource usage across the organization and will assist in Schedule Development since the resource calendar may put additional constraints on when resources are available to be scheduled.

Activity Duration Estimates

This is another important input into the process of Schedule Development. The activity duration estimates, created earlier in Activity Duration Estimating, specify how long an activity will take, which has a direct bearing on the schedule.

Project Management Plan

The project management plan is the single, unified document that guides execution, monitoring, control, and closure. Of particular interest in the process of Schedule Development are the schedule management plan and the risk register. The schedule management plan describes how the schedule will be managed and how changes to the schedule will be managed. The risk register lists specific risks and responses. Because this process is all about developing the schedule, the risks related to the schedule would be of highest interest here.

Tools

Schedule Network Analysis

This technique actually refers to a group of techniques used to create the schedule. Any of the other specific tools or techniques that are part of the process of Schedule Development may be used as part of this general tool.

Critical Path Method (CPM)

Before trying to understand the critical path method, it is important to understand what the critical path is. A project's critical path is the combination of activities that, if any are delayed, will delay the project's finish.

The critical path method is an analysis technique with two main purposes:

1. To calculate the project's finish date.
2. To identify how much individual activities in the schedule can slip (or "float") without delaying the project.

A more detailed explanation of the critical path method appears later in this chapter under the heading, "Special Focus: Critical Path Method." The section shows specific techniques relevant to the exam and provides exercises that you will need to be able to perform to pass the exam.

Key Fact

Schedule Compression

On many projects, there are ways to complete the project schedule earlier without cutting the project's scope. That is the purpose of schedule compression.

Two types of questions that you will probably encounter on the exam involving schedule compression are crashing and fast tracking. Crashing involves adding resources to a project activity so that it will be completed more quickly. Crashing almost always increases costs.

Original Estimate

Activity	Resources	Estimated days
200 yards of pipeline construction	1	12

Crashed Estimate

Activity	Resources	Estimated days
200 yards of pipeline construction	4	4

An example of crashing the schedule by adding more resources to an activity

Note that in the example above, as is often the case, increasing the number of resources does decrease the time but not by a linear amount. This is because activities will often encounter the law of diminishing returns when adding resources to an activity. The old saying "Too many cooks spoil the broth" applies to projects as well as cooking.

Fast tracking means that you re-order the sequence of activities so that some of the activities are performed in parallel, or at the same time. Fast tracking does not necessarily increase costs, but it almost always increases risk to the project since discretionary dependencies are being ignored and additional activities are happening simultaneously. (Discretionary dependencies were discussed under the process of Activity Sequencing.)

Original Estimate

Original duration of 31 days

Fast Tracked Estimate

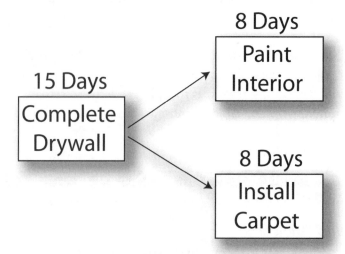

Fast tracked duration of 23 days

Note that fast tracking often results in some individual activities taking longer, and it increases the risk. In the example above, the workers may have a harder time moving around each other, thus increasing the time to paint and install carpet. Also, there is an increased risk associated with these activities. For example, the painters could damage the carpet, or the carpet installers could be hampered by the fresh paint.

What-If Schedule Analysis

"What-if analysis" typically uses Monte Carlo analysis to predict likely schedule outcomes for a project and identify the areas of the schedule that are the highest risk.

This analysis is performed by computer and evaluates probability by considering a huge number of simulated scheduling possibilities, or a few selected likely scenarios. A computer employing Monte Carlo Analysis can perform what-if analysis and identify the highest risk activities that may not otherwise be apparent, showing the impact of these changes on the schedule.

Schedule Development

Key Fact

Resource Leveling

When many people think about the technique of resource leveling, they may mistakenly consider only what their project management software does to level resources. Resource leveling is when your resource needs meet up with the organization's ability to supply resources.

In order to resource-level the project, you first use the critical path method to calculate and analyze all of the network paths for the project. Then you apply resources to that analysis to see what effect it has on schedule outcome.

Consider the following scenario. After performing the processes of Activity Duration Estimating and Activity Resource Estimating, you end up with the following project schedule network diagram.

Activity ID	Activity	Preceding Activity	Resources needed	Quantity of Resource Required	Estimated Duration (in days)
A	Database Design	Start	Database Administrator	2	8
B	Data Entry	A	Data Entry Clerk	10	5
C	Write stored procedures	A	Programmer	8	5
D	Test stored procedures	B,C	Quality Control Engineer	1	2

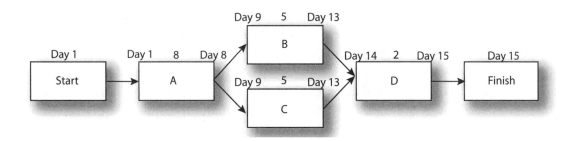

The project network diagram above was created using the critical path method. Now, however, consider what would happen if the organization

Schedule Development

could not provide eight programmer resources as reflected in this scenario. Instead, they could only supply two. The scenario must be resource leveled, resulting in a longer overall network diagram as follows:

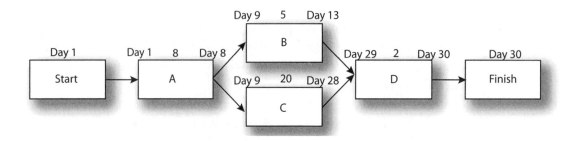

After the resource calendar has been applied and the schedule has been leveled, a schedule is created based on the resources applied, where each activity is assigned a projected start and finish date.

Critical Chain Method

Although it is not yet widely used, the critical chain method is considered to be one of the most significant potential advancements to project management theory in the past thirty years. Based on the theories of Eliyahu Goldratt, critical chain provides a new way to view and manage uncertainty when building the project schedule.

The traditional way, using the critical path method, puts the primary managerial focus on making sure no activity exceeds its float. If you are successful at that, the project will finish on time. With the critical chain method, you first determine latest possible start and finish date for each activity, and then add schedule "buffers" between activities. The goal is to manage the project so that no matter what uncertainties or problems occur, you do not exceed your buffers. If you are successful, the project will finish on time or early.

To use the critical chain method, you first perform normal critical path analysis and then analyze resource constraints and probabilities in order to build the schedule and the buffers.

Project Management Software

The tool of project management software simply helps to facilitate the other tools and techniques listed in this section (in addition to cost and other knowledge areas). Project management software can relieve the project manager of many of the routine calculations.

Applying Calendars

Calendars may be thought of as a sort of constraint. These may be calendars for the organization, such as corporate holidays or periods when work cannot be performed, or they could be calendars related to specific resources or groups.

For instance, a large manufacturing organization may have the ability to run shifts around the clock, while a project spanning international boundaries will probably have non-working holidays in one country that do not apply in other countries. Another example might be an engineering department's unavailability during a particular week due to training.

Adjusting Leads and Lags

Leads and lags can significantly affect the critical path as well as other components of the schedule. Adjusting leads and lags amounts to fine tuning the schedule so that they are as accurate and realistic as possible.

Schedule Model

The schedule model precedes the project schedule. The project manager uses the activity attributes and estimates along with a schedule tool or method to create the project's schedule. The schedule model allows the project manager to experiment with different allocations and scenarios in order to produce the project schedule.

Outputs

Project Schedule

The project schedule shows when each activity is scheduled to begin and end, as well as showing a schedule start and finish for the overall project. The schedule is typically represented graphically, and there are different forms it may take. The most common forms are covered as follows:

Project Network Diagram

The project network diagram is a useful detail-driven tool that provides a powerful view of the dependencies and sequences of each activity. It is the best representation for calculating the critical path and showing dependencies on the project.

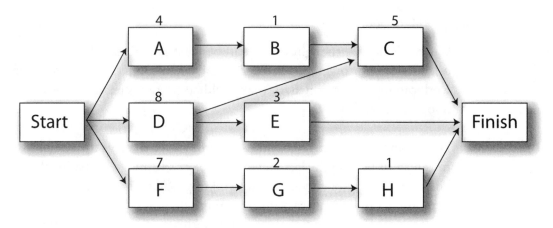

Bar Charts (also called Gantt Charts)

Bar charts, or Gantt charts, show activities represented as horizontal bars and typically have a calendar along the horizontal axis. The length of the bar corresponds to the length of time the activity should require.

A bar chart, or Gantt chart, can be easily modified to show percentage complete (usually by shading all or part of the horizontal bar). It is considered to be a good tool to use to communicate with management, because unlike the project network diagram, it is easy to understand at a glance.

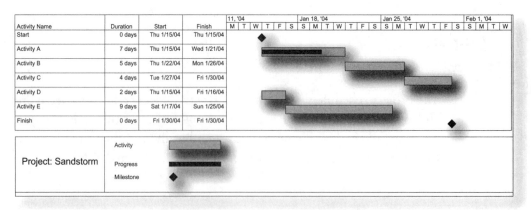

Milestone Chart

A milestone chart, as the name implies, only represents key events (milestones) for the project. Milestones may be significant events or deliverables by you or external parties on the project.

Milestone charts, because of the general level of information they provide, should be reserved for brief, high level project presentations where a lot of schedule detail would be undesirable or even distracting.

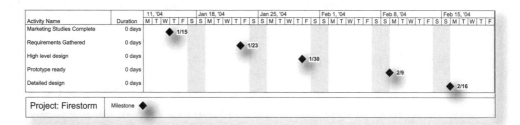

Schedule Model Data

The schedule model data means the information the project team used to model and create the project schedule. It would include schedule templates that were used, the activities and their attributes, estimated durations, and any constraints and assumptions.

This output is simply the data which supports how this schedule was developed.

Schedule Baseline

Any baseline (whether scope, schedule, or cost) is the original plan plus all approved changes. In this example, the schedule baseline is created at the point at which the schedule is approved by the customer, the sponsor, and the project manager (as well as possibly others such as the functional managers and the team). When schedule change requests are approved, they become part of the schedule baseline.

Resource Requirement Updates

Updates to the resource requirements are a very common output in Schedule Development, especially in the case of the tool of resource leveling, which adjusts the resources that are required in light of the organization's ability to supply them.

Schedule Development

Activity Attribute Updates

Any time attributes such as the resource requirements or start and finish dates are changed for an activity, these need to be updated in the activity attributes documentation.

Project Calendar Updates

The project calendar is brought into this process as an input, and any schedule changes that change project calendars, such as resource usage that would affect a resource calendar, should be updated back to that calendar.

Requested Changes

Change requests are a normal output of Schedule Development. For instance, if the project team determined that it was impossible to perform the scope of work within the allotted time, a change request to eliminate certain unnecessary components of the scope may be entered.

Project Management Plan Updates

The project management plan contains the information on how the project will be managed. Of specific interest here is the schedule management plan, which details how the schedule will be managed and how changes to the schedule will be managed.

Schedule Control

What it is:

As you can tell from its name, Schedule Control is a controlling process. The concept behind controlling processes in general is to compare the work results to the plan and ensure that they line up. In this process, the schedule is controlled to make sure that time-related performance on the project is in line with the plan.

One of the more important concepts to master with Schedule Control (and most controlling processes in general) is that schedule changes are not only reacted to, but the schedule is controlled proactively. That is, the project manager should be out in front of the project, influencing changes before they affect the project. Of course, at times, changes to the schedule may occur, and the project manager will have to react to them, but the project manager should be proactive whenever possible.

Why it is important:

Any time the schedule changes or a change request that affects the schedule occurs, the change should be evaluated and planned. The schedule should be monitored continuously against the actual work performed to ensure that things stay on target.

When it is performed:

The process of Schedule Control is performed throughout the life of the project.

How it works:

Inputs

Schedule Management Plan

The schedule management plan is an essential input into Schedule Control, since this is the portion of the project management plan that defines how the schedule will be managed and changed, and Schedule Control is the process that processes and manages those changes.

Schedule Baseline

The schedule baseline is another essential input into this process. It is the latest approved version of the project schedule. As changes are made or change requests are approved, the schedule baseline is updated to reflect those changes.

Performance Reports

For the process of Schedule Control, we are most interested in the performance reports that relate to the schedule. This would include information such as which activities and milestones had been met and which were slipping.

Approved Change Requests

Requested changes can, and usually do, affect the project schedule. They are factored into this controlling process, since Schedule Control is where the schedule changes are analyzed and managed.

Tools

Progress Reporting

The project schedule shows planned start and finish dates for each activity; however, it is the actual dates that determine when the project is delivered. Progress reports are used to show how the project is progressing against the schedule.

Schedule Change Control System

The schedule change control system is part of the integrated change control system. It includes all of the procedures that are used to approve or reject a change.

Performance Measurement

The performance measurement tool uses actual schedule data to compare against planned schedule data. Any differences between the plan and reality must be carefully analyzed and understood.

Project Management Software

Software simply automates and simplifies the analysis used in the other tools and techniques described for Schedule Control.

Variance Analysis

Variance analysis looks at the difference between what was scheduled and what was executed in order to understand any differences. These differences are analyzed to determine whether or not corrective action is required.

Schedule Comparison Bar Charts

Bar charts, also known as Gantt charts, are an effective way to communicate the schedule and the actual results. With this tool, one bar shows the plan for each schedule activity and the other shows the actual data to date.

Outputs

Schedule Model Data Updates

The schedule model data is used to build the schedule. As the underlying data are affected by change requests, slippage, etc., these updates need to be reflected in the schedule model data updates.

Schedule Baseline Updates

A baseline (whether scope, schedule, or cost) is the original plan plus all approved changes. In this case, when a change to the schedule is approved, this change becomes part of the schedule baseline.

Performance Measurements

The updated schedule performance index (SPI), schedule variance (SV) and other earned value measurements relevant to the schedule need to be calculated and communicated out.

Requested Changes

As the schedule is analyzed in detail, it is normal for change requests to be entered. For instance, if it were determined that the project was substantially ahead of schedule, it might be appropriate to reconsider scope items that had been omitted earlier in the interest of time.

Recommended Corrective Action

Corrective action is not about fixing past mistakes; they are considered to be water under the bridge. Instead, it is defined as anything done to bring future results in line with the plan. In the process of Schedule Control, after variance analysis has taken place, the recommended corrective action would be to evaluate ways that future performance and the schedule baseline could be made to align.

Organizational Process Assets Updates — See Chapter 2, Common Outputs

Activity List Updates — See this chapter, Activity Definition, Outputs

Activity Attribute Updates — See this chapter, Activity Definition, Outputs

Project Management Plan Updates — See Chapter 2, Common Outputs

As a general note regarding the four preceding outputs, updates to the organizational process assets, the activity list, the activity attributes, and the project management plan are normal results of the process of Schedule Control. Any time one of these is added to or changes in any way, these updates need to be formally captured.

Free float – Also known as "free slack," free float is the amount of time an activity can be delayed without affecting the early start date of subsequent dependent activities. If this leaves you scratching your head, consider the diagram below:

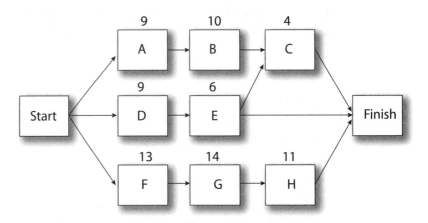

The free float of activity E would be determined by calculating how long it could slip before it impacted the early start of activity C. In this example, activity E has 4 units of free float. Note that this is different from its float, which is 19 units.

Negative Float – Negative float is a situation that occurs when an activity's start date occurs before a preceding activity's finish date. For instance, suppose that there is a constraint for an activity (Activity D) that involves a 1 day final inspection of a building that is to begin and be completed on July 15th; however, a preceding activity (Activity C) that encompasses testing the electrical components of the project does not finish until July 25th. If work is scheduled 7 days per week, then it could be stated that Activity D has a negative float of 10 days.

Technically, negative float exists when an activity's finish date happens before its start date. In the example above, Activity D is supposed to finish at the end of the 15th; however, it cannot even begin until 10 days later. There Activity D has 10 days of negative float.

Negative float for an activity tells you that your schedule has problems. It most often occurs when immovable constraints or milestones are imposed by forces outside the project, causing an impossible situation. Negative float may be resolved by several methods, such as reworking the logic of the schedule, crashing, or fast-tracking.

Summary of Key Terms

You must understand each of the following key terms. You do not have to memorize every term word for word, but you should be able to recall the general definition and apply them on the exam.

Activity on Arrow Diagram - A type of network diagram where the activities are represented by the arrows. The nodes (usually circles) are used to connect or show dependencies. Activity on arrow diagrams are always shown "finish to start," where one activity is finished before the next one begins. This is the diagramming method that uses dummy activities (usually represented by dashed lines).

Activity Decomposition – Activity decomposition is similar to scope decomposition (remember the asteroids metaphor), except that the final result here is an activity list instead of the WBS.

Activity List – A list of every activity that will be performed on the project.

Activity Duration Estimates – Probable number of periods (weeks, hours, days, months, etc.) this activity should take with the probable range of results. Example:

Activity Duration Estimate	Explanation
1 week +/- 3 days	The activity should take between 2 and 8 days, assuming a 5 day work week
1 month + 20% probability it will be accomplished later	There is an 80% likelihood that the activity will be completed within a month and a 20% chance that it will exceed a month.

Analogous Estimating – A form of expert judgment often used early on when there is little information available. Example: "This project is similar to one we did last year, and it took three months." It is performed from the top down, focusing on the big picture.

Backward Pass – The method for calculating late start and late finish dates for an activity.

Critical Path – The paths through the network diagram that show which activities, if delayed, will affect the project finish date. For schedule, the critical path represents the highest risk path in the project.

Dependencies – Activities that must be completed before other activities are either started or completed.

Dependencies	Description	Example
Mandatory	Also called "hard logic," these activities must be followed in sequence.	Clearing the lot on a construction site before pouring the foundation.
Discretionary	Also called "soft logic." Expert judgment and best practices often dictate that particular activities are performed in a particular order. The dependencies are discretionary because they are based on expert opinion rather than mandatory or hard logic.	Painting the interior before putting down carpet.
External	Dependencies relying on factors outside of the project.	Zoning approval for a new building. Weather for a rocket launch.

Dummy Activity – An activity on a network diagram that does not have any time associated with it. It is only included to show a relationship, and is usually represented as a dotted or dashed line. Dummy activities only exist in activity on arrow diagrams.

Duration compression - This technique is primarily made up of two means of compressing the schedule: crashing and fast-tracking, described in the table below.

Technique	Description	Example
Crashing	Applying more resources to reduce duration. Crashing the schedule usually increases cost.	If setting up a computer network takes one person 6 weeks, three resources may be able to do it in two weeks. Note – Crashing usually does not reduce the schedule by a linear amount.
Fast tracking	Performing activities in parallel that would normally be done in sequence. Fast tracking activities usually increases project risk, and these activities have a higher probability of rework.	Example: In XYX Corp, no coding on software modules is allowed until after the database design is complete, but when fast tracking, the activities could be done in parallel if it is not a mandatory dependency.

Delphi Technique - A means of gathering expert judgment where the participants do not know who the others are and therefore are not able to influence each other's opinion. The Delphi technique is designed to prevent groupthink and to find out a participant's real opinion.

Expert Judgment – A method of estimating in which experts are asked to provide input into the schedule. Combining expert judgment with other tools and methods can significantly improve the accuracy of time estimates and reduce risk.

Float – How much time an activity can be delayed without affecting the project's finish date. Also known as "slack."

Forward Pass – The method for calculating early start and early finish dates for an activity.

Free float – Also known as "free slack." How much time an activity can be delayed without affecting the early start date of subsequent dependent activities.

Heuristics – Rules for which no formula exists. Usually derived through trial and error.

Lag – The delay between the activity and the next one dependent upon it. For example, if you are pouring concrete, you may have a 3 day lag after you have poured the concrete before your subsequent activities of building upon it can begin.

Lead – Activities with finish to start relationships cannot start until their predecessors have been finished; however, if you have 5 days of lead time on an activity, it may begin 5 days before its predecessor activity has finished. Think of it as getting a head start, like runners in a relay race. Lead time lets the subsequent task begin before its predecessor has finished.

Mathematical Analysis – A technique to show scheduling possibilities where early and late start and finish dates are calculated for every activity without looking at resource estimates.

Milestones – High level points in the schedule used to track and report progress. Milestones usually have no time associated with them.

Key Terms

Monte Carlo Analysis – Computer simulation that throws a high number of "what if" scenarios at the project schedule to determine probable results.

Network Diagram – (also called network logic diagram or project network diagram). A method of diagramming project activities to show sequence and dependencies.

Negative Float – Occurs when an activity's start date occurs before a preceding activity's finish date. Technically, negative float exists when an activity's finish date happens before its start date. Negative float for an activity indicates a schedule with problems. Reworking the logic of the schedule, crashing, or fast-tracking are potential solutions.

Precedence Diagramming Method – (also called Activity on Node). A type of network diagram where the boxes are activities, and the arrows are used to show dependencies between the activities.

Reserve Time (Contingency) – A schedule buffer used to reduce schedule risk. The chart below represents the most common types of reserve for a project.

Contingency	Example
Project %	Add 15% to the entire project schedule
Project lump sum	Add 2 months calendar schedule to the project
Activity %	Add 10% to each activity (or to key, high-risk activities)
Activity lump sum	Add 1 week to each activity (or to key, high risk activities)

Schedule Baseline – The approved schedule that is used as a basis for measuring and reporting. It includes the originally approved project schedule plus approved updates.

Slack – See "Float."

Variance Analysis – Comparing planned versus actual schedule dates.

Time Management Questions

1. You are the project manager for the construction of a commercial office building that has very similar characteristics to a construction project performed by your company two years ago. As you enter Activity Definition, what is the BEST approach?

   A. Use the activity list from the previous project as your activity list.

   B. Generate your activity list without looking at the previous project's list and compare when your project's list is complete.

   C. Use the gap analysis technique to identify any differences between your project and the previous project.

   D. Use the previous activity list to help construct your list.

2. The customer has called a project team member to request a change in the project's schedule. The team member asks you what the procedure is for handling schedule changes. Where should you refer the team member to help him understand the procedure?

   A. The project office.

   B. The change control board.

   C. The schedule management plan.

   D. Inform the team member that the customer is always right.

3. If you were creating duration estimates for a schedule activity, which of the following tools or techniques would NOT be appropriate to use?

   A. Expert judgment.

   B. Reserve analysis.

   C. Three-point estimating.

   D. Least-squares estimating.

4. Senior management has called you in for a meeting to review the progress of your project. You have been allocated 15 minutes to report progress and discuss critical issues. Which of the following would be BEST to carry with you in this case?

A. Milestone chart.

B. The project network diagram.

C. An expert from each functional area of the project so that all questions may be answered.

D. Project status reports from your team members.

5. How does activity on node differ from activity on arrow?

A. Activity on arrow is superior to activity on node.

B. Activity on node is superior to activity on arrow.

C. Activity on arrow may have dummy activities.

D. Activity on node may have dummy activities.

6. The amount of time that an activity may be delayed without extending the critical path is:

A. Lag.

B. Grace period.

C. Free factor.

D. Slack.

7. Crashing differs from fast tracking because crashing:

A. Usually increases value.

B. Usually increases the cost.

C. Usually saves more time.

D. Usually saves more money.

8. If senior management tells you "The last project we did like this cost us almost five million dollars," what estimating method is being used?

    A. Delphi technique.

    B. Principle of equivalency of activities.

    C. Analogous estimating.

    D. Bottom-up estimating.

9. You are advising a project manager who is behind schedule on his project. The sponsor on his project is very unhappy with the way things have progressed and is threatening to cancel the project. The sponsor has accepted a revised due date from the project manager but did not allow any increased spending. Which of the following would represent the BEST advice for the project manager in this case?

    A. Fast track the schedule.

    B. Ask senior management for a new sponsor within the organization.

    C. Crash the schedule.

    D. Talk with the customer to see if budget may be increased without the sponsor's involvement.

10. Which Schedule Development tool inserts non-working buffer time between schedule activities?

    A. Critical chain method.

    B. Critical path method.

    C. Resource leveling.

    D. Schedule modeling.

11. What is the BEST tool to use to calculate the critical path on a project?

    A. Work breakdown structure.

    B. GERT diagram.

    C. Gantt chart.

    D. Project network diagram.

12. Which of the following choices best fits the description of a project manager applying the technique of What-if Scenario Analysis?

    A.   Using project management software to build three versions of the project schedule.

    B.   Using Monte Carlo analysis to identify what would happen if schedule delays occurred.

    C.   Using critical path method to analyze what would happen if the critical path actually occurred.

    D.   Discussing with the functional managers what they would do if certain project team members quit the project early.

13. How do the activity list and activity attributes relate to each other?

    A.   The activity list focuses on schedule activities, while the activity attributes apply to WBS activities.

    B.   The activity attributes are created prior to the activity list.

    C.   The activity list may be substituted for the activity attributes in most processes.

    D.   Activity attributes provide additional information for each activity on the activity list.

14. Which of the following is the BEST description of the critical path?

    A.   The activities that represent critical functionality.

    B.   The activities that represent the largest portions of the work packages.

    C.   The activities that represent the highest schedule risk on the project.

    D.   The activities that represent the optimal path through the network.

15. Your project schedule has just been developed, approved, and distributed to the stakeholders and presented to senior management when one of the resources assigned to an activity approaches you and tells you that her activity cannot be performed within the allotted time due to several necessary pieces that were left out of planning. Her revised estimate would change the schedule but would not affect the critical path. What would be the BEST way for the project manager to handle this situation?

    A.   Stick with the published schedule and allow for any deviation by using schedule reserve.

    B.   Go back to Activity Duration Estimating and update the schedule and other plans to reflect the new estimate.

    C.   Hire an independent consultant to validate her claim.

    D.   Replace the resource with someone who says they can meet the published schedule.

Answers to Time Management Questions

1.   D. The previous activity list would make an excellent tool to help you ensure that you are considering all activities. Any historical information such as this is thought of as an organizational process asset. 'A' is incorrect because you cannot simply substitute something as intricate as a complete activity list. 'B' is incorrect because the other activity list would provide a good starting point and should be considered before you create your activity list. 'C' (gap analysis) is a tool that is used in the real world that is not defined by PMI, nor is it used in activity list definition.

2.   C. The schedule management plan, which becomes part of the project plan, would be the best source of information on how changes to the schedule are to be handled. 'A' is incorrect because the project office's job is to define standards – not to make decisions on tactical items such as this. 'B' is incorrect because the change control board may or may not even exist, and if it does exist, it usually approves or rejects scope changes. Answer 'D' would be the worst choice. The customer is not always right when it comes to requesting changes. Procedures should be defined and followed in order to improve the project's chances of success.

3   D. Since we are creating activity duration estimates, we are performing the process of Activity Duration Estimating. Answers 'A', 'B', and 'C' are all tools used in Activity Duration Estimating, but 'D' is a made up term.

4.   A. Milestone charts show the high level status, which would be appropriate given the audience and time allocated for this update.

5.   C. Activity on arrow project network diagrams may have dummy activities, while activity on node diagrams cannot show dummy activities. While some debate over which method is superior may exist, answer 'C' is the most appropriate choice here.

6.   D. The slack (or float) is the amount of time an activity may be delayed without affecting the critical path.

7.   B. Crashing adds more resources to an activity. This usually increases the cost due to the law of diminishing returns which predicts that 10 people usually cannot complete an activity in half the time that 5 people can. The savings from crashing are rarely linear. 'A' is incorrect because crashing does not directly affect the project's value. 'C' is incorrect because crashing may or may not save more time than fast tracking – depending on the situation. 'D' is incorrect because crashing usually costs more money than fast tracking.

8. C. In this example management is providing you with analogous estimates. These estimates use actual costs from previous projects (historical information or organizational process assets) to produce estimates for a similar project.

9. A. In this case, you must compress the schedule without increasing the costs. Fast tracking does not directly add cost to the project and is the best choice in this case. 'B' is incorrect. The sponsor is paying for the project. Do this, and your sponsor will probably be asking for a new project manager instead! 'C' is incorrect because crashing usually adds cost to the project, and that is not allowed in this scenario. 'D' is incorrect because the sponsor authorizes budget. Doing an end-run around the sponsor and going to the customer would be very inappropriate.

10. A. The critical chain method uses buffers, which are non-working times, to help prevent the activities themselves from slipping.

11. D. The project network diagram shows duration and dependencies which would help you calculate the critical path. 'A' is incorrect because the WBS does not show durations or activity dependencies. 'B' is incorrect because GERT is most helpful for showing conditions and branches. 'C' is incorrect because a Gantt chart is very useful for showing percentage complete on activities but is not the best tool for showing activity dependencies or calculating the critical path.

12. B. What-if analysis can take on many forms, but the form you are most likely to see on the exam is Monte Carlo analysis, which throws a large number of scenarios at the schedule to see what would happen if one or more bad scenarios occurred.

13. D. The activity attributes simply expand on the information for each activity. 'A' is incorrect since the activity attributes tie back to the activity list and not the WBS. 'B' is incorrect since the activity attributes may be created at the same time or after the activity list, but not before. 'C' is incorrect since the activity attributes may never be substituted for the activity list. Instead the activity attributes accompany the activity list, providing additional information on each activity.

14.   C. This one may have been difficult for you, because it is a non-traditional definition of the critical path. The critical path is the series of activities, which if delayed, will delay the project. This makes these activities the highest schedule risk on the project. 'A' is incorrect because the critical path has no relationship with functionality. 'B' is incorrect because the size of the work packages does not directly correlate to the critical path. 'D' is incorrect because the critical path does not represent the optimal path through the network.

15.   B. Changes happen. Some of them are submitted as change requests, and some of them come out of nowhere. In this case, you would want to return to planning and update the plans. The project will not be delayed, and the resource has given a good reason why the dates need to be revisited (a common occurrence in the real world). 'A' is incorrect, because the plan should reflect reality – not an unrealistic estimate. 'C' is incorrect, because you cannot possibly get an outside opinion every time a resource needs to change a date. 'D' is incorrect, because the resource gave a good reason for the adjustment. It was not that she was lacking in training or ability, but that pieces were left out of planning. Therefore, 'B' represents the all-around best answer.

Cost Management

Difficulty	Memorization	Exam Importance
High	High	High

7

The topic of Cost Management, like time management, has critical formulas that must be learned and understood. This chapter will explain these formulas clearly and provide methods and exercises for quick retention.

Most of the principles and techniques explained here, such as earned value, did not originate with PMI but were derived from long-standing practices in the fields of cost accounting, managerial accounting, and finance.

From the indicators at the top of the page, you can tell that most people find this chapter to be one of the more difficult ones. In order to help you prepare for this topic, this book has clearly broken down the practices and outlined the techniques and formulas needed to ace the questions on the exam.

Philosophy

While the actual tools and techniques behind Cost Management may be different from time management, the driving philosophy has several similarities. Costs should be planned, quantified, and measured. The project manager should tie costs to activities and resources and build the estimates from the bottom up.

It is common practice for high-level budgets to be determined prior to knowing costs. The reason for this is that many companies use fiscal year planning cycles that must be done far in advance of their project planning. Budgetary

The processes of Project Cost Management with their *primary* outputs

Cost Management

Cost Estimating
Activity Cost Estimates

Cost Budgeting
Cost Baseline
Funding Requirements

Cost Control
Performance Measures
Forecasted Completion

constraints are a fact of life, but instead of blindly accepting whatever budget is specified by management, the project manager carefully reviews the scope of work and the duration estimates and then reconciles them to the scope and projected costs. Adjustments to the project scope, the budget, or the schedule are much easier to justify by working up from a detailed level instead of from the top down. Although summary budgets are often the first thing created in the real world, when it comes to detailed planning, the overall approach advocated here is scope first, schedule second, and budget third.

Throughout this book, you will see that estimates should be built from the bottom up. At the point in the process where budgets are created, you should have a well-defined work breakdown structure, an activity list with resource and duration estimates for each activity, and a schedule. Now budgeting becomes a task of applying rates against those resources and activities to create activity cost estimates, a cost baseline, and a cost management plan.

It is the project manager's job to constantly monitor and control cost against time, scope, quality, and risk to ensure that all projections remain realistic and clearly defined.

Importance

The topic of Cost Management is of high importance for the exam, both in the understanding of PMI's processes and in the application of key formulas, which play a part here as well.

Preparation

Learning the 12 key formulas for Cost Management is a must. Learning to apply them is equally as important. The good news is that none of the formulas are overly difficult, and there are plenty of explanations and examples in this book to help cement the concepts.

As mentioned briefly above, memorization is important; however, understanding the formulas is even more important. Once you grasp the formulas and concepts, the memorization will be a snap. In fact, some people studying for the exam only memorize the concepts and reconstruct the formulas as needed. This is possible because each formula does make sense, so read and reread this chapter until they are clear to you.

Important Concepts

Process Group	Cost Management Process
Initiating	(none)
Planning	Cost Estimating, Cost Budgeting
Executing	(none)
Controlling	Cost Control
Closing	(none)

In the knowledge area of Cost Management, it is also essential that you know the main outputs that are produced during each process. The different tasks that are performed in each process are summarized in the chart that follows.

Process	Key Output(s)
Cost Estimating	Activity cost estimates
Cost Budgeting	Cost baseline, Funding requirements
Cost Control	Performance measurements, Forecasted completion, Recommended corrective actions

Life-Cycle Costing

Instead of simply asking "How much will this product cost to develop?" life-cycle costing looks at the total cost of ownership from purchase or creation, through operations, and finally to disposal. It is a practice that encourages making decisions based on the bigger picture of ownership costs.

For instance, it may be less expensive for the project to use generic computer servers to develop a software product; however, if the organization will have to maintain those servers, and if that organization has expertise and service contracts with IBM, then the project has made a short-sighted decision that will have adverse effects downstream.

Cost Mgt Processes

Value Engineering

Value engineering is the practice of trying to get more out of the project in every possible way. It tries to increase the bottom line, decrease costs, improve quality, shorten the schedule, and generally squeeze more benefit and value out of each aspect of the project. The key to value engineering is that the scope of work is not reduced by these other efforts.

Cost Estimating

What it is:

One of the biggest improvements evident in this edition of the PMBOK Guide is that most of the processes are intuitively named, making it that much easier to understand them. Cost Estimating is an example of that. Its name indicates exactly what it does.

In Cost Estimating, each activity is analyzed to evaluate the activity time estimates and the resource estimates associated with them, and a cost estimate is produced.

Why it is important:

If you've heard the old saying that the devil is in the details, then you know why Cost Estimating is important. In this process, you gain a detailed understanding of the costs involved in performing a project.

When it is performed:

It may be misleading to suggest that Cost Estimating is only performed once. This process, like many others, may be performed over and again throughout the project; however, there are a few essential predecessor processes that must be completed before it can be performed adequately.

At the time of this publication, the 3rd Edition PMBOK Guide specifies that only the processes of Scope Definition and Create WBS must be performed ahead of Cost Estimating; however, this appears to be an incomplete list and will most likely be corrected in future revisions of the PMBOK Guide. It is normal to perform Activity Definition, Activity Resource Estimating, and Activity Duration Estimating before estimating the costs. The reason for this is that costs are estimated against schedule activities.

It is also helpful to know the number of resources and how long they are expected to work on the project. Even though the current publication of the PMBOK does not list these preceding processes or inputs, you will be better prepared for the exam if you understand the way this is explained in the preceding paragraph rather than the way it is explained in the PMBOK Guide.

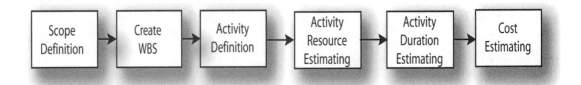

The order of certain processes from Scope Definition through Cost Estimating

How it works:

Cost estimates, prepared for each activity, are thought of in terms of their accuracy. In other words, how much leeway are you giving yourself with your estimating?

When it comes to estimates that result from this process, there are many options. Consider the table that follows:

Estimate type	Range
Order of Magnitude Estimate	-50% to +100%
Conceptual Estimate	-30% to +50%
Preliminary Estimate	-20% to +30%
Definitive Estimate	-15% to +20%
Control Estimate	-10% to +15%

These five different types of estimating are used, depending on the need. For instance, in the initiation of a project, an order of magnitude estimate may suffice, while later in the project, a definitive estimate may be in order. For activities with relatively few unknowns, a control estimate may be appropriate. Typically, the closer in time you get to actually spending money for an activity, the more precise you want that activity's estimate to be.

Inputs

Enterprise Environmental Factors — See Chapter 2, Common Inputs

Organizational Process Assets — See Chapter 2, Common Inputs

Project Scope Statement

The project scope statement, created earlier in Scope Definition, defines the scope and ties each element of the scope back to the underlying need it was designed to address. Also, the project scope statement provides information on constraints and assumptions related to the scope, and these can dramatically affect the cost estimates.

All of this information found in the project scope statement should be carefully considered as the cost estimates are being created.

Work Breakdown Structure

The work breakdown structure contains everything in scope and the how these deliverables are organized. Costs are mapped back to work packages on the WBS.

WBS Dictionary

Any time you see the WBS, you are likely to see the WBS dictionary. It provides additional attributes and expanded information about the WBS that may prove helpful.

Project Management Plan

The project management plan provides the plan for how the project will be executed and controlled. Specifically, the schedule, cost, and staffing management plans, which are all part of the project plan, should be considered. Also, the risk register should be carefully considered since risks and cost estimates are typically tightly linked.

Tools

Analogous Estimating

The tool of analogous estimating uses the actual results of projects that have been performed by your organization as the estimates for your activities. Analogous estimates are typically easier to use, and their accuracy depends on how similar the two projects actually are.

Determine Resource Cost Rates

The resource cost rates are applied to the activity resource estimates, determined earlier. For instance, if it were determined that a senior Java programmer would be needed for 120 hours on an activity, then the hourly rate for that resource would be needed in order to know the full cost of those 120 hours. These resource cost rates may be actual or estimated.

Bottom-Up Estimating

The technique of bottom-up estimating produces a separate estimate for each schedule activity. These individual estimates are then aggregated up to summary nodes on the WBS.

Cost Estimating

Bottom-up estimating is considered to be highly accurate; however, it can also be time consuming and labor-intensive.

Parametric Estimating

Parametric estimating is a tool often used on projects with a high degree of historical information, and it works best for linear, scalable projects. For instance, if you knew that it cost $4,000,000 to build a mile of roadway, then you could estimate that it would cost $32,000,000 to build 8 miles of road.

Project Management Software

The tool of project management software is most useful in facilitating the other tools and techniques, performing the routine calculations, and organizing and storing the large amounts of information used to build the cost estimates.

Vendor Bid Analysis

Bids should be analyzed, and most specifically the winning bid, if for no other reason than to improve the project team's understanding of costs.

Reserve Analysis

It is normal for the cost estimates that will be produced as a result of this process to include reserve amounts, also called contingency. This is simply a buffer against slippage on the project.

The reserve amounts should be analyzed as part of the Cost Estimating process simply to ensure that the amount of reserve being planned properly reflects the risk associated with the project.

Cost of Quality

The technique of evaluating the cost of quality, often abbreviated as COQ, looks at all of the costs that will be realized in order to achieve quality. This tool is also used in the Quality Planning process. The costs of items that are not conformant to quality standards are known as "cost of poor quality," often abbreviated as COpQ.

Outputs

Activity Cost Estimates

The activity cost estimates are the primary output of this process. These estimates address how much it would cost to complete each schedule activity on the project.

Activity Cost Estimate Supporting Detail

When it comes to the PMBOK Guide, you can never have too much supporting detail. Here, especially, it is important to include enough information on how you derived the activity cost estimates.

Requested Changes

When costs are estimated, it is normal that change requests to the project scope or schedule would be made. For instance, if the cost estimates came in higher than the allowable cost constraint, then the project team might elect to review elements of the scope to determine whether there were any non-essential elements that could be cut in order to get costs back on track.

Cost Management Plan Updates

The cost management plan (discussed in the Integration chapter), details how the project costs will be managed and how change or requested changes to the project costs will be managed. As the activity cost estimates are created, it is normal that this plan would be updated, sometimes significantly.

Cost Estimating

Cost Budgeting

What it is:

In order to understand this process, it is necessary to understand what a budget is.

A budget, also known as the cost baseline, takes the estimated project expenditures and maps them back to dates on the calendar. In other words, the Cost Budgeting process time phases the costs so that the performing organization will know how to plan for cash flow and likely expenditures.

Why it is important:

A good cost baseline will help the organization plan their expenditures appropriately and will prevent the organization from tying up too much money throughout the life of the project. For instance, a construction project may have relatively low costs early on, but these costs may rise dramatically in the construction phase. The cost baseline will reflect this, helping the organization to plan accordingly.

Although a high-level budget, similar to a cost constraint, may be determined early in the project, this cost baseline describes a detailed budget that shows costs and timelines for each work package or activity.

When it is performed:

Because the budget typically maps back to schedule activities, it should be performed after Activity Definition, Activity Duration Estimating, and Activity Resource Estimating have been performed. Additionally, because it is time-phased, it should be performed after Schedule Development, since that is where the project's timeline is determined, and since it is based on the activity costs estimates, it should be performed after the process of Cost Estimating.

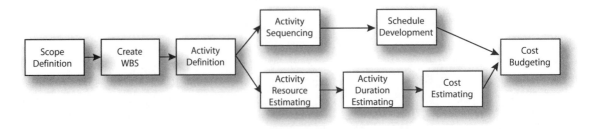

Cost Budgeting

How it works:

Inputs

Project Scope Statement

The project scope statement contains information on why the scope was set where it was, what its limits are, and what other scope-related constraints exist. For instance, certain elements of scope may be non-negotiable since they are required by contract, while other requirements may be easily changed. As the project's budget is being created, the scope should be carefully considered.

Work Breakdown Structure

Most often, the budget is not only mapped back to the schedule (that is, time-phased), but costs are also tied back to a node on the work breakdown structure.

WBS Dictionary

The WBS dictionary is almost inseparable from the WBS. It provides expanded attributes, information, and details on the work packages.

Activity Cost Estimates

The activity cost estimates are a primary input into this process. They provide details on what each schedule activity is estimated to cost. Because every schedule activity maps back to a single work package, these activity cost estimates are added together to get the cost for their parent work package.

Activity Cost Estimate Supporting Detail

As in other areas, you can never have too much supporting detail. The supporting detail for the activity cost estimates describes how you derived the cost estimates you are using here.

Project Schedule

The project's budget is time-phased, meaning that it shows what costs will be incurred and when they will be incurred. The schedule helps tie these costs back to periods of time for planning purposes.

Chapter 7

Resource Calendars

Resource calendars show when resources are going to be utilized and when they will be available. This, along with the project schedule, will help plan for when costs will be incurred.

 Contract

The contract may provide information on what costs the project is contractually obliged to incur. For instance, the contract may specify that only a specific brand of computer server may be used in a data center, or that the project is obligated to use at least five of these servers. Any contractual information that affects the cost or expenditures should be factored into the Cost Budgeting process.

 Cost Management Plan

The cost management plan is created during Develop Project Management Plan, and it describes how the cost baseline will be created and managed and how changes to the cost baseline will be managed.

Tools

 Cost Aggregation

Even though costs are estimated at an activity level, these cost estimates should be aggregated to the work package level where they will be measured, managed, and controlled during the project.

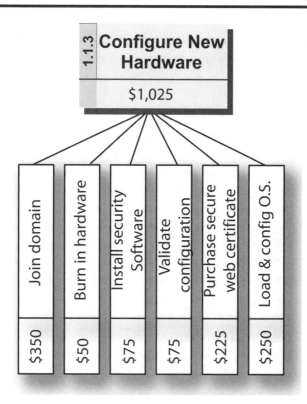

Individual cost estimates aggregating back to a single work package

Reserve Analysis

The tool of reserve analysis is related to risk. Almost all projects maintain a financial reserve to protect them against cost overrun. How much they keep, and how they track it vary from project to project. These buffers go by various names such as management reserve and contingency reserve.

For instance, one project may decide to pad each activity cost estimate by 10% across the board, while another project may only pad the activities that are considered to be at highest risk for cost overrun. Still another project may add a total cost buffer of 20% as a lump sum to the entire project cost baseline.

There is no one prescribed way to perform reserve analysis; however, the reserve amount should be in keeping with the risk levels and tolerances on the project.

Parametric Estimating

Parametric estimating typically uses simple formulas to estimate costs. It may be used for an individual activity, as in Cost Estimating, or for the entire cost baseline, as is the case here.

Cost Budgeting

An example of parametric estimating would be basing the cost of the development of a software application on the estimated number of lines of code or screens involved or the cost of an airport runway based on its planned length.

Parametric estimates work best when the project being undertaken is highly similar to previous projects and there is significant historical information available within your organization or industry.

Funding Limit Reconciliation

Because companies typically operate on fiscal years, they are required to budget for projects long before the actual scope is known. Because of that, it is normal for a project to receive a funding limit or constraint as the project is begun.

It is important for the project to reconcile planned spending with these funding limits. For instance, the organization may specify that they will only be able to provide $200,000 in the first month of a project, but $450,000 in the second month. The project's cost baseline ultimately needs to be compatible with these limitations.

Outputs

Cost Baseline

The cost baseline is another term for the project's budget, and you should expect to see questions related to it on the exam. It not only specifies what costs will be incurred, but when they will be incurred. Larger projects may be divided into multiple cost baselines. For instance, one cost baseline may track domestic labor costs, while a second cost baseline is used to track international labor costs.

Project Funding Requirements

It would be impractical for most projects to petition management for authorization on each individual cost, so instead the project determines funding requirements. The cost baseline is used to determine the project's funding requirements. The funding requirements are almost always related to the planned expenditures, but they are not identical to them. For instance, a project may request $20,000 per month throughout the life of the project, or they may require a larger portion early on in order to purchase equipment or incur other fixed costs.

The funding requirements should also include any planned contingency or reserve funds, since these must be available to the project as soon as they are needed.

Cost Management Plan Updates

Often times performing the process of Cost Budgeting results in changes to the project's scope, schedule, or costs. If any of these changes affect the way in which costs are managed (or the way change requests to the costs are managed) then the cost management plan should be updated to reflect this.

Requested Changes

As with most processes, performing this process may result in changes that should be channeled back through the appropriate change control process.

Cost Control

What it is:

Cost Control, in many ways, is the quintessential monitoring and controlling process. There are two important things to keep in mind about controlling processes:

1. They are proactive. They do not merely wait for changes to occur. Instead, they try to influence the factors that lead to change.
2. Controlling processes measure what was executed against what was planned. If the results of what was executed do not match the cost baseline, then appropriate steps are taken to bring the two back in line. This could either mean changing future plans or changing the way the work is being performed.

Cost Control is primarily concerned with cost variance. In project management, cost variances are described as either being positive (good) or negative (bad). It is important to understand that even a positive cost variance needs to be understood and the plan must be adjusted. Accurate planning is paramount.

Why it is important:

Cost Control is an essential process for ensuring that costs are carefully monitored and controlled. It ensures that the costs stay on track and that change is detected whenever it occurs.

When it is performed:

Cost Control is not a process that is performed only once. Instead, it is performed regularly throughout the project, typically beginning as soon as project costs are incurred. The activities associated with Cost Control are usually performed with more frequency as project costs increase. For instance, many projects will perform Cost Control monthly during planning phases and weekly (or even more frequently) during construction phases, where costs typically peak.

How it works:

Inputs

Cost Baseline

> The cost baseline is a primary input into the process of Cost Control. A baseline is the original plan plus all approved changes. The cost baseline (also known as the budget) shows what costs are projected and when they are projected to be incurred. The cost baseline is the plan against which the actual costs are measured.

Project Funding Requirements

> Like the preceding input of the cost baseline, the project funding requirements are also part of the plan against which the actual funding is measured. In this case, positive or negative variances from the planned funding requirements will be evaluated so that corrective action may be taken if necessary.

Performance Reports

> The performance reports provide a summary of how costs are progressing against the plan for work completed. Performance reports are covered in greater detail in Chapter 10 - Communication Management.

Work Performance Information — See Chapter 2, Common Inputs

Approved Change Requests

> Any change requests that are approved should be evaluated for their impact on the cost baseline.

Project Management Plan

> The project management plan contains the cost management plan, which guides the Cost Control process. The cost management plan tells how costs will be managed and how changes or variances to the costs will be managed.

Tools

Cost Change Control System

The cost change control system describes how the cost baseline may be changed. Like any other system described here, it can include people, departments, systems, policies, forms, etc.

Performance Measurement Analysis

There are numerous performance measurement techniques used within project management, most of them originating in the field of cost accounting. These fall under the heading of Earned Value, discussed later in this chapter, and include Earned Value (EV), Planned Value (PV), Actual Cost (AC), Estimate To Complete (ETC), Estimate At Completion (EAC), Cost Variance (CV), Schedule Variance (SV), Cost Performance Index (CPI), Schedule Performance Index (SPI), and the Cumulative CPI (CPI^C). Each of these formulas and concepts are covered in detail later in this chapter.

Forecasting

The technique of forecasting uses current and previous cost information to predict future costs. This focuses on the concepts of Estimate At Completion (EAC) and Estimate To Completion (ETC), covered later in this chapter under the heading of Earned Value.

Project Performance Reviews

Periodic reviews of the project performance are meetings held to measure actual performance against the plan. As part of Cost Control, particular attention is paid to cost performance.

Project Management Software

Because the calculations involved in Cost Control (especially the earned value calculations) can be tedious and complex, project management software is typically used to calculate actual values and assist with "what if" analysis.

Variance Management

How you will handle variances is determined in the cost management plan (part of the overall project management plan). Keep in mind that positive variance is considered to be good, while negative variance is bad, but even positive variances need to be managed, and the cost baseline should be adjusted to accurately reflect anticipated costs.

Outputs

Cost Estimate Updates

As previous cost estimate changes are detected and understood, it may be appropriate to update future cost estimates. For instance, if a contractor has been producing every deliverable at half the estimated cost, and there is reason to believe that will continue, then the project manager may decide to adjust future cost estimates to reflect this performance increase.

Cost Baseline Updates

It is a common misconception that baselines may not be updated, but they can. Once a change becomes approved, it becomes part of the baseline. You should understand that if a change was not approved, it does not become part of the baseline.

Performance Measurements

Performance measurements show how the project is performing against the plan. For the process of Cost Control, the performance measurements of CV, SV, CPI, SPI, and CPI^C are especially applicable, since they help show variances and trends on how the project is performing against the plan.

Forecasted Completion

The two values that relate most closely to completion are EAC and ETC. These numbers are used to help forecast a likely completion date for the project.

Requested Changes

As Cost Control is performed, requested changes are a normal output. For instance, if the process of Cost Control showed that the project was going to cost significantly less or more than the cost baseline, then certain changes would likely result to bring the project back in line. These changes could take the form of reducing the scope, increasing the budget, or changing factors related to execution.

Recommended Corrective Actions

Corrective action is anything done to bring future results in line with the plan. For the process of Cost Control, if the actual costs did not line up with the cost baseline and the activity cost estimates, then corrective action could mean changing the plan or changing something with the execution (e.g. training or changing vendors) to help control costs.

Cost Control

Organizational Process Assets Updates

Every mistake is potentially an asset if it is documented in the form of lessons learned, but lessons learned can document more than mistakes. Organizational process assets could also include things done well that resulted in costs falling into line.

Project Management Plan Updates

Anything that changes the project plan, such as changes to the cost baseline, changes to the cost management plan, or changes to any other parts of the project management plan, should be updated back into the project management plan.

Special Focus: Earned Value

 The following section is of key importance

If you are wrestling with your understanding of earned value, think about the concept of debits and credits. In a double entry accounting system, for every debit to one account, there is a corresponding credit to another account. Earned value is similar in that if you spend a dollar on labor for your project, that dollar doesn't just evaporate into thin air. You are "earning" a dollar's value back into your project. If you buy bricks or computers, write code or documentation, or perform any work on the project, those activities earn value back into your project.

There are 12 key formulas associated with earned value management that often appear on the test, and they require both memorization and understanding. Following is a chart that presents a summary of the key terms used in earned value calculations.

Note that for Planned Value, Earned Value, and Actual Cost, there are older, equivalent terms that still show up on the exam. These older terms and their associated abbreviations are shown along with the current terms on the chart on the following page, and you must be able to recognize and apply either one on the exam.

Term	Abbreviation	Description	Formula
Budgeted At Completion	BAC	How much was originally planned for this project to cost.	No one formula exists. BAC is derived by looking at the total budgeted cost for the project.
Planned Value (also known as Budgeted Cost of Work Scheduled)	PV (or BCWS)	How much work should have been completed at a point in time based on the plan. (Derived by measuring where you had planned to be in terms of work completed at a point in the schedule).	Planned % Complete X BAC
Earned Value (also known as Budgeted Cost of Work Performed)	EV (or BCWP)	How much work was actually completed during a given period of time. Derived by measuring where you actually are in terms of work completed during a given period of time in the schedule.	EV = Actual % Complete X BAC
Actual Cost (also known as Actual Cost of Work Performed)	AC (or ACWP)	The money spent during a given period of time.	Sum of the costs for the given period of time.
Cost Variance	CV	The difference between what we expected to spend and what was actually spent.	CV = EV-AC
Schedule Variance	SV	The difference between where we planned to be in the schedule and where we are in the schedule.	SV = EV-PV
Cost Performance Index	CPI	The rate at which the project performance is meeting cost expectations during a given period of time.	CPI = EV ÷ AC
Cumulative CPI	CPI^C	The rate at which the project performance is meeting cost expectations from the beginning up to a point in time. CPI^C is also used to forecast project costs at completion.	$CPI^C = EV^C ÷ AC^C$
Schedule Performance Index	SPI	The rate at which the project performance is meeting schedule expectations up to a point in time.	SPI = EV ÷ PV
Estimate At Completion	EAC	Projecting the total cost at completion based on project performance up to a point in time.	$EAC = BAC ÷ CPI^C$ (Note that there are over 25 ways to calculate the EAC, but this one should be sufficient for the exam.)
Estimate To Completion	ETC	Projecting how much will be spent on the project, based on past performance.	ETC = EAC - AC
Variance At Completion	VAC	The difference between what was budgeted and what will actually be spent.	VAC = BAC - EAC

Earned Value

EVM Example

Consider the following example:

You are the project manager for the construction of 20 miles of sidewalk. According to your plan, the cost of construction will be $15,000 per mile and will take 8 weeks to complete.

2 weeks into the project, you have spent $55,000 and completed 4 miles of sidewalk, and you want to report performance and determine how much time and cost remain.

Below, we will walk through each calculation to show how we arrive at the correct answers.

Budgeted at Completion

In the approach outlined by this book, we will always begin by calculating BAC. Budgeted at completion simply means, "how much we originally expected this project to cost". It is typically very easy to calculate. In our example, we take 20 miles of sidewalk * $15,000 / mile. That equates to a BAC of $300,000.

BAC = $300,000

Planned Value

The planned value is how much work was planned for this point in time. The value is expressed in dollars.

Planned Value = Planned % complete * BAC

We do this by taking the BAC ($300,000) and multiplying it by our % complete. In this case, we are 2 weeks complete on an 8 week schedule, which equates to 25%. $300,000 * .25 = $75,000. Therefore, we had planned to spend $75,000 after two weeks.

PV = $75,000

Earned Value

If you have been intimidated by the concept of earned value, relax. Earned value is based on the assumption that as you complete work on the project, you are adding value to the project. Therefore, it is simply a matter of calculating how much value you have "earned" on the project.

Planned value is what was planned, but earned value is what actually happened.

EV = Actual % Complete * BAC

In this case, we have completed 4 miles of the 20 mile project, which equates to 20%. We multiply that percentage by the BAC to get EV. It is $300,000 * 20% = $60,000. This tells us that we have completed $60,000 worth of work, or more accurately, we have earned $60,000 of value for the project.

EV = $60,000

Actual Cost

Building on the above illustration, we will calculate our actual costs. Actual cost is the amount of cost you have incurred at this point, and we are told in the example that we have spent $55,000 to date. In this example, no calculation is needed.

AC = Actual Cost

AC = $55,000

Cost Variance

Cost variance (CV) is how much actual costs differ from planned costs. We derive this by calculating the difference between EV and AC. In this example, it is EV of $60,000 – AC of $55,000. A positive variance (as in this case), reflects that the project is doing better on cost than expected.

For those who are curious, the reason we use EV in this formula instead of PV is that we are calculating how much the actual costs have varied. If we used PV, it would give us the variance from our plan, but the cost variance measures *actual* cost variance, and EV is based on actual performance, whereas PV is based on planned performance.

A positive CV is a good thing. It indicates that we are doing better on costs than we had planned. Conversely, a negative CV indicates that costs are running higher than planned.

CV = EV-AC

CV = $5,000

Schedule Variance

Schedule variance (SV) is how much our schedule differs from our plan. Where people often get confused here is that *this concept is expressed in dollars.* SV is derived by calculating the difference between EV and PV. In this example, the schedule variance is EV of $60,000 – PV of $75,000. A negative variance (as in this case) reflects that we are not performing as well as we had hoped in terms of schedule. A positive SV would indicate that the project is ahead of schedule.

SV = EV-PV

SV = -$15,000

Cost Performance Index

The cost performance index gives us an indicator as to how much we are getting for every dollar. It is derived by dividing Earned Value by the Actual Cost. In this example, Earned Value = $60,000, and our Actual Cost = $55,000. $60,000 ÷ $55,000 = 1.09.

This figure tells us that we are getting $1.09 worth of performance for every $1.00 we expected. A CPI of 1 indicates that the project is exactly on track. A closer look at the formula reveals that values of 1 or greater are good, and values less than 1 are undesirable.

CPI = EV ÷ AC

CPI = 1.09

Schedule Performance Index

A corollary to the cost performance index is the schedule performance index, or SPI. The schedule performance index tells us how fast the project is progressing compared to the project plan. It is derived by dividing earned value by the planned value. In this example, earned value = $60,000, and our planned value = $75,000. $60,000 ÷ $75,000 = 0.8. This tells us that the project is progressing at 80% of the pace that we expected it to, and when we look at the example, this conclusion makes sense. We had expected to lay 20 miles of sidewalk in 8 weeks. At that rate, after 2 weeks, we should have constructed 5 miles, but instead the example tells us that we had only constructed 4 miles. That equates to 4/5 performance, which is 80%. Like the cost performance index, values of 1 or greater are good, and values that are less than 1 are undesirable.

Earned Value

$SPI = EV \div PV$

$SPI = 0.8$

A common way for the cost performance and schedule performance index to be used is to track them over time. This is often displayed in the form of a graph, as illustrated below. This graph may be easily interpreted if you consider that a value of 1 indicates that the index is exactly on plan.

Schedule Performance Index Over Time
(same view with Cost Performance Index)

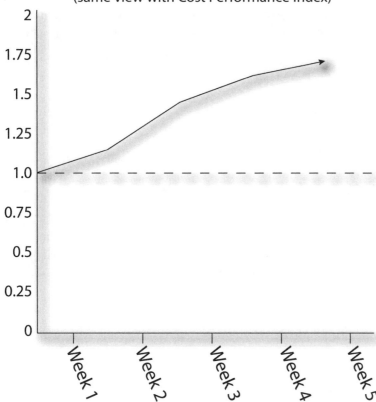

Estimate At Completion

Estimate at completion is the amount we expect the project to cost, based on where we are relative to cost and schedule. If that sounds confusing, think of it this way. If you know you are half way through the project, and you are currently 20% over budget, then the estimate at completion factors that variance out to the end of the project. There are many ways to calculate EAC; for the exam, the most straightforward way to calculate it is to take the BAC and divide it by our cost performance index. In this example, we expected to spend (BAC) $300,000 and our CPI is 1.09.

$300,000 \div 1.09 = \$275,229.36$. This should make sense. We are doing better on costs than we had originally planned, and this value reflects that.

$$EAC = BAC \div CPI$$

$$EAC = \$275,229.36$$

Estimate To Completion

Estimate to completion is simply how much more we expect to spend from this point forward based on what we've done so far. It can be easily backed into by taking our estimate at complete (what we expect to spend) and subtracting what we have spent so far (Actual Cost). Given the numbers above, it would be EAC of $275,229.36 - AC of $55,000 = $220,229.36. This tells us that we expect to spend $220,229.36 more, given our performance thus far.

$$ETC = EAC - AC$$

$$ETC = \$220,229.36$$

Variance at Completion

Variance at completion is the difference between what we originally budgeted and what we expect to spend. A positive variance indicates that we are doing better than projected, and a negative variance indicates that we expect the project to run over on costs.

In this example, our BAC was $300,000; however, our EAC is now $275,229.36. $300,000 - $275,229.36 = $24,770.64.

$$VAC = BAC - EAC$$

$$VAC = \$24,770.64$$

Cumulative CPI (CPI^c)

Once you understand the concept of earned value, the cumulative cost performance index (expressed as CPI^c) is not as intimidating as it may first look. Recall that the regular CPI is simply EV/AC, the efficiency indicator of performance during a given period of time. The CPI^c is simply all of the periodic earned value calculations added together (EV^c) and divided by all of the periodic actual cost calculations added together (AC^c).

Consider a company that took earned value measurements at monthly intervals for the past three months as summarized in the table below.

	EV	AC
Month 1	$22,000	$13,700
Month 2	$151,000	$137,900
Month 3	$107,000	$98,400

The following table, using the same example, conveys the usefulness of CPI and CPI^c.

	EV	EV^c	AC	AC^c	CPI	CPI^c
Month 1	$22,000	$22,000	$13,700	$13,700	1.61	1.61
Month 2	$151,000	$173,000	$137,900	$151,600	1.09	1.14
Month 3	$107,000	$280,000	$98,400	$250,000	1.09	1.12

Given this information, the CPI^c would be calculated by adding up all of the earned value figures ($280,000) and dividing by the sum of the actual costs ($250,000). This yields a cumulative CPI of 1.12.

Cost Performance Index (CPI) was calculated by applying the formula $CPI = EV \div AC$, which gave us a calculation of the monthly performance. For the Cumulative Cost Performance Index (CPI^c), we applied the formula $CPI^c = EV^c \div AC^c$, which calculates the project's performance up to a point in time.

These values are useful, because the monthly CPI only provided a snapshot of your earned value performance at a point in time, but the cumulative CPI can show a number that factors in performance efficienty in all months up to a point in time. The cumulative CPI has been shown to be a good predictor of performance at completion, even when used very early in the project.

Earned Value

Types of Cost

Several types of questions regarding cost may appear on the exam. It is important to understand the difference between the different types of cost presented below:

Cost type	Explanation
Fixed	Costs that stay the same throughout the life of a project. An example is a piece of heavy equipment, such as a bulldozer.
Variable	Costs that vary on a project. Examples are hourly labor, and fuel for the bulldozer.
Direct	Expenses that are billed directly to the project. An example is the materials used to construct a building.
Indirect	Costs that are shared and allocated among several or all projects. An example could be a manager's salary. His people might be direct costs on a project, but his salary is overhead and would be considered an indirect cost.
Sunk	Costs that have been invested into or expended upon the project. Sunk costs are like spilt milk. If they are unrecoverable, they are to be treated as if they are irrelevant! This is difficult for many people to understand, but the statement "we've spent over 10 million dollars on this project, and we're not turning back now" is not good decision-making if the costs are unrecoverable, or "sunk."

Exercises

Example 1

You are constructing 6 additional rooms on an office building. Each of the six rooms is identical, and the projected cost for the project is $100,000 and is expected to take 5 weeks.

At the end of the 2nd week, you have spent $17,500 per room and have finished 2 rooms; you are ready to begin on the 3rd.

1. Based on the information provided in the example above, fill in the values for the following table:

	Value
Budgeted At Completion	
Planned Value	
Earned Value	
Actual Cost	
Cost Variance	
Schedule Variance	
Cost Performance Index	
Schedule Performance Index	
Estimated At Completion	
Estimated To Completion	
Variance At Completion	

2. Is the project ahead of or behind schedule?

3. Is the project going to be completed over or under budget?

Example 2

Here is another example to test your understanding of these concepts.

You have planned for a project to write a software application to take 1 year. The costs to this project are budgeted at $12,500 per month.

Six months into the project, you find that the software application is 50% completed, and you have spent $70,000.

4. Based on the information provided, fill in the values for the following table:

	Value
Budgeted At Completion	
Planned Value	
Earned Value	
Actual Cost	
Cost Variance	
Schedule Variance	
Cost Performance Index	
Schedule Performance Index	
Estimated At Completion	
Estimated To Completion	
Variance At Completion	

5. Is the project ahead of or behind schedule?

6. Is the project going to be completed over or under budget?

7. Mark one value in each column that shows the most desirable value given the information provided. (Note that some of these attributes are covered in Chapter 4 – Project Scope Management)

IRR	SPI	CPI	NPV	Payback Period	BCR	ROI
22%	1	.5	$25,000	16 mos	2	9%
0%	0	1	$95,000	2 yrs	1.5	12%
12%	.8	1.2	$50,000	16 wks	1	-2%
-3%	1.2	1.15	$71,000	25 mos	.2	3%

8. Project X was projected to take four months and cost $70,000 per month. At the end of month one, the project was 20% complete, and had spent $89,000. At the end of month two, it was 40% complete and had spent $151,000. What is the cumulative CPI for Project X at the end of month two?

Cost Exercises

Answers to Exercises

1. Your answers should look like these:

	Value
Budgeted At Completion	$100,000
Planned Value	$40,000.00
Earned Value	$33,333.33
Actual Cost	$35,000.00
Cost Variance	-$1,666.67
Schedule Variance	-$6,666.67
Cost Performance Index	0.95
Schedule Performance Index	0.83
Estimated At Completion	$105,263.15
Estimated To Completion	$70,263.15
Variance At Completion	-$5,263.15

- BAC = $100,000.00
- PV = 2 weeks ÷ 5 weeks = 40% complete * 100,000 = $40,000
- EV = 2 rooms ÷ 6 rooms = 33.3% complete * 100,000 = $33,333.33
- AC = $17,500 per rooms * 2 rooms = $35,000
- CV = (EV) $33,333.33 – (AC) $35,000.00 = -$1,666.67
- SV = (EV) $33,333.33 – (PV) $40,000.00 = -$6,666.67
- CPI = (EV) $33,333.33 ÷ (AC) $35,000.00 = 0.95
- SPI = (EV) $33,333.33 ÷ (PV) $40,000.00 = 0.83
- EAC = (BAC) $100,000.00 ÷ (CPI) 0.95 = $105,263.15
- ETC = (EAC) $105,263.15 – (AC) $35,000.00 = $70,263.15
- VAC = (BAC) $100,000.00 – (EAC) $105,263.15 = -$5,263.15

2. Is the project ahead of or behind schedule?

   The project is behind schedule. The easiest way to determine this is by looking at the SPI. Since it is less than 1, we can determine that the project is not doing well in terms of the schedule.

3. Is the project going to be completed over or under budget?

   There are two ways to see that the project is going to run over budget. First, the CPI is less than 1. Second, the VAC is negative.

4. Check your answers against these:

	Value
Budgeted At Completion	$150,000.00
Planned Value	$75,000.00
Earned Value	$75,000.00
Actual Cost	$70,000.00
Cost Variance	$5,000.00
Schedule Variance	$0
Cost Performance Index	1.07
Schedule Performance Index	1
Estimated At Completion	$140,186.91
Estimated To Completion	$70,186.91
Variance At Completion	$9,813.09

- BAC = $150,000.00
- PV = 6 months ÷ 12 months = 50% complete * 150,000 = $75,000
- EV = Project is 50% complete * 150,000.00 = $75,000.00
- AC = $70,000 .00
- CV = (EV) $75,000.00 – (AC) $70,000.00 = $5,000.00
- SV = (EV) $75,000.00 – (PV) $75,000.00 = $0
- CPI = (EV) $75,000.00 ÷ (AC) $70,000.00 = 1.07
- SPI = (EV) $75,000.00 ÷ (PV) $75,000.00 = 1
- EAC = (BAC) $150,000.00 ÷ (CPI) 1.07 = $140,186.91
- ETC = (EAC) $140,186.91 – (AC) $70,000.00 = $70,186.91
- VAC = (BAC) $150,000.00 – (EAC) $140,186.91 = $9,813.09

5. Is the project ahead of or behind schedule?

   This would be classified as a "trick" question, as neither answer is correct. Since the SPI is 1, we can see that the project is exactly on schedule.

6. Is the project going to be completed over or under budget?

   The project is projected to finish ahead of budget, due to the cost performance index being greater than 1.

7. The most desirable project attributes for each column are shaded in the chart below. Note that some of these formulas came from Chapter 4, Scope Management:

IRR	SPI	CPI	NPV	Payback Period	BCR	ROI
22%	1	.5	$25,000	16 mos	2	9%
0%	0	1	$95,000	2 yrs	1.5	12%
12%	.8	1.2	$50,000	16 wks	1	-2%
-3%	1.2	1.15	$71,000	25 mos	.2	3%

Did you notice that for most of these measurements, the bigger value is the best one? That is true for all except for the payback period, where you want the shortest time to recoup project costs.

8. If you got this one, give yourself a big pat on the back! In order to answer it, you first had to calculate the earned value for months one and two.

> Month 1 EV = 0.2 X $280,000 = $56,000
> Month 2 EV = 0.2 X $280,000 = $56,000
> Month 2 AC = $151,000

After getting these values, the CPI^C is a snap. It is simply the sum of the earned value numbers divided by the sum of the actual costs. Since you already know the sum of the actual costs is $151,000, all you have to do is add the earned values together and divide. This yields $112,000 ÷ $151,000 = a cumulative CPI (CPI^C) of 0.74.

Cost Management Questions

1. Your schedule projected that you would reach 50% completion today on a road construction project that is paving 32 miles of new highway. Every 4 miles is scheduled to cost $5,000,000. Today, in your status meeting, you announced that you had completed 20 miles of the highway at a cost of $18,000,000. What is your Planned Value?

    A. $12,800,000.

    B. $18,000,000.

    C. $20,000,000.

    D. $40,000,000.

2. Activity cost estimates are used as an input into which process?

    A.   Cost Estimating.

    B.   Cost Budgeting.

    C.   Cost Analysis.

    D.   Cost Control.

3. The difference between present value and net present value is:

    A.   Present value is expressed as an interest rate, while net present value is expressed as a dollar figure.

    B.   Present value is a measure of the actual present value, while net present value measures expected present value.

    C.   Present value does not factor in costs.

    D.   Present value is more accurate.

4. Which of the following process sequences is correct?:

    A.   Create WBS, then Cost Budgeting, then Cost Estimating.

    B.   Create WBS, then Cost Estimating, then Cost Budgeting.

    C.   Cost Budgeting, then Cost Estimating, then Create WBS.

    D.   Cost Estimating, then Cost Budgeting, then Create WBS.

5.   One of your team members makes a change to the budget with your approval. In what process is he engaged?

   A.   Cost Planning.

   B.   Cost Estimating.

   C.   Project Cost Management.

   D.   Cost Control.

6.   Your project office has purchased a site license for a computerized tool that assists in the task of cost estimating on a very large construction project for a downtown skyscraper. This tool asks you for specific characteristics about the project and then provides estimating guidance based on materials, construction techniques, historical information, and industry practices. This tool is an example of:

   A.   Bottom-up estimating.

   B.   Parametric modeling.

   C.   Analogous estimating.

   D.   Activity duration estimating.

7.   You are managing a project that is part of a large construction program. During the execution of your project you are alerted that the construction of a foundation is expected to experience a serious cost overrun. What would be your FIRST course of action?

   A.   Evaluate the cause and size of the overrun.

   B.   Stop execution until the problem is solved.

   C.   Contact the program manager to see if additional funds may be released.

   D.   Determine if you have sufficient budget reserves to cover the cost overrun.

8. If earned value = $10,000, planned value = $8,000, and actual cost = $3,000, what is the schedule variance?

    A. -$2,000

    B. $2,000

    C. $5,000

    D. $-5,000

9. Estimate to complete indicates:

    A. The total projected amount that will be spent, based on past performance.

    B. The projected remaining amount that will be spent, based on past performance.

    C. The difference between what was budgeted and what is expected to be spent.

    D. The original planned completion cost minus the costs incurred to date.

10. If a project has a CPI of .95 and an SPI of 1.01, this indicates:

    A. The project is progressing slower and costing more than planned.

    B. The project is progressing slower and costing less than planned.

    C. The project is progressing faster and costing more than planned.

    D. The project is progressing faster and costing less than planned.

11. 16. As a project manager, your BEST use of the project cost baseline would be to:

    A. Measure and monitor cost performance on the project.

    B. Track approved changes.

    C. Calculate team performance bonuses.

    D. Measure and report on variable project costs.

12. The value of all work that has been completed so far is:

    A. Earned value.

    B. Estimate at complete.

    C. Actual cost.

    D. Planned value.

13. If you have a schedule variance of $500, this would indicate:

    A. Planned value is less than earned value.

    B. Earned value is less than the estimate at complete.

    C. Actual cost is less than earned value.

    D. The ratio of earned value to planned value is 5:1.

14. If budgeted at complete = $500, estimate to complete = $400, earned value = $100, and actual cost = $100, what is the estimate at complete?

    A. $0.

    B. $150.

    C. $350.

    D. $500.

15. You have spent $322,168 on your project to date. The program manager wants to know why costs have been running so high. You explain that the resource cost has been greater than expected and should level out over the next six months. What does the $322,168 represent to the program manager?

    A. Earned value

    B. Actual cost

    C. Planned value

    D. Cost performance index

Answers to Cost Management Questions

1. C. Planned value is calculated by multiplying the Budgeted At Completion by planned % complete. Our cost per mile is planned at $1,250,000 ($5,000,000 ÷ 4 miles), and our Budgeted At Completion is 32 miles * 1,250,000/mile = $40,000,000. We planned to be 50% complete. Therefore, $40,000,000 * .50 = $20,000,000.

2. B. Cost Budgeting takes the activity cost estimates and uses them (along with other inputs) to create a budget. 'A' is incorrect because Cost Estimating is the process that creates the activity cost estimates, so it stands to reason that they would be an output and not an input. 'C' sounds like a decent guess, but it is not a real process. 'D' is incorrect because the process of Cost Control is not concerned with just the individual activity cost estimates. Instead, it uses inputs of the cost baseline.

3. C. This question was drawn on material covered in chapter 2. There is a difference between present value and net present value. Present value tells the expected value of the project in today's dollars. Net present value is the same thing, but it subtracts the costs after calculating the present value.

4. B. This question may not look like it is about inputs and outputs, but it actually is. Create WBS is performed first out of the three processes, and the output is the Work Breakdown Structure (WBS). The WBS is used as an input for the next process of the three, Cost Estimating, where the costs of the activities are estimated and aggregated back to the WBS. Finally, the output of that process, the Activity Cost Estimates, is used as an input into Cost Budgeting, which occurs last out of the three processes listed. By understanding how the outputs of one process become the inputs into another, it becomes simpler to understand the logical order of many of these processes.

5. D. The main clue here is "change." If they are making approved changes, they are in a control process. 'A' is not a real process. 'B' is incorrect since Cost Estimating is the process where the original estimates are developed and not where they are updated. 'C' is the knowledge area (careful not to get these confused with processes).

6. B. This is an example of parametric modeling. Parametric modeling is common in some industries, where you can describe the project in detail, and the modeling tool will help provide estimates based on historical information, industry standards, etc.

7.	A. This illustrates one of PMI's biggest biases on these questions. Your job as a project manager is almost always to evaluate and understand first. Know what you are dealing with before you take action, and don't just accept anyone's word for it - verify the information yourself!

8.	B. Schedule Variance is calculated as EV-PV. In this example, $10,000 - $8,000 = $2,000.

9.	B. The estimate to complete is what we expect to spend from this point forward, based on our performance thus far.

10.	C. Did the wording trip you up on this one? Make sure you read the questions and answers carefully since things were switched around on this one. A schedule performance index greater than 1 means that the project is progressing faster than planned. A cost performance index that is less than 1 means that the project is costing more than planned. Therefore choice 'C' is the only one that fits.

11.	A. The cost baseline is used to track cost performance based on the original plan plus approved changes.

12.	A. Earned value is defined as the value of all work completed to this point.

13.	A. This is another tricky question because of the way it is worded. Schedule variance is calculated as earned value – planned value. In this case, schedule variance could only be positive if earned value is greater than planned value (or stated otherwise, if planned value is less than earned value). 'A' is the only choice that has to be true.

14.	D. The estimate at complete is what we expect to have spent at the end of the project. It is calculated by taking our budgeted at complete and dividing it by our cost performance index. Step 1 is to calculate our cost performance index. It is earned value ÷ actual cost, and in this case, it equals 1. Budgeted at complete is $500, and $500 ÷ 1 = $500. Therefore, 'D' is the correct answer, indicating that we are progressing exactly as planned.

15.	B. Look at the first sentence "You have spent $322,168…" Actual cost is what you have spent to date on the project.

Cost Mgt Answers

Chapter 7

Quality Management

Difficulty	Memorization	Exam Importance
Medium	Medium	High

The topics on the CAPM borrow from numerous business disciplines such as psychology, math, accounting, and even law. Previous formal study of these disciplines is beneficial but not necessary to pass the exam. This is especially true for the topic of quality management. The study of quality and its effect on business and projects has been the focus of considerable research, especially since the end of World War II. Volumes of research, usually focused on a few central theories, have been conducted and documented. Quality borrows heavily from the field of statistics, and a high-level explanation of some of the statistical tools and techniques is provided here.

The quality processes presented in the PMBOK Guide and on the CAPM Exam come largely from the theories of Deming, Crosby, and Juran.

There are numerous theories on quality, how it should be implemented, how it should be measured, and what levels of quality should be attained. You need to have a solid grasp of the theories presented in this chapter before taking the exam.

Please note that the statistics and statistical examples here are greatly simplified, but they are adequate to get you through the exam. Topics on the CAPM Exam, such as sampling, distribution, and deviations from the mean are built on underlying assumptions that you do not need to know in order to pass, but you do need to know how to apply them.

The processes of Project Quality Management with their *primary* outputs

Quality Management

Quality Planning

Quality Management Plan
Metrics
Checklists

Perform Quality Assurance

Requested (process) Changes

Perform Quality Control

Quality Control Measures
Validated Defect Repair

Philosophy

PMI's philosophy of quality is derived from several leading quality theories, including TQM, ISO-9000, Six Sigma, and others. The foundational work in this field performed by PMI looks at each of these theories in terms of the tools and techniques they provide.

PMI's philosophy of quality is also a very proactive approach. Whereas early theories on quality relied heavily on inspection, current thinking is focused on prevention over inspection. This evolution of thought is based on the fact that it costs more to fix an error than it does to prevent one.

The responsibility of quality in PMI's philosophy falls heavily on the project manager. Everyone on the team has an important contribution to make to project quality; however, it is management's responsibility to provide the resources to make quality happen, and the project manager is ultimately responsible and accountable for the quality of the project.

The PMI process, as it relates to quality, is perhaps more important here than most other places. Quality Planning, Perform Quality Assurance, and Perform Quality Control map closely to the Plan-Do-Check-Act cycle as described by Deming, and several questions on the exam rely heavily on your understanding of how quality activities flow and connect.

It is also important to understand that some of the investment in quality is usually borne by the organization, since it would be far too expensive for each project to have its own quality program. An example would be a company investing in a site license for a software testing product that can be used across numerous projects.

Importance

Project quality management is one of the slimmer chapters both in this book and in the PMBOK Guide, but it is of high importance on the exam. You should expect to see several exam questions that will relate directly to this chapter, so it will be necessary to become acquainted with the terms and theories as prescribed below. Then reread this chapter to ensure that you have mastered the topic.

In real world practice, quality formulas abound; however, the CAPM does not currently require you to memorize or apply them. This chapter focuses, instead, on the processes, concepts and terms.

Some parts of this topic will be revisited in later chapters in order to show how quality fits into the overall project management context.

Preparation

The quality processes, tools and techniques, and outputs found in this chapter must be learned and understood. You should expect to see questions on the CAPM Exam that relate directly to these concepts. Special attention will be paid to the key quality theories that show up on the exam, as well as terminology that you need to know.

Pay careful attention to the differences between Quality Planning, Perform Quality Assurance, and Perform Quality Control. This distinction is a tricky area for many people on the exam.

Quality Management Processes

Definition of Quality

The definition of quality you should know for the exam is "the degree to which a set of inherent characteristics fulfill requirements." It is also important to realize that the requirements or needs of the project may be stated or implied.

Quality Processes

There are only three processes within project quality management, as listed in the table below. In the PMI framework, these processes touch three process groups: planning (Quality Planning), executing (Perform Quality Assurance), and monitoring & controlling (Perform Quality Control).

Process Group	Quality Management Process
Initiating	(none)
Planning	Quality Planning
Executing	Perform Quality Assurance
Monitoring & Controlling	Perform Quality Control
Closing	(none)

The primary outputs associated with the three quality management processes are shown in the table below.

Process	Primary Outputs
Quality Planning	• Quality management plan • Quality baseline
Perform Quality Assurance	• Requested changes • Recommended corrective action
Perform Quality Control	• Quality control measurements • Defect repair

Quality Terms and Philosophies

 All of these quality management terms are important for the exam.

Total Quality Management (TQM)

A quality theory popularized after World War II that states that everyone in the company is responsible for quality and is able to make a difference in the ultimate quality of the product. TQM applies to improvements in processes and in results. TQM also includes statistical process control.

TQM shifts the primary quality focus away from the product that is produced and looks instead at the underlying process of how it was produced.

Continuous Improvement

Also known as "Kaizen," from the Japanese Management term. A philosophy that stresses constant process improvement, in the form of small changes in products or services.

Kaizen

(See Continuous Improvement)

Just-In-Time (JIT)

A manufacturing method that brings inventory down to zero (or near zero) levels. It forces a focus on quality, since there is no excess inventory on hand to waste.

ISO 9000

Part of the International Standards Organization to ensure that companies document what they do and do what they document. ISO 9000 is not directly attributable to higher quality, but may be an important component of Perform Quality Assurance, since it ensures that an organization follows their processes.

Statistical Independence

When the outcomes of two processes are not linked together or dependent upon each other, they are statistically independent. Rolling a six on a die the first time neither increases nor decreases the chance that you will roll a six the second time. Therefore, the two rolls would be statistically independent.

Mutually Exclusive

A statistical term that states that one choice excludes the others. For example, painting a house yellow and painting it blue or white are mutually exclusive events.

Standard Deviation

The concept of standard deviation is an important one to understand for the exam. Standard deviation is a statistical calculation used to measure and describe how data is organized. The following graphic of a standard bell curve illustrates standard deviation:

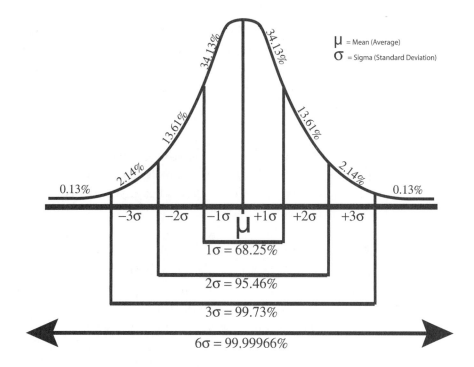

The standard deviation, represented by the Greek symbol σ, is calculated first by averaging all data points to get the mean, then calculating the difference between each data point and the mean, squaring each of the differences, and dividing the sum of the squared differences by the number of data points minus one. Finally, take the square root of that number, and you have the standard deviation of the data set. If the data set is "normally distributed," as it is in the preceding chart, the following statistics will be true:

- 68.25% of the data points (or values) will fall within 1 σ from the mean.
- 95.46% of the values will fall within 2 σ from the mean.
- 99.73% of the values will fall within 3 σ from the mean.
- 99.99966% of the values will fall within 6 σ from the mean.

The standard deviation may be used in a few different ways in quality. For instance, the higher your standard deviation, the more diverse your data points are. It is also used to set quality levels (see the Six Sigma topic later in this chapter), and to set control limits to determine if a process is in control (see the control charts topic later in this chapter).

Even though you should not expect to have to perform standard deviation calculations for the exam, you will likely see questions related to the application of the standard deviation. The more you understand about this concept, the more prepared you will be for the exam.

Six Sigma

Six sigma is a popular philosophy of quality management that focuses on achieving very high levels of quality by controlling the process and reducing defects (a defect is defined as anything that does not meet the customer's quality standards).

As you will remember from the section on standard deviation, a σ (sigma) is defined as 1 standard deviation from the mean. At the level of one sigma quality, 68.25% of all outputs will meet quality standards. At the three sigma quality level, that number jumps to 99.73% of all outputs that meet quality standards. At the six sigma level, the number is 99.99966% of all outputs that meet quality standards. This means that when quality reaches six sigma standards, the results will be such that only 3.4 out of every 1,000,000 outputs do not meet quality standards. Six sigma quality strives to make the overwhelming majority of the bell curve fall within customer quality limits.

Six sigma puts a primary focus on quantifying, measuring, and controlling the quality of products, services, and results. It is based on the underlying theory that anything will vary if measured to a fine enough level. The goal is to refine the process so that human error and outside influence no longer exist, and these variations are completely random. If done properly, the statistical outcome should follow the bell curve illustrated previously under the topic of standard deviation. The goal is to make six standard deviations (sigmas) of the outputs fall within the customer's quality limits.

If this seems like a lot of information, the most important things to know for the exam are that six sigma is a quality management philosophy that sets very high standards for quality, and that one sigma quality is the lowest quality level, allowing 317,500 defects per 1,000,000 outputs, three sigma quality is higher, allowing 2,700 defects per 1,000,000, and six sigma quality is the highest of these, allowing only 3.4 defects per 1,000,000.

Also know that six sigma quality levels may not be high enough for all projects or all industries. For instance, the pharmaceutical industry, the airline industry, and power utilities typically strive for higher levels of quality than six sigma would specify in some areas of their operations.

Prevention vs. Inspection

Prevention is simply keeping defects from occurring, while inspection is about catching the errors that have occurred before they impact others outside the project.

Attribute Sampling vs. Variable Sampling

Attribute sampling is binary; either a work result conforms to quality or it does not. Variable sampling, on the other hand, measures how well something conforms to quality. Consider, for example, a production facility making prescription drugs. Using attribute sampling, they would define tolerances, a batch of product would be tested, and it would either pass or fail that inspection. Using variable sampling, however, the batch of product would be rated on a continuous scale (perhaps on parts per million) that showed how well the batch conformed to ideal quality.

Special Causes vs. Common Causes

Within the topic of statistical process control (see control charts later in this chapter), there is a concept of special causes and common causes. Special causes are typically considered unusual and preventable, whereas common causes are normal. For instance, if your manufacturing process produced 250 defects per 1,000,000 due to assembly errors, that might be considered a special cause, whereas if your manufacturing process produced one defect in a million due to bad raw materials, that might be considered a common cause. In general, special causes are considered preventable by process improvement, while common causes are generally accepted.

Quality Terms

Tolerances vs. Control Limits

Tolerances deal with the limits your project has set for product acceptance. For instance, you may specify that any product will be accepted if it weighs between 12 and 15 grams. Those weights would represent your tolerances for weight. Control limits, on the other hand, are a more complex concept. Typically, control limits are set at three standard deviations above and below the mean. As long as your results fall within the control limits, your process is considered to be in control. Control limits are discussed further under the topic of control charts, covered later in this chapter.

If that explanation still leaves you scratching your head, consider that tolerances focus on whether the product is acceptable, while control limits focus on whether the process itself is acceptable.

Quality Terms

Quality Planning

What it is:

Quality Planning is named appropriately. It is the process where the project team identifies what the quality specifications are for this project and how these specifications will be met.

Why it is important:

As stated earlier in this chapter, quality is planned in from the start, and not inspected in after the product has been constructed. Quality Planning is the process where this planning is performed to make sure that the resulting product is of acceptable quality.

When it is performed:

Quality Planning begins early in the project planning phase of the project. In fact, it typically is performed concurrently with other planning processes and the development of the project management plan.

The reason Quality Planning is performed early in the project planning is that decisions made about quality can have a significant impact on other decisions such as scope, time, cost, and risk.

How it works:

Inputs

Enterprise Environmental Factors — See Chapter 2, Common Inputs

Organizational Process Assets

Assets such as quality management plans from previous projects should be considered and used as part of the project plan. Also, the performing organization's quality policy should be brought into this process. The quality policy is usually brief and defines the performing organization's attitudes about quality across all projects. It must be considered if it exists. If it does not exist, the project team should write one for this project.

Project Scope Statement

Many project management practitioners view scope and quality as inseparable. The PMBOK Guide also views them as tightly linked, and this is why the project scope statement is a primary input into Quality Planning. The project scope statement defines the requirements, and it also specifies the acceptance criteria for these requirements.

Project Management Plan — See Chapter 2, Common Inputs

Tools

 Cost-Benefit Analysis

Quality can be expensive to achieve; however, there is a golden rule in quality that all benefits of quality activities must outweigh the costs. No activities should be performed that cost more (or even the same) as the expected benefits. These benefits potentially include acceptance, less rework, and overall lower costs.

 Benchmarking

The technique of benchmarking is where a project's quality standards are compared to those of other projects which will serve as a basis for comparison. These other projects may be from the industry, such as an automaker setting quality standards based on those of other automobiles in their class, or it may be based on projects previously executed by the performing organization.

 Design of Experiments

The technique of design of experiments, often abbreviated as DOE, is an important technique in Quality Planning. It uses data analysis to determine optimal conditions. For instance, rather than conducting a series of individual trials, an information technology project may use design of experiments analysis and optimize hardware and bandwidth needed to run an Internet-based application, finding the optimal match of system response time and overall cost.

 Cost of Quality

The technique of evaluating the cost of quality (often abbreviated as COQ) looks at all of the costs that will be realized in order to achieve quality. The costs of items that do not conform to quality are known as "cost of poor quality," often abbreviated as COpQ.

Quality Planning

Additional Quality Planning Tools

There are nearly countless additional Quality Planning tools that are designed by specific industries or for use with specific types of manufacturing processes. For the exam, focus energy on the tools presented here.

Outputs

Quality Management Plan

The quality management plan is a key output of the Quality Planning process. It describes how the quality policy will be met.

Quality Metrics

Quality metrics specifically define how quality will be measured. For instance, it is not adequate for the team to say that the system needs to have a rapid response time. Instead, a quality metric might specify that a system must respond within two seconds to 99% of all requests up to 1,000 simultaneous users. Quality metrics may relate to any quality measure.

Quality Checklists

A checklist is a Quality Planning output created to ensure that all steps were performed, and that they were performed in the proper sequence. They are created here and used in the process of Perform Quality Control.

Process Improvement Plan

The concept of process improvement is tightly linked to quality, and the process improvement plan (part of the project management plan), deals with how quality activities will be streamlined and improved.

Quality Baseline

A baseline is the original plan plus approved changes. The quality baseline is the quality objectives and the plan for achieving those objectives. The quality baseline, like other baselines, may be changed through the change control process.

Project Management Plan Updates

As Quality Planning is performed, it is normal to update the project management plan (specifically the process improvement plan and the quality management plan).

Perform Quality Assurance

What it is:

For many people, Perform Quality Assurance can be a tricky process to understand. One of the most common mistakes exam takers make is to confuse Perform Quality Assurance with Perform Quality Control (covered next), and the difference between the two can appear subtle.

Perform Quality Assurance is an executing process, and the most important thing for you to remember about this process is that it is primarily concerned with overall process improvement. It is not about inspecting the product for quality or measuring defects. Instead, Perform Quality Assurance is focused on steadily improving the activities and processes undertaken to achieve quality. Numerous questions on the exam are missed because of a misunderstanding of this key distinction!

Why it is important:

Too often, people think of quality as simply measuring, testing, and inspecting the final product; however, quality management should be about improving the process as well as the product.

Perform Quality Assurance is important because if the quality of the process and activities are improved, then quality of the product should also improve, along with an overall reduction of cost.

When it is performed:

The process of Perform Quality Assurance is performed as an ongoing activity in the project management lifecycle. It typically begins early and continues throughout the life of the project. Because Perform Quality Assurance uses many of the outputs of Quality Planning, it is not undertaken until after Quality Planning has been performed.

How it works:

Inputs

Quality Management Plan

The quality management plan gives guidance as to how the process of Perform Quality Assurance will be executed. As changes are made to the way quality is managed, they should be documented back into the quality management plan.

Quality Metrics

The quality metrics created earlier in Quality Planning are used here. Since Perform Quality Assurance is primarily concerned with process improvement, the metrics provide an objective means of measurement.

Process Improvement Plan

The process improvement plan is one of the primary inputs into the process of Perform Quality Assurance, as it defines much of what this process is about. It describes how the quality process will be improved and how these improvements will be measured and managed.

Work Performance Information

Since Perform Quality Assurance is primarily about process improvement, the work performance information is a key input. It will help identify areas where process improvement is needed, as well as areas where process improvements have worked.

Approved Change Requests

Any change requests should be evaluated for their impact on the quality of the project (among other things). A change in scope or schedule can potentially have a significant effect on the quality of the project.

Quality Control Measurements

The quality control measurements can be thought of as a feedback loop. As changes are evaluated here in the process of Perform Quality Assurance, they are measured in Perform Quality Control and fed back into this process for evaluation.

Implemented Change Requests; Implemented Corrective Actions; Implemented Defect Repair; Implemented Preventive Actions

This applies to the four preceding inputs. As a change or correction is implemented, it should be brought back into Perform Quality Assurance. The reason for this is that Perform Quality Assurance is constantly monitoring the quality process to ensure that it is working, and any change, positive or negative, needs to be a part of that evaluation.

Tools

Quality Planning Tools and Techniques

The same tools and techniques used for Quality Planning are used in Perform Quality Assurance.

Quality Audits

Quality audits are the key tool in Perform Quality Assurance. The reason for this is that audits review the project to evaluate which activities taking place on the project should be improved and which meet quality standards. The goal of the audits is both to improve acceptance of the product and the overall cost of quality.

Process Analysis

The process analysis carefully reviews the quality process to ensure that it is working efficiently and effectively.

Outputs

Requested Changes

When this much analysis and evaluation is taking place, requested changes are a normal and expected outcome of this process.

Recommended Corrective Actions

Corrective action is anything done to bring future results in line with the plan. In Perform Quality Assurance, the recommended corrective actions are going to be focused on adjusting the use of the tools in this process.

Organizational Process Assets Updates

These assets are anything that can be borrowed, built-upon, and reused for future projects within this organization. Any such assets should be updated as new practices are implemented or new information is learned.

Project Management Plan Updates

As the process of Perform Quality Assurance changes the way in which the project is managed, the project management plan (and specifically the quality management plan) should be updated.

Perform Quality Control

What it is:

Perform Quality Control looks at specific results to determine if they conform to the quality standards. It involves both product and project deliverables, and it is done throughout the project – not just at the end.

Perform Quality Control typically uses statistical sampling rather than looking at each and every output. Many volumes have been written about sampling techniques, and the practice is often very complex and is highly tailored to industry.

This process uses the tool of inspection to make sure the results of the work are what they are supposed to be. Any time you find a part being inspected for quality, you can be sure that you are in the control process.

Why it is important:

Perform Quality Control is the process where each deliverable is inspected, measured, and tested. This process makes sure everything produced meets quality standards.

When it is performed:

This process typically takes place throughout much of the project. It is performed beginning with the production of the first product deliverable and continues until all of the deliverables have been accepted.

How it works:

Inputs

Quality Management Plan

The quality management plan, a component of the project management plan, is a primary input into Perform Quality Control. This provides the plan for how Perform Quality Assurance and Perform Quality Control will be carried out.

Quality Metrics

The quality metrics will be used to measure whether the work results meet quality specifications.

Quality Checklists

The quality checklists show the steps that were taken to achieve quality on the product. Now that the product is in Perform Quality Control, the checklists will assist in assessing its conformance to quality.

Organizational Process Assets Updates

Any informational assets (or other types of assets) should be brought into this process. For instance, if a company invested in a license for a tool that assisted in software testing, that would be appropriate to bring into this process.

Work Performance Information

The work performance information can shed light on the current state of the deliverable and where it should be. For example, if a software project is scheduled to have the database completed by this date, and the work performance information shows that it is still in design, that will affect the Perform Quality Control process. In this example, you would likely use the work performance information to alter your testing scenarios to reflect the database's unfinished state.

Approved Change Requests

Change requests can not only change the product, but also the way the product is constructed, and either of these types of changes will affect quality management.

Deliverables

The project's deliverables are a primary input into this process. The deliverables are inspected and measured to ensure that they conform to quality standards.

Tools

Cause and Effect Diagram

Cause and effect diagrams are also known as Ishikawa diagrams or fishbone diagrams. In Quality Control, these are used to show how different factors relate together and might be tied to potential problems.

In Quality Control, cause and effect diagrams are used as part of an approach to improve quality by identifying quality problems and trying to uncover the underlying cause.

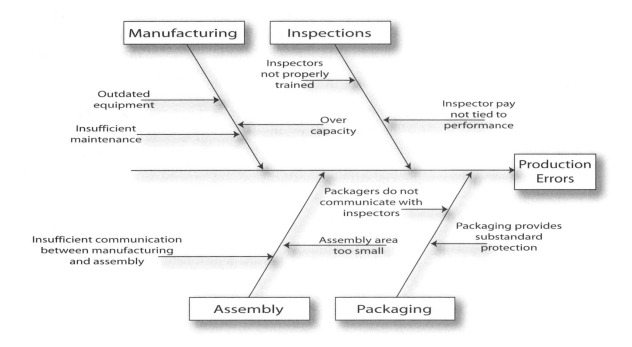

An example of a Cause and Effect (or Ishikawa or Fishbone) Diagram

Cause and Effect Diagrams, or Ishikawa Diagrams, are also known as fishbone diagrams due to the way the chart appears like a fish's skeleton.

Control Charts

Control charts are part of a set of quality practices known as Statistical Process Control. If a process is statistically "in control," it does not need to be corrected. If it is "out of control," then there are sufficient variations in results that must be brought back statistically in line. A control chart is one way of depicting variations and determining whether or not the process is in control.

Control charts graph the results of a process to show whether or not they are in control. The mean of all of the data points is represented by a line drawn through the average of all data points on the chart. The upper and lower control limits are set at three standard deviations above and below mean.

If measurements fall outside of the control limits, then the process is said to be out of control. The assignable cause should then be determined.

An interesting rule that is used with control charts is known as the rule of seven. It states that if seven or more consecutive data points fall on one side of the mean, they should be investigated. This is true even if the seven data points are within the control limits.

Some control charts, especially those used in a manufacturing environment, represent the upper and lower limits of a customer's specification for quality as lines on the control chart. Everything between those lines would be considered within the customer's quality specification.

Perform Quality Control

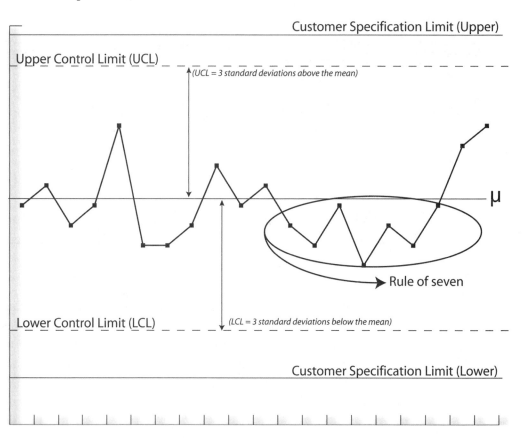

Customer Specification Limit (Upper)

Upper Control Limit (UCL)

(UCL = 3 standard deviations above the mean)

μ

Rule of seven

Lower Control Limit (LCL)

(LCL = 3 standard deviations below the mean)

Customer Specification Limit (Lower)

An example of a control chart

Key Fact

Flowcharting

Flowcharts show how various components relate in a system. Flowcharting can be used to predict where quality problems may happen. In addition to traditional flow charts, Cause and Effect Diagrams are another type of flowcharting.

Histogram

A histogram is another word for a column chart. Histograms show how often something occurs, or its frequency. A Pareto chart (see next tool) is one example of a type of histogram.

Pareto Chart

Another type of chart used as a tool of Perform Quality Control is the Pareto diagram. This is a histogram showing defects ranked from greatest to least. It is used to focus energy on the problems most likely to change results.

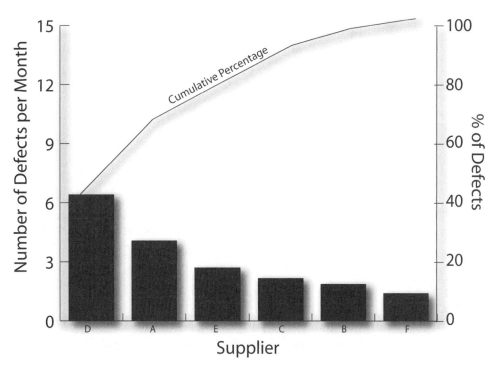

Sample Pareto chart showing a ranking of problems by supplier

Pareto's Law

Pareto diagrams are based on Pareto's Law, which is also known as the 80/20 rule. This rule states that 80% of the problems come from 20% of the causes, but there are variations on this theme. For the exam, know that Pareto's Law is also known as the 80/20 rule and that a Pareto chart is used to help determine the few root causes behind the majority of the problems on a project.

Run Chart

When you measure quality, it is somewhat like taking a snapshot of the way things are at a point in time. This can be useful as a stand-alone tool, but when those snapshots are compiled over time, they can provide excellent information on trends. Using the tool of a run chart, such as the one pictured here, the project manager can analyze how quality is trending over time.

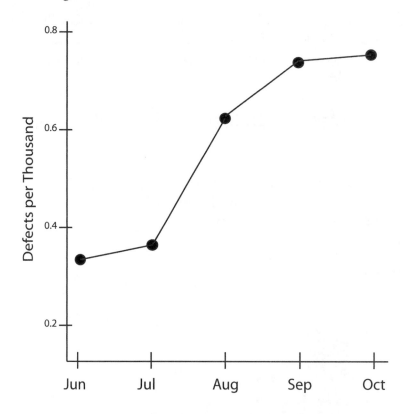

Scatter Diagram

Scatter diagrams are a particularly powerful tool for spotting trends in data. Consider the following three scatter diagrams:

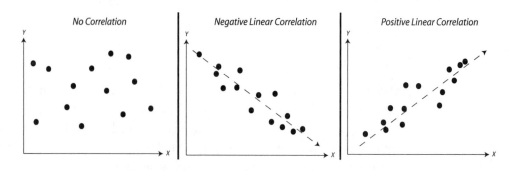

Perform Quality Control

Scatter diagrams are made using two variables (a dependent variable and an independent variable). What you are looking for is correlation between the two variables. Considering the previous examples, suppose that the horizontal, or X axis, represented hours of study, which is your independent variable. The vertical, or Y axis, represented your score on the CAPM Exam, which is the dependent variable. In that case, the third graph would make sense, since the more people studied, the higher their scores tended to be. When you see a graph that looks like the second graph, where the more the person studied, the lower their score, you might deduce that the book they are reading is actually having a negative effect. The first example graph below might lead you to deduce that the study material being used has no effect at all and therefore there is no correlation.

Statistical Sampling

Statistical sampling is a powerful tool where a random sample is selected instead of measuring the entire population. By sampling properly, you can dramatically cut down on the number of measurements you need to take. Note that you will not need to know how to statistically sample for the CAPM Exam. Opinion on statistical sampling varies widely among experts and industries.

Inspection

The tool of inspection is exactly what it sounds like. Inspection may be testing a module of a software application or performing a walkthrough on a building.

Defect Repair Review

When defects are noted, they must be fixed. The tool of the defect repair review is used to ensure that the defects were fixed and meet quality specifications.

Outputs

Quality Control Measurements

As the process of Perform Quality Control is performed, important measurements of quality levels and compliance are a normal output and should be documented.

Validated Defect Repair

Defects need to be corrected, and as they are corrected, they need to be inspected again to validate that they now meet quality standards.

Quality Baseline Updates

The quality baseline, like other baselines, may be changed. This quality baseline is the quality management plan and standards that must be achieved, and as either the quality limits or the plan on how to achieve or manage that quality changes, the baseline should be officially modified.

Validated Deliverables

The validated deliverables are the key output of Perform Quality Control.

Recommended Corrective Actions — See Chapter 2, Common Outputs

Recommended Preventive Actions — See Chapter 2, Common Outputs

Requested Changes — See Chapter 2, Common Outputs

Recommended Defect Repair — See Chapter 4, Monitor and Control Project Work, Outputs

Organizational Process Assets Updates — See Chapter 2, Common Outputs

Project Management Plan Updates — See Chapter 2, Common Outputs

Quality Management Questions

1. You are a project manager, and your manager wants to meet with you to evaluate your project's performance in order to see how it is meeting the quality standards supplied by the company. In what process is your boss engaged?

    A. Total Quality Management.

    B. Perform Quality Control.

    C. Quality Planning.

    D. Perform Quality Assurance.

2. If you were using a fishbone diagram to determine root causes of problems, you would you be involved in:

    A. Quality Inspection.

    B. Quality Prevention.

    C. Quality Control.

    D. Quality Audits.

3. Quality Planning includes all of the following outputs EXCEPT:

    A. Quality management plan.

    B. Acceptance.

    C. Operational definitions.

    D. Checklists.

4. In a control chart, the mean is represented as a horizontal line. This represents:

    A. The average of the control limits.

    B. The average of all data points.

    C. The average of all data points that are within control limits.

    D. A means of identifying assignable cause.

5. Quality audits are an important part of quality management because:

   A. They allow for quantification of the risk.

   B. They randomly audit product results to see if they are meeting quality standards.

   C. They check to see if the quality process is being followed.

   D. They are conducted without prior notice and do not allow team members time to cover up defects.

6. If the results of activity A have no bearing on the results of activity B, the two activities would be considered:

   A. Statistically unique.

   B. Statistically independent.

   C. Correlated, but not causal.

   D. Mutually exclusive.

7. The BEST tool to use to look for results that are out of control is:

   A. Pareto chart.

   B. Control chart.

   C. Ishikawa diagram.

   D. Statistical sampling.

8. You are a project manager with limited resources on the project. Several quality defects have been discovered, causing the stakeholders concern. You wish to begin by attacking the causes that have the highest number of defects associated with them. Which tool shows defects by volume from greatest to least?

   A. Pareto chart.

   B. Control chart.

   C. Ishikawa diagram.

   D. Cause and effect diagram.

9. In the process of managing a construction project, you discover a very serious defect in the way one particular section has been built. Your engineers analyze the section of the building and decide that the problem is actually relatively minor. In which process are you involved?

    A. Quality Planning.

    B. Perform Quality Assurance.

    C. Perform Quality Control.

    D. Quality Management.

10. You are performing a project that has a lot in common with a project completed by your company two years ago. You want to use the previous project to help you determine quality standards for your project. Which of the following tools would be the BEST one to help you with this?

    A. Benchmarking.

    B. Control chart.

    C. ISO 9000.

    D. Total Quality Management.

11. Which of these quality standards is the highest?

    A. It is impossible to determine without further information.

    B. 99% quality.

    C. Three sigma quality.

    D. Six sigma quality.

12. Which quality process is performed first?

    A. Quality Planning.

    B. Perform Quality Assurance.

    C. Perform Quality Control.

    D. Quality Definition.

13. A project team is having their first quality meeting and plans to review the organization's quality policy when it is discovered that the company has never developed an organizational quality policy. The project manager is very concerned about this discovery. What would be the BEST course of action?

   A. Document the absence of a quality policy in the quality management plan and take corrective action.

   B. Write a quality policy just for this project.

   C. Substitute benchmark data for the quality policy.

   D. Suspend execution until the organization provides a quality policy.

14. On a control chart, the customer's acceptable quality limits are represented as:

   A. Control limits.

   B. Mean.

   C. Specification.

   D. Normal distribution.

15. A customer is concerned that the quality process is not being followed as laid out in the quality management plan. The best way to see if this claim is accurate is:

   A. Random sampling.

   B. Kaizen.

   C. Personally participate in the quality inspections.

   D. Audits.

Answers to Quality Management Questions

1. D. In this example your boss is auditing you to see if you are following the process. Remember that audits are a tool of Perform Quality Assurance.

2. C. Quality Control is the correct answer here.

3. B. Acceptance is not an output of Quality Planning. It is an output of Perform Quality Control.

4. B. The mean represents the average of all of the data points shown on the chart, calculated simply by adding the values together and dividing by the number of values. 'C' is not correct because the mean includes everything. If only the values that were within the control limits were used, it could make the mean look better than it should.

5. C. Audits are a tool of Perform Quality Assurance that checks to see if the process is being followed. Choices 'A' and 'D' are incorrect, and choice 'B' is referring to inspection, which is a tool of Perform Quality Control.

6. B. If two events have no bearing on each other, they are statistically independent. Choice 'D' is when two events cannot both happen at the same time.

7. B. That is how a control chart is used. It visually depicts whether a process is in or out of control. Choice 'A' is used in Perform Quality Control to rank problems by frequency. 'C' is used in Quality Planning to anticipate problems in advance. Choice 'D' is used in Perform Quality Control to pick random samples to inspect.

8. A. Pareto charts rank defects from greatest to least, showing you what should get the most attention.

9. C. Perform Quality Control is the best choice here. Your clue here was the fact that your engineers had inspected something specific. This wasn't related to planning or process – it was a physical inspection of a work result, and that is what happens during the Perform Quality Control process.

10. A. Benchmarking takes results from previous projects and uses them to help measure quality on your project. Benchmarks give you something against which you can measure.

11. D. Six sigma represents 99.99966% of all work results that will be of acceptable quality in the manufacturing process. This is higher than 99% or 3 sigma, which represents a 99.73% quality rate.

12. A. Quality Planning should always happen first. Perform Quality Assurance and Perform Quality Control would come after the quality management plan is in place. 'D' is not a PMI process. Keep in mind that the quality processes do run in a cycle, but planning should always happen first.

13. B. If no organizational quality policy exists, you should develop one for this project. 'A' and 'C' are incorrect since you should not proceed without a quality policy. 'D' would be a good way to lose your job! You should try to fix this problem yourself rather than force your organization to write a quality policy.

14. C. The quality specification is the customer's quality requirements. 'A' represents the limits for what is in and out of statistical control, typically set at three standard deviations from the mean. 'B' is the average of all of the data points. 'D' is a statistical term relating to the way the data points are scattered.

15. D. Audits, part of the Perform Quality Assurance process, review the process and make sure that the process is being followed.

Human Resource

Difficulty	Memorization	Exam Importance
Low	Medium	Medium

Although the PMBOK Guide treats the subject of human resource management lightly, you should expect several questions on the exam that cover a variety of theories, including leadership, motivation, conflict resolution, and roles within a project.

The content for this area of the test is drawn from basic management theory, organizational behavior, psychology, and of course, the field of human resources. If you have ever formally studied these subjects, you have probably been exposed to many of the theories in this chapter.

In managing a project, the project manager must also lead people. Some project managers may excel at organizing tasks and planning activities and be dismal at motivating other people.

This chapter covers the processes, inputs, tools, and outputs you will need to know in order to pass the exam.

Philosophy

PMI's approach to the area of human resource management is to define a role for everyone on the project and to define the responsibilities for each of these roles. Many people make the mistake of only understanding the role of the project manager, and never understanding the proper role of senior management, the sponsor, or the team. Instead of merely looking at their own role on the project, project managers must help define the roles and influence everyone who has a role on the project.

The processes of Project HR Management with their *primary* outputs

Human Resource Management

Human Resource Planning
Roles and Responsibilities
Staffing Management Plan

Acquire Proj. Team
Staff Assignments

Develop Proj. Team
Team Performance Assessment

Manage Proj. Team
Requested Changes
Recom. Corrective Action

PMI's philosophy of leadership and power are based on the realization that the project manager is rarely given complete and unquestioned authority on a project. Instead, he must be able to motivate and persuade people to act in the best interest of the project and must be able to build a team and lead members to give their best effort to the project.

Importance

After professional responsibility, human resource management questions are considered by many people to be the easiest questions on the exam. This is because this is one of the few sections where many of the questions can often be answered by using common sense. Unless you find these questions particularly difficult, it is a good idea to get comfortable with the information in this chapter and focus your attention on more challenging subject matter. A careful review of the theories and content prior to taking the exam should be adequate to help you through this section.

Preparation

The focus of this chapter will be on roles and responsibilities, motivational theories, forms of power, and leadership styles. While this knowledge area is considered to be one of the easiest ones, take the time to learn it. Questions from this section will appear on the exam.

This chapter, in particular, contains a significant amount of content that is not found in the PMBOK Guide.

Human Resource Management Processes

There are four processes within project human resource management. In the PMI framework, these processes touch three process groups: planning (Human Resource Planning), executing (Acquire Project Team and Develop Project Team), and monitoring & controlling (Manage Project Team).

Process Group	Human Resource Management Process
Initiating	(none)
Planning	Human Resource Planning
Executing	Acquire Project Team, Develop Project Team
Monitoring & Controlling	Manage Project Team
Closing	(none)

The primary outputs associated with the four human resource management processes are shown in the table below.

Process	Primary Outputs
Human Resource Planning	• Roles and responsibilities • Project organizational chart • Staffing management plan
Acquire Project Team	• Staff assignments
Develop Project Team	• Team performance assessment
Manage Project Team	• Change requests • Recommended corrective actions • Recommended preventive actions

Human Resource Planning

What it is:

It is a common pattern throughout the PMI processes to have a knowledge area that starts off with a planning process to set the tone for the remaining processes in that area. This is the case with Human Resource Management, which begins with Human Resource Planning. This process gives guidance to the rest of the human resource processes, defining the roles and responsibilities and creating the staffing management plan.

Why it is important:

This process lays out how you will staff, manage, team-build, assess, and improve the project team.

When it is performed:

Human Resource Planning typically takes place very early on the project, and it may be performed iteratively. In other words, you may do some work on the scope, some work on the schedule, and then plan human resources, and then do more work on the scope, returning again to human resources, and so on. It should not be thought of as a process that is tackled only one time.

How it works:

Inputs

Enterprise Environmental Factors — See Chapter 2, Common Inputs

Organizational Process Assets — See Chapter 2, Common Inputs

Project Management Plan — See Chapter 2, Common Inputs

Tools

Organization Charts and Position Descriptions

There are many ways to represent who will be working on the project and what they will be responsible for doing. For the exam, you need to know about three primary formats:

Hierarchical

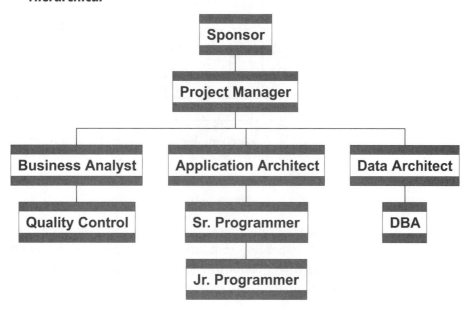

Matrix

Matrix charts are used to illustrate which roles on the project will be working with which work packages and what their responsibilities will be. One of the most popular categories is the Responsibility Assignment Matrix (RAM), which displays work packages in the rows and the roles in the columns. Each cell shows how that role will work on that particular work package.

One popular type of the RAM is known as the RACI chart (pronounced "ray-cee"). RACI charts, such as the one that follows, list each work package in the rows and list the roles in the columns. RACI charts derive their name from the way each cell is assigned either an 'R' for Responsible, 'A' for Accountable, 'C' for Consult, or 'I' for Input. Generally, only one person is assigned accountability for a work package, but more than one person may be responsible for performing the work on a work package.

Role Work Package	Project Manager	Business Analyst	Data Architect	Application Architect	Jr. Programmer	Sr. Programmer	Quality Control
Document scope	C	A					R
Review scope	A	I	C	C	C	C	C
Approve scope	A	R	R	R	R	R	R
Create database	C	C	A	I			
Design application	I	I	I	A	I	R	C
Code application	I	I	I	I	R	A	C
Application testing	I	I	I	I	I	I	A

R = Responsible, **A** = Accountable, **C** = Consult, **I** = Inform

Text

Text formats basically follow the format of a position description, detailing out what responsibilities each position on the project will involve and what qualifications will be needed to fill these positions. This tool is particularly useful in recruiting.

Networking

Networking is the process of communicating with others within your "network" of contacts. By tapping into his network of contacts, a project manager can leverage his expertise on issues related to human resources on the project.

Organizational Theory

Groups behave differently than individuals, and it is important to understand how organizations and teams behave. Familiarizing yourself with the vast amount of work that has been done to understand organizational theory can pay dividends throughout the project.

Outputs

Roles and Responsibilities

Each role on the project should be defined with a title, its level of responsibility, authority, and the skill level or competency needed to be able to perform this role.

Project Organization Charts

A project organization chart shows how team members relate on a project. This is particularly important since reporting relationships that exist on a project will often be different than those which exist in the organization.

Staffing Management Plan

The staffing management plan, which is part of the project management plan, is the plan which details how and when the project will be staffed, how and when the staff will be released, and other key human resources components such as how they will be trained.

One common component of the staffing management plan is a resource histogram. A resource histogram (see example below) simply shows the usage for resources for a given period of time. On most projects, resources increase from planning through executing, falling off in monitoring and control and closure.

Database Programmers

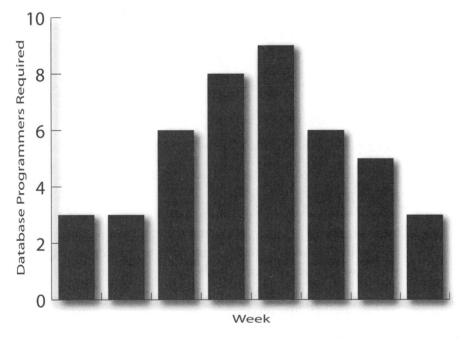

Sample Resource Histogram

Acquire Project Team

What it is:

Acquire Project Team is another process that sounds exactly like what it is. This process focuses on staffing the project. Because it is an executing process, you can think of it as the process that carries out the staffing management plan.

Why it is important:

This process gets the right people working on the project. Careful attention to this process should pay off in the form of the quality of staff you bring on.

When it is performed:

Make sure that you understand that the process of Acquire Project Team is typically performed throughout the project, as you may need different skill sets throughout the life of the project. For instance, you may need business analysts early on in the life of the project, while you may need more quality engineers later in the project. Acquire Project Team would be performed as long as the project was adding new staff.

How it works:

Inputs

Enterprise Environmental Factors — See Chapter 2, Common Inputs

Organizational Process Assets — See Chapter 2, Common Inputs

Roles and Responsibilities

As you are staffing the project, the roles and responsibilities you defined earlier in Human Resource Planning (usually in the form of position descriptions) will be indispensable here.

Project Organization Charts

The organization charts show the number of people, how they will relate to each other on the project, and how they fit into the overall project organization.

Staffing Management Plan

The staffing management plan details when resources will be needed and how long they will be needed. Other human resources information that would be useful to functional managers and the team may be included, such as whether the resources will be internal or external, how they will be released, etc.

Tools

Pre-Assignment

It is normal on project for the roles to be defined first. Later, resources are assigned to perform those roles and fulfill the responsibilities; however, occasionally specific resources will be pre-assigned to fill a role. This may occur before the staffing management plan has been created and even before the project formally begins.

Negotiation

Negotiating is an important skill for project managers to cultivate. Project managers often have to negotiate for resources, both inside and outside the organization.

Acquisition

The tool of acquisition, as used here, can be a bit misleading, since the overall process is "Acquire Project Team." The tool of acquisition refers to looking outside the organization for resources when they cannot be provided by your organization.

Virtual Teams

Virtual teams have become much more popular over recent years. A virtual team is a group of individuals who may or may not see each other in person. Instead, they typically use communication tools to meet online, share information, and collaborate on deliverables.

Outputs

Project Staff Assignments

The assigned staff is the primary output of this process. Each role that was defined should have a resource assigned to it. Understand that these assignments may happen several times throughout the process as resources are needed. For instance, it would typically be difficult to assign a particular person to a role that will not be needed for a year.

Key Fact

Resource Availability

As resources are assigned to the project, the time they are assigned to work on activities should be documented. Each resource's forecasted time on the project should be documented.

Staffing Management Plan Updates

It is normal for the staffing management plan to undergo revisions and updates as staff members are assigned. Specifically, as things work or do not work when staffing a project, elements of the staffing management plan may be updated to reflect re-planning and corrective action.

Develop Project Team

What it is:

Where the exam is concerned, Develop Project Team is the most important process in Project Human Resource Management. It is an executing process that focuses on building a sense of team and improving its performance.

Why it is important:

A team performs better than a group of disconnected individuals. This is true not only for sports teams, but also for project teams.

When it is performed:

The process of Develop Project Team is performed throughout the project. In other words, as long as there is a team on the project, you should perform this process, but it is considered to be most effective when done early.

How it works:

Inputs

Project Staff Assignments

The staff assignments, which were made as part of the Acquire Project Team process, are brought into this. The rationale behind this is that the staff assignments contain a list of all team members for the project.

Staffing Management Plan

The staffing management plan provides the guidance for this entire process. It outlines how project team members will be trained and how Develop Project Team will be conducted. This may include such things as offering flex time, bonus pay, or options of telecommuting.

Resource Availability

The resource availability specifies, for each resource, when project team members would be available to take part in team building activities.

Tools

General Management Skills

General management skills cover a whole host of topics, but are particularly focused on producing key results by driving and managing tasks and motivating team members.

There is a difference between leading and managing on a project. Managing has been defined as being about producing key results, while leading involves establishing direction, aligning people to that direction, and motivating and inspiring.

There are several different styles of leading that are recognized throughout the field of project management. The following graphic may prove very helpful for the exam. In the early phases of the project, the project manager should take a very active role in the leadership of the project, usually directing the activities and providing significant leadership. As the project progresses, however, other styles of leading may be more appropriate. These styles of leading are less heavy-handed. Of course, the particular style of leading needed will vary from one project to the next.

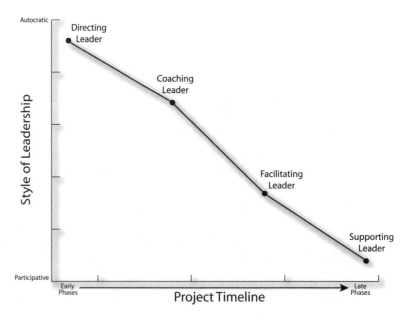

Punishment

Training

Training can include a wide range of activities, but it may be thought of as any instruction or acquisition of skills that increases the ability of the team or individuals to perform their jobs.

If a team member does not have the skills needed to carry out his responsibilities, then training may be a good option. In general, training is highly favored for the exam, but in most cases it should be paid for by the performing organization or the functional manager and not by the customer or the project.

Team-Building Activities

A team-building activity is any activity that enhances or develops the cohesiveness of the team. This usually occurs by focusing on building bonds and relationships among team members. It is important to keep in mind that although team-building may be treated as a special event, it can occur while performing regular project responsibilities, and it actually becomes more important as the project progresses.

Team-building cannot be forced. It should be modeled by the project manager, who should work to include all members of the team and create a shared goal.

Ground Rules

A project's ground rules are the formal or informal rules that define the boundaries of behavior on the project. For instance, a project may lay down ground rules that say that everyone on the project shares responsibility for protecting the security of project data. In this case, everyone on the project would be expected to treat information with the same general caution. It is important that ground rules be defined and communicated to the team members.

Co-Location

Co-location is the act of physically locating team members in the same general space. The most common example of this is to create a war room where all the team members work, or to co-locate the project team at the customer's site.

Recognition and Rewards

Recognition and reward systems are typically defined as part of the staffing management plan. In general, desirable behaviors should be rewarded and recognized. For the exam, you should focus on win-win rewards as the best choices for team building. Win-lose rewards, such as a contest where one team member wins and the others do not, can be detrimental to the sense of team.

Outputs

Team Performance Assessment

The output of team performance assessment focuses on measuring and evaluating how the team is doing. For instance, you may measure the work performance, the experience the team is acquiring, the turnover rate, or even such factors as the schedule performance index and similar metrics.

Develop Project Team

Manage Project Team

What it is:

Keep in mind that any time you encounter a controlling process, you are generally going to be making sure that the plan matches up with the results. That holds true here, where you are managing the team. You need to ensure that the staffing management plan is working and change it where it must be changed. You need to handle changes to your team, performance problems, and anywhere the plan does not match up with reality.

But keep in mind that even if the differences are positive, you still need to document the differences between the plan and the results. For instance, if you planned for 7% turnover and had no turnover on the project, you would want to document that so that a future team could use your lessons learned to build on your successes.

Why it is important:

Out of all the areas on the project, the human resource side often has the most trouble matching the plan. People don't perform as expected. Some leave the project, teams experience unexpected conflict, individuals suffer from low morale, and all of these events directly affect objective measures such as the budget, the schedule, and quality.

This uncertainty becomes even more challenging when you consider that team members often report to a different functional manager and have "dotted line" responsibilities to the project manager.

In the Manage Project Team process, the project manager considers all of these factors and works to keep the team at their optimal performance.

When it is performed:

Manage Project Team is performed as long as there is a team on the project.

How it works:

Inputs

The first five inputs are basic ingredients for making this process work.

Organizational Process Assets — See Chapter 2, Common Inputs

Project Staff Assignments — See Acquire Project Team, Outputs

Roles and Responsibilities — See Human Resource Planning, Outputs

Project Organization Charts — See Human Resource Planning, Outputs

Staffing Management Plan — See Human Resource Planning, Outputs

Team Performance Assessment

The team performance assessment is an important and ongoing input into the Manage Project Team process. The project manager should regularly assess the performance of the team so that issues can be identified and managed. The format and frequency of the assessment may vary.

Work Performance Information

While the project work is being performed, the project manager monitors the performance of team members. How the team members perform their job, how they handle their responsibilities, and how they meet their deadlines are all considered and brought into the process of Manage Project Team.

Performance Reports

The performance reports are an objective measure of progress against the plan. Such items as scope, time, and cost are measured carefully, and any difference between these and the plan is documented.

Tools and Techniques

Observation and Conversation

These informal tools are used to monitor team morale and identify problems, whether potential or real.

Project Performance Appraisals

A project performance appraisal is where the project manager and other personnel managers on the project meet with the people who report to them on the project and provide feedback on their performance and how they are conducting their job.

Manage Project Team

In recent years, the tool of 360 degree feedback has gained in popularity. Using this tool, feedback is provided from all directions and often from individuals both internal and external to the project, and occasionally even vendors and external contractors.

Conflict Management

Managing conflict in a constructive way helps improve team morale and performance. As discussed earlier in this chapter, conflict may occur between any individuals or groups on the project, but it most often occurs between project managers and functional managers. It is important to manage and resolve conflict; however, if conflict cannot be resolved among the parties involved, it should be escalated.

Conflict that hurts the project should be dealt with in progressively more official channels, such as escalation to the project manager, escalation to the functional managers, and ultimately escalation to the human resources department.

Sources of Conflict

One last area of conflict management you should understand is based on research that suggests that the greatest project conflict occurs between project managers and functional managers. Most conflict on a project is the result of disagreements over schedules, priorities, and resources. This finding runs contrary to a commonly held belief that most conflicts are the result of personality differences.

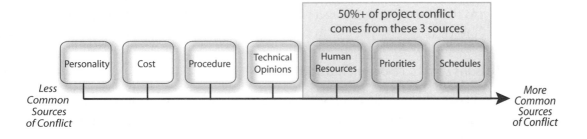

Issue Log

An issue may be thought of as anything that threatens project progress. It could be specific, such as a technical concern, or general, such as a personality conflict among team members. A documented log of issues is important, since it gives the project team a place to record issues that require resolution. Along with each issue, the person or people responsible for resolving the issue should be documented, as well as due dates for the desired resolution.

Manage Project Team

Manage Project Team

Outputs

Requested Changes

Requested changes to the staff could occur for a number of reasons. The team could be dysfunctional, the workers could be under-qualified or over-qualified, or you may need to augment the staff with more resources than previously planned. Any of these or other scenarios that change the staffing management plan should be documented and processed through the change control system.

Recommended Corrective Action

Corrective action is anything done to bring future results in line with the plan. Where the Manage Project Team process is concerned, this would include anything that helps the team perform as planned. This might include incentives, changing staff members, or getting them more training to augment their skills.

Recommended Preventive Action

Preventive action is all about helping to prevent a problem from occurring. For instance, the development of attendance policies could be viewed as preventive action that can help prevent attendance problems.

Organizational Process Assets Updates — See Chapter 2, Common Inputs

Input to Organizational Performance Appraisals

The project manager's feedback on the performance of team members to their functional managers is valuable and will help in planning future projects.

Lessons Learned Documentation

Lessons learned focus on variances between what was planned and what occurred. Here, your lessons learned would document things that you would do differently if you had the project to do again. The lessons learned can be a valuable input for future projects. They help ensure that the organization keeps learning from historical information.

Project Management Plan Updates — See Chapter 2, Common Outputs

Human Resource Management Questions

1. Who manages the resources in a matrix organization?

    A. Senior management.

    B. Functional managers.

    C. Project manager.

    D. Human resources.

2. The staffing management plan:

    A. Must be created by the human resources department.

    B. Is a part of the resource management plan.

    C. Is a tool of team development.

    D. Is an output of the Human Resource Planning process.

3. Which technique produces the most lasting results?

    A. Problem-solving.

    B. Smoothing.

    C. Compromising.

    D. Withdrawing.

4. The most important role of the project sponsor is to:

    A. Manage and resolve conflicts between the team and upper management.

    B. Provide and protect the project's financial resources.

    C. Provide and protect the project's human resources.

    D. Balance the project's constraints regarding time, scope, and cost.

5. Human resource management encompasses:

    A. Organizational Planning, Staff Acquisition, Performance Reporting, and Manage Project Team.

    B. Human Resource Planning, Staff Acquisition, Performance Reporting, and Develop Project Team.

    C. Human Resource Planning, Staff Acquisition, Develop Project Team, and Release Project Team.

    D. Human Resource Planning, Acquire Project Team, Develop Project Team, Manage Project Team.

6. Which of the following is NOT an input into Human Resource Planning?

    A. Enterprise environmental factors.

    B. Roles and responsibilities.

    C. Organizational process assets.

    D. Project management plan.

7. Team building is primarily the responsibility of:

    A. The project team.

    B. The project manager.

    C. Senior management.

    D. The project sponsor.

8. Which of the following is NOT a process of human resources management?

    A. Human Resource Planning.

    B. Acquire Project Team.

    C. Team Performance Reporting.

    D. Develop Project Team.

9. A project coordinator is distinguished from a project manager in that:

    A. A project coordinator has no decision-making power.

    B. A project coordinator has less decision-making power.

    C. A project coordinator has no authority to assign work.

    D. A project coordinator takes on larger projects than a project manager.

10. Which of the following is not a tool used in Develop Project Team?

    A. General Management Skills.

    B. Training.

    C. Ground Rules.

    D. Encouragement.

11. One potential disadvantage of a matrix organization is:

    A. Highly visible project objectives.

    B. Rapid responses to contingencies.

    C. Team members must report to more than one boss.

    D. The matrix organization creates morale problems.

12. A project manager in Detroit is having difficulty getting the engineers in his company's Cleveland office to complete design documents for his project. He has sent numerous requests to the VP of Engineering (also in Cleveland) for assistance in getting the design documents, but so far his efforts have been unsuccessful. What kind of organization does this project manager work in?

    A. Functional.

    B. Hierarchical.

    C. Strong matrix.

    D. Projectized.

13. Which of the following is not true about a project's ground rules?

    A. Ground rules should be communicated to all team members.

    B. Ground rules should be consistent across projects in an organization.

    C. Ground rules should be clearly defined.

    D. Ground rules define behavioral boundaries on a project.

14. A war room is an example of:

    A. Contract negotiation tactics.

    B. Resource planning tools.

    C. A functional organization.

    D. Collocation.

15. Which statement is TRUE concerning project performance appraisals?

    A. Project performance appraisals focus on the project's performance against the plan.

    B. Project performance appraisals focus on the performance of the team members against the plan.

    C. Project performance appraisals focus on the earned value against the planned value.

    D. Project performance appraisals are most important early in the project.

Answers to Human Resource Management Questions

1. B. The functional manager has resource responsibilities in a matrix organization. In this type of organizational structure, the project manager must work with the functional managers to secure resources for a project. If you were tempted to choose 'C', keep in mind that the project manager primarily manages the project. The benefit of a matrix organization is that the project manager does not need to divert as much attention to managing the resources as he or she would in a projectized organization.

2. D. The staffing management plan is created during the Human Resource Planning process.

3. A. Problem-solving (sometimes referred to as confrontation) is getting to the root of the problem and is the best way to produce a lasting result and a real solution.

4. B. This question comes from Chapter 2 – Foundational Terms and Concepts. The project sponsor provides the funds for the project. He may or may not take on other roles, but this is his defining role on the project.

5. D. The four processes are Human Resource Planning, Acquire Project Team, Develop Project Team, Manage Project Team, and yes, you do need to know all of them before taking the CAPM Exam.

6. B. Role and responsibility assignments are the result, or output, of human resource planning. An even easier way to answer this question, however, was to realize that enterprise environmental factors, organizational process assets, and the project management plan are inputs into almost every planning process.

7. B. Team building must be carried out under the direction of a strong leader. The project manager has the only project role that allows for regular, direct interaction with the team.

8. C. Team Performance Reporting is not a real process. It does sound similar to the Communications process of Performance Reporting, but this question asked which of the processes did not belong to the knowledge area of human resources management.

9. B. A project coordinator has some authority and some decision making power, but less than a project manager.

10.   D. Encouragement may be a great idea, but it is not specified as a tool of Develop Project Team. 'A', 'B', and 'C' all are. If you missed this question keep in mind that you should favor the terms, vocabulary, and phrases you see here on the exam. Few people can commit all 592 inputs, tools and techniques, and outputs to memory, but you should learn to recognize them and pick out the ones that do not belong.

11.   C. In a matrix organization, team members report to both the project manager and the functional manager. This can sometimes cause confusion and can lead to conflict on a project and within the organization.

12.   A. The clue in the question that indicates a functional organization is the project manager's low authority; he must appeal to the head of the engineering department rather than making his request directly to the team members.

13.   B. Ground rules may be unique to the project, and they certainly don't have to be the same across all projects in an organization. For instance, a project that has high security might have more stringent ground rules than a less secure one. 'A' and 'C' are incorrect, because clearly defining ground rules and communicating them to everyone helps to make sure they are understood and will be followed. 'D' is incorrect, because that is exactly what ground rules do – they define the boundaries of behavior that team members should respect.

14.   D. Collocation is the practice of locating all team members in a central location, or collocation. Another variation of a war room is a conference room devoted exclusively to use by a particular project team. It is a tool of Develop Project Team used in human resource management.

15.   B. Project performance appraisals, used in the Manage Project Team process, help to measure how team members are performing against the plan. This feedback is typically provided by the project manager to the functional manager(s). Answer 'D' is incorrect since these performance appraisals typically become more important as execution ramps up and peaks on a project, and not at the very beginning.

Communications Management

10

Many consider communications management to be one of the easiest knowledge areas to study for the CAPM. Although project communications management can be very political and tricky in an organization, the volume of material for the test is moderate and not exceedingly difficult.

Many people who study this material are surprised that it is not related to the skill of communication through verbal and written media, in areas such as project writing styles, persuasion, and presentation methods. Rather, communications management covers all tasks related to producing, compiling, sending, storing, distributing, and managing project records. This knowledge area is made up of four processes to determine what to communicate, to whom, how often, and when to reevaluate the plan. It involves understanding who your stakeholders are and what they need to know.

Communications management also requires that you accurately report on the project status, performance, change, and earned value, and that you pay close attention to controlling the information to ensure that the communication management plan is working as intended.

Philosophy

There is an old joke in project management circles about "mushroom project management," in which you manage projects the same way you grow

The processes of Project Communications Management with their *primary* outputs

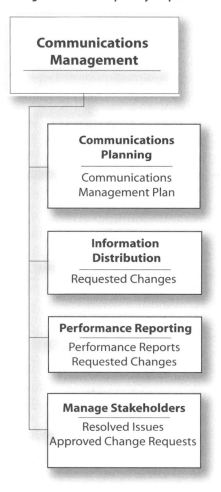

Communications Management

Communications Planning

Communications Management Plan

Information Distribution

Requested Changes

Performance Reporting

Performance Reports
Requested Changes

Manage Stakeholders

Resolved Issues
Approved Change Requests

mushrooms – by keeping everyone buried in manure, leaving them in the dark, and checking back periodically to see what has popped up.

PMI's philosophy is, as you may have guessed, quite different. It focuses on keeping the stakeholders properly informed throughout the project. Communication under PMI's philosophy may be a mixture of formal and informal, written and verbal, but it is always proactive and thorough. It is essential that the project manager distribute accurate project information in a timely manner and to the right audience.

Importance

Communications management is of medium importance on the exam, bordering on high. You may see several questions that relate directly to this chapter, so it will be necessary to become acquainted with the terms and theories presented here.

Preparation

Although the volume of material in communications management is smaller than most of the other areas, there are key concepts that must be learned. Be prepared for several questions on the test specifically related to the inputs, tools and techniques, and outputs for each process. The reason the focus is on these areas is that they are critical to the smooth operation of the processes, and most test takers do not find them intuitive.

Two other areas of key importance are the communications model and understanding channels of communication. You can expect to see questions about these on the exam.

There are not as many exam questions related to this section as there are to some of the others, and by carefully reviewing this chapter, and the exercises, you should be in good shape for the exam.

There are four processes within project communications management. In the PMI framework, these processes touch three process groups: planning (Communications Planning), executing (Information Distribution), and monitoring and controlling (Performance Reporting, and Manage Stakeholders).

Process Group	Communications Management Process
Initiating	(none)
Planning	Communications Planning
Executing	Information Distribution
Monitoring & Controlling	Performance Reporting, Manage Stakeholders
Closing	(none)

The primary outputs associated with the four communications management processes are shown in the table below.

Process	Primary Outputs
Communications Planning	• Communications management plan
Information Distribution	• Requested changes
Performance Reporting	• Performance reports • Forecasts • Requested changes
Manage Stakeholders	• Resolved issues • Approved change requests • Approved corrective actions

Project Manager's Role in Communications

The project manager's most important skill set is that of communication. It is integral to everything the project manager does. You may see questions on your exam asking you what the project manager's most important job or most important skills are, or how most of the project manager's time is spent. The answer is almost always related to communications. It is estimated that an effective project manager spends about 90% of his time communicating, and fully 50% of that time is spent communicating with the project team.

Also note that while communications take up a majority of the project manager's working day, one individual cannot control everything communicated on a project, nor should he try. Project managers who ask that every single e-mail or conversation be filtered through them first are generally demonstrating that they are *not* in control on the project. Instead, the project manager should be in control of the communications *process*. This is done by creating a strong communications management plan, adhering to it, and regularly monitoring and controlling.

Communications Processes

Communications Planning

What it is:

For the exam, you should consider that Communications Planning is all about the communications management plan, its sole output. The communications management plan is, as you might guess, the plan that drives communication on the project. It defines:

- How often communications will be distributed and updated
- In what format the communications will be distributed (e.g. e-mail, printed copy, web site, etc.)
- What information will be included in the project communications
- Which project stakeholders will receive these communications

Why it is important:

This plan sets stakeholder expectations on the project, letting them know what information they will receive and when and how they will receive it. If the project manager invests time in defining these lines of communication up front, conflict should be less than if it were undefined. Keep in mind that projects will vary greatly in how formally they define the communications management plan. On a small project, it may not make sense for the project manager to go to great lengths to define an overly formal communications management plan.

When it is performed:

Like many planning processes, Communications Planning is typically performed early on the project, before regular project communications commence; however, it may be revisited as often as needed.

How it works:

Inputs

Enterprise Environmental Factors — See Chapter 2, Common Inputs

Organizational Process Assets — See Chapter 2, Common Inputs

Project Management Plan — See Chapter 2, Common Inputs

Project Scope Statement

One of the important components of the communications management plan is to communicate with the project's stakeholders. Since the stakeholders were identified during the Scope Definition process and documented in the project scope statement, the list of identified stakeholders should be brought into this process.

Tools & Techniques

Communications Requirements Analysis

This one tool can cover quite a bit of ground. It is relatively simple to define, but sometimes quite tricky to perform on an actual project. The goal of this technique is to identify which stakeholders should receive project communications, what communications they should receive, how they should receive these communications, and how often they should receive them.

Communications Technology

Technology is a tool, and the right tool should be selected for a given communications need. Whereas formal face-to-face meetings may be needed for some projects, a project web site may be more appropriate for others. The technology should be tailored to the need.

Outputs

Communications Management Plan

The communications management plan is part of the project management plan, and it defines the following:

- Who should receive project communications
- What communications they should receive
- Who should send the communication
- How the communication will be sent
- How often it will be updated
- Definitions so that everyone has a common understanding of terms

Information Distribution

What it is:

It is easiest to consider the process of Information Distribution as the execution of the communications management plan. In other words, the communications management plan lays out how communications will be handled, and the process of Information Distribution carries that out.

Keep in mind that while Information Distribution is performed according to the communications management plan, it must also be flexible so that unplanned information requests may be handled.

Why it is important:

Information Distribution is the process where the bulk of project communications takes place.

When it is performed:

Information Distribution generally updates stakeholders on the progress of the project according to the communications management plan. It may start quite early on the project, but typically elevates in importance and activity during the construction phase of the project.

How it works:

Inputs

Communications Management Plan

The communications management plan is the only input into this process. It is indispensable to this process since it defines how this process will be carried out.

Tools & Techniques

Communications Skills

A project manager relies on good communication skills throughout the life of the project. These skills may be written, oral, formal, and informal.

Whether the project manager is the sender or the receiver, he should work to make sure the information is understood between all parties. The sender encodes a message, and it is the job of the receiver to to decode it.

Information Gathering and Retrieval Systems

Regardless of what system you select and implement for information gathering and retrieval, it is important to be able to organize and access material quickly and easily.

Information Distribution Methods

Information on the project may be distributed to the stakeholders in many ways - oral or written, electronic or paper, live or taped. The important thing about these methods is that they are used to distribute accurate information in a timely fashion.

Lessons Learned Process

The oddly-named tool "lessons learned process" describes meetings that help facilitate the gathering of the lessons learned. These then become an organizational process asset for use in future projects.

All lessons learned generally focus on one simple question: "Where were the variances on the project, and what would we do differently to avoid those variances if we had the project to do over again?" This question is evaluated across all components of the project.

Outputs

Organizational Process Assets Updates

All of the information coming out of the Information Distribution process is potentially valuable to the organization for use in future projects.

Requested Changes

The changes described here typically represent changes to the types of information that are distributed or the way in which it was distributed. These requested changes should be processed back through the Integrated Change Control process.

Performance Reporting

What it is:

The process of Performance Reporting is another one that lives up to its name. This process reports to the stakeholders how the project is progressing against the plan. It is easy to confuse this process with its cousin, Information Distribution; however, they are different. For instance, Performance Reporting belongs to the monitoring and controlling process group (Information Distribution, as you remember, is an executing process), and it is specifically focused on reporting against the performance baseline. In other words, performance reporting tracks how the project is doing against the plan, which is more specific than Information Distribution.

Why it is important:

Performance reporting is important because it updates stakeholders on how the project is doing against the plan, and this kind of communication is especially beneficial.

When it is performed:

Like its cousin, Information Distribution, Performance Reporting begins early on the project and takes on increasing importance as the project enters the construction phase where more resources and costs are expended.

How it works:
Inputs

Work Performance Information

This input comes from the process Direct and Manage Project Execution, and it covers practically all aspects of the project. Work performance information can include performance updates on scope, schedule, costs, quality, and the use of resources. This work performance information is brought in as the primary input into Performance Reporting, since it is compared with the various baselines to measure progress against the plan.

Performance Measurements

Performance measurements specifically refer to the cost variance (CV), schedule variance (SV), cost performance index (CPI), the cumulative CPI (CPI^C), and the schedule performance index (SPI). They are used to determine how the project is performing against the plan.

Forecasted Completion

This input typically describes the estimate at completion (EAC) or the estimate to completion (ETC). It provides the best estimate as to how much the project will cost based on past performance.

Quality Control Measurements

How a project is performing against the quality specifications is an important aspect of its overall performance. Measurements from quality control are brought into this process so the results may be compared with the plan.

Project Management Plan

The project management plan is brought into this process, because it provides the planned baseline against which the actual performance is measured and reported.

Approved Change Requests

Approved changes to the project which affect the baseline (whether scope, schedule, cost, or quality) should be factored into Performance Reporting. Note that this applies to approved changes and not to all changes. The reason for this is that approved changes become part of the baseline, while changes that were not approved do not. Performance reporting is done against the baseline, so changes that were not approved would show up negatively on the reporting.

Deliverables

This one is a bit unusual here and probably won't show up on the exam. It is an input here, presumably so that performance may be measured against what was actually completed, but the more important input of work performance information (listed earlier in this process) would cover this more completely.

Tools & Techniques

Information Presentation Tools

The use of the word "information" here primarily means graphical information. Project information, and specifically performance information, may be presented in a number of different ways, including text, graphics, animation, etc., and this type of presentation can make the information more readily understood. Tools that assist with this should be leveraged as part of Performance Reporting.

Performance Information Gathering and Compilation

Numerous sources may be used for gathering and compiling the information, including electronic, paper, and other sources. The takeaway from this tool is that information must be gathered and compiled before it is reported.

Status Review Meetings

Status meetings to review progress should happen at regular intervals.

Time Reporting Systems

A system should be used to track actual time spent on activities or work packages and on the project as a whole.

Cost Reporting Systems

A cost reporting system should be used to track actual costs spent on activities or work packages and on the project as a whole. These systems can be especially useful in breaking down or summarizing costs and comparing actual results with the plan.

Outputs

Performance Reports

This is the essential output from Performance Reporting. The performance reports show how the project is progressing against the various baselines (scope, time, cost, quality). The performance reports are tailored to the audience. For instance, the project manager may produce only a one page executive summary for the sponsor, while a more detailed report may be prepared and distributed for the team.

Key Fact

Forecasts

Forecasts are future predictions combined with expert judgment based on past performance. Estimate at completion (EAC) and estimate to completion (ETC) are the most common financial forecasts, while the project's schedule is typically used to forecast a projected completion date.

Requested Changes

Changes to the project are a normal output of Performance Reporting. For example, if the project is progressing slower than anticipated or is costing more than planned, the project manager may elect to eliminate certain pieces of non-essential scope to get the project back on track. These changes should be factored back into the integrated change control system.

Recommended Corrective Actions

Corrective actions are anything done to bring future results in line with the plan. In the process of Performance Reporting, needed corrective actions will often become apparent.

Organizational Process Assets Updates

Anything that may be reused on this project or on future projects should be considered an organizational process asset and should be updated and archived appropriately.

Performance Reporting

Manage Stakeholders

What it is:

As you spend time studying the PMBOK Guide, you will find that many knowledge areas (such as Communications Management) contain one or more planning processes, sometimes an executing process, and are often followed by a monitoring and controlling process.

Monitoring and controlling processes ensure that the executed results match up with the plan. In the case of Manage Stakeholders, you are ensuring that the stakeholders are heard and that their needs are addressed.

Why it is important:

This process helps to ensure that no issues raised by stakeholders mushroom into problems that could jeopardize the project. Instead, Manage Stakeholders works to identify and resolve stakeholder concerns in a timely manner.

When it is performed:

This process will be performed throughout the project, as soon as you begin communicating on the project (typically quite early).

How it works:

Inputs

Communications Management Plan

The project manager uses the communications management plan to set and manage stakeholder expectations in regards to project communications. This plan drives communication on the project, defining the who, what, when, where, and how of informational flow.

Organizational Process Assets

Any examples from previous projects of how stakeholder issues were resolved or records of issues being handled would be of benefit to bring into this process.

Tools & Techniques

Communications Methods

The important take-away from this tool is that face-to-face meetings are the best ones to use where stakeholder issues are concerned.

Effective Meetings

While meetings are an important part of good communication, effective and productive meetings are rare in the real world. Meetings should be held for a clear purpose and should involve only the people necessary. Their main purpose is to make decisions and communicate decisions. Meetings with no clear purpose simply should not be held.

Following are ingredients to an effective meeting. Most of these should be intuitive, and test takers should focus on understanding the list rather than memorizing it:

- Clearly define the reason, issues, and processes for the meeting
- Establish clear objectives for the meeting
- Publish and follow a written agenda
- Have a structure for conducting the meeting
- Foster creative thinking
- Drive toward making decisions and not only toward discussion
- Listen and communicate collaboratively
- Control communication during the meeting. This does not mean that you micro-manage every detail of every discussion, but rather that you keep the discussion relevant and aligned with the topics
- Include all of the necessary people and only the necessary people. Meetings are important, but can be a tremendous waste of time.
- Document the meeting through written minutes

Kickoff Meeting

The kickoff meeting is an opportunity to bring the team together, along with key stakeholders, the sponsor, the customer, and senior management to discuss the project plan. Additionally it is considered a good practice to share lessons learned from previous projects during the kickoff meeting.

Issue Logs

A log of all issues is indispensable to the project manager for two reasons:

1. It helps keep track of all issues so that none are lost.
2. It gives stakeholders a way of seeing that their issue is being actively tracked and managed.

Note that an issue log is also a tool of Manage Project Team in Human Resource Management.

Outputs

Resolved Issues

In an ideal world, all issues are resolved, and the identified resolutions are documented in the issue log.

Organizational Process Assets Updates

Any information that could help future projects avoid issues your project had to resolve should be properly archived.

Approved Change Requests — See Chapter 2, Common Outputs

Approved Corrective Actions — See Chapter 2, Common Inputs

Project Management Plan Updates — See Chapter 2, Common Outputs

Manage Stakeholders

Communications Management Questions

1. The process to create a plan showing how all project communication will be conducted is known as:

    A.   Communications Modeling.

    B.   Communications Planning.

    C.   Information Method.

    D.   Communication Distribution Planning.

2. The responsibility of decoding the message rests with:

    A.   The sender.

    B.   The receiver.

    C.   The communications management plan.

    D.   The communications model.

3. Which of the following is FALSE regarding Information Distribution?

    A.   Information Distribution is an executing process.

    B.   Information Distribution ends when the product has been accepted.

    C.   Information Distribution may involve unexpected requests from stakeholders.

    D.   Information Distribution carries out the communications management plan.

4. Your latest review of the project status shows it to be more than three weeks behind schedule. You are required to communicate this to the customer. This message should be:

    A.   Formal and written.

    B.   Informal and written.

    C.   Formal and verbal.

    D.   Informal and verbal.

5. Which of the following statements is TRUE regarding issues?

    A. All issues must be resolved in order for the project to be closed.

    B. The issue log is a tool for stakeholders to manage project issues.

    C. Each issue should be assigned to a single owner.

    D. Issue management may be treated as a sub-project on larger, more complex projects.

6. Communications skills would be used most during which of the following processes?

    A. Information Distribution.

    B. Status Meetings.

    C. Performance Reporting.

    D. Communications Change Control.

7. The communications management plan typically contains all of the following EXCEPT:

    A. The expected stakeholder response to the communication.

    B. The stakeholder communication requirements.

    C. What technology will be used to communicate information.

    D. A glossary of terms.

8. You are about to attend a bi-weekly status meeting with your program manager when she calls and asks you to be certain to include earned value analysis in this and future meetings. Why is earned value analysis important to the communications process?

    A. It communicates the project's long term success.

    B. It communicates how the project is doing against the plan.

    C. It communicates the date the project deviated from the plan.

    D. It communicates the value-to-cost ratio.

9.   The MOST important skill for a project manager to have is:

    A.   Good administrative skills.

    B.   Good planning skills.

    C.   Good client-facing skills.

    D.   Good communication skills.

10.   The best definition of noise is:

    A.   Any unsupportable information that finds its way onto written or verbal project communications.

    B.   Anything that interferes with transmission and understanding of a message.

    C.   Any communication that takes place through unofficial project channels.

    D.   A communications acronym for Normal Operational Informing of Select project Entities.

11.   A project manager is holding a meeting with stakeholders related to the status of a large project for constructing a new runway at a major airport. The runway project has a CPI of 1.2 and an SPI of 1.25, and the manager is going to have to deliver the message to the stakeholders that a crucial quality test has failed. What kind of communication does this meeting represent?

    A.   Formal verbal.

    B.   Informal verbal.

    C.   Paralingual.

    D.   Non-verbal.

Communication Questions

12.   You have just taken over as the project manager for a new runway for a major airport. The project is already in progress, and there are over 200 identified stakeholders on the project. You want to know how to communicate with these stakeholders. Where should you be able to find this information?

    A.   It depends on the type of project.

    B.   The stakeholder management plan.

    C.   The communications management plan.

    D.   Communication requirements.

13.   Mary is using forecasting to determine her project's estimate at complete. What would be the most likely place to include this information?

    A.   The communications management plan.

    B.   The project activity report.

    C.   The performance reports.

    D.   The stakeholder management report.

14.   Lessons learned should contain:

    A.   The collective wisdom of the team.

    B.   Feedback from the customer as to what you could have done better.

    C.   Information to be used as an input into administrative closure.

    D.   Analysis of the variances that occurred from the project's baseline.

15.   In which process would earned value analysis be used?

    A.   Communications Planning.

    B.   Information Distribution.

    C.   Performance Reporting.

    D.   Report Project Value.

Answers to Communication Questions

1. B. Communications Planning is the process for determining how the overall communication process will be carried out. It is the general plan for communications. None of the other three answers were terms used in this book, but the real giveaway was that only one answer 'B' was even the name of a process.

2. B. In the communications model, it is the sender that encodes, and the receiver decodes the message.

3. B. Did you get tricked by this one? Information Distribution doesn't always end when acceptance has occurred, so this is the answer that doesn't fit. Some stakeholders will need information distributed on the closure of the contracts and projects. 'A' is true, because Information Distribution is an executing process. 'C' is true because Information Distribution carries out predetermined communication, but also will be used to respond to unplanned requests from stakeholders. 'D' is true because Information Distribution is the process that executes the communications management plan.

4. A. Communication on schedule slippage, cost overruns, and other major project statuses should be formal and in writing. That doesn't mean you can't pick up the phone to soften the blow, but the formal and written aspects of the communication are what count here.

5. C. Each issue should be assigned to an owner and be assigned a target completion date. 'A' is incorrect since a project could be closed (successfully) and still have outstanding issues. Sometimes the issues are out of the project manager's control. 'B' is incorrect since the issue log is not for the stakeholders – it is for the project manager to use to manage issues. 'D' is incorrect because issues are managed within the context of a project. If you were even considering creating a separate project to manage issues, your project is probably beyond hope.

6. A. Your communications skills are used as a tool in Information Distribution. You should have eliminated 'B' and 'D' because they were not real processes. 'C' might have been tricky for you, but it is incorrect because the process of Performance Reporting mainly produces the performance reports, which factually state the status of the project, while Information Distribution, which can cover many more topics, requires more in the way of skill and communication ability.

7. A. The expected response you will receive is not part of the communications management plan. The communications management plan focuses on how you will communicate to stakeholders and not how they will communicate to you. 'B', 'C', and 'D' are all typically part of the communications management plan.

8. B. Earned value analysis is a communication tool, and it's all about how the project is doing against the plan.

9. D. Good communication skills are the most important skills a project manager can have! Project managers spend more time communicating than anything else.

10. B. Noise is anything that interferes with the transmission and understanding of a message. If you guessed 'D', then you were indeed guessing.

11. B. Many people incorrectly guess 'A' for this question, but meetings are classified as informal verbal - even when the subject matter is important!

12. C. The stakeholder's communication needs are all contained in the communications management plan.

13. C. Performance Reporting uses the tool of forecasting and produces the performance reports. These performance reports often contain the estimate at complete and the estimate to complete, as well as the cost and schedule performance indexes. 'A' was the only other answer that contained a term that is used in this book, and it is not an appropriate match for this question.

14. D. This is important! Lessons learned focus on variances from the plan and what would be done differently in the future in order to avoid those variances.

15. C. Earned value analysis is a tool of Performance Reporting, since earned value analysis factors in the difference between what was planned and the work that was actually accomplished. This information can then be distributed out to the appropriate stakeholders.

Risk Management

Difficulty	Memorization	Exam Importance
High	Medium	Medium

Risk management is a very rich field, full of information and tools for statistical analysis. In the real world, actuaries anticipate risk and calculate the probability of risk events and their associated cost, and entire volumes are written on risk analysis and mitigation. In this section, you do not need to know every tool and technique associated with risk. Instead, focus your study on the high level interactions within the different risk processes.

Risk is one of the rare sections of the PMBOK Guide where the names and basic functions of the processes have not changed from the previous editions of the PMBOK Guide. That is not to suggest that the material has not changed. There are significant differences in the details of the processes, but the good news is that this section has actually been significantly pared down, streamlined and simplified from the prevision edition of the PMBOK Guide!

Philosophy

By this time, you should have picked up on the fact that very little in PMI's methodology is reactive. The overriding philosophy is that the project manager is in control and proactively managing events, avoiding as many problems as possible. The project manager must understand how to anticipate and identify areas of risk, how to quantify and qualify them, and how to plan for them.

Importance

Risk is one of the areas many people find difficult on the exam. The material may be new or unfamiliar, and the techniques may take some work in order to master.

Preparation

In order to pass this section of the exam, you need to understand the risk management plan and the terms related to risk. The 6 risk management processes contain 25 inputs, 23 tools and techniques, and 13 outputs. All of these components to the processes are important, but

The processes of Project Risk Management with their *primary* outputs

Risk Management

Risk Mgt. Planning
Risk Management Plan

Risk Identification
Risk Register

Qualitative Analysis
Risk Register Updates

Quantitative Analysis
Risk Register Updates

Risk Response Planning
Risk Register Updates
Contract Agreements

Risk Monitoring and Control
Risk Register Updates
Requested Changes

the secret is that most of them are either common sense or they rarely show up on the exam. This chapter puts more emphasis on the essential elements that you need to know. Material is organized around these six processes, building upon the different components that go with each one.

There are six processes within project risk management. In the PMI framework, these processes touch two process groups: planning (Risk Management Planning, Risk Identification, Qualitative Risk Analysis, Quantitative Risk Analysis, Risk Response Planning), and monitoring and controlling (Risk Monitoring and Control).

Process Group	Risk Management Process
Initiating	(none)
Planning	Risk Management Planning, Risk Identification, Qualitative Risk Analysis, Quantitative Risk Analysis, Risk Response Planning
Executing	(none)
Monitoring & Controlling	Risk Monitoring and Control
Closing	(none)

The primary outputs associated with the six risk management processes are shown in the table below.

Process	Primary Outputs
Risk Management Planning	• Risk management plan
Risk Identification	• Risk register
Qualitative Risk Analysis	• Risk register updates
Quantitative Risk Analysis	• Risk register updates
Risk Response Planning	• Risk register updates
Risk Monitoring and Control	• Risk register updates • Requested changes • Recommended corrective actions • Recommended preventive actions

Risk

PMI's usage of the word "risk" is different than many project managers and organizations may have encountered before. Risk has two characteristics that must be understood for the exam:

1. Risk is related to an uncertain event.
2. A risk may affect the project for good or for bad. Although risk usually has negative connotations, it may well have an upside.

Risk Management Planning

What it is:

Risk Management Planning is the process that is concerned with one thing: creating the risk management plan. Your understanding of that plan is the key to unlocking this process.

In Risk Management Planning, the remaining five risk management processes are planned. How they will be conducted is documented in the risk management plan, which is typically general and high-level in nature. This means that Risk Management Planning usually doesn't concern itself with specific project risks. Instead, it focuses on how risk will be approached on the project.

Why it is important:

Think of this process as creating your roadmap for the five processes of Risk Identification, Qualitative Risk Analysis, Quantitative Risk Analysis, Risk Response Planning, and Risk Monitoring and Control. By creating a plan (the Risk Management Plan) for these five processes, you are being deliberate and proactive with risk on the project.

The more risk that is inherent on the project, and the more important the project is to the organization, the more resources you would typically apply to performing this process.

When it is performed:

This process is general and high-level in nature and therefore takes place early on the project, usually before many of the other planning processes are performed. The reason it usually takes place very early is that the results of this (and other risk processes) can significantly influence decisions made about scope, time, cost, quality, and procurement.

How it works:

Inputs

Enterprise Environmental Factors — See Chapter 2, Common Inputs
Organizational Process Assets — See Chapter 2, Common Inputs
Project Scope Statement — See Chapter 5, Scope Definition, Outputs
Project Management Plan — See Chapter 2, Common Inputs

Tools and Techniques

Planning Meetings and Analysis

As is stressed in this process, the risk management plan outlines the project's overall approach to risk, and this is not to be determined in a vacuum. As this tool suggests, the approach is plotted out through meeting with all appropriate stakeholders. This is followed up with a careful analysis to determine the appropriate level of risk and the approach warranted on the project.

Outputs

Risk Management Plan

As stated in the introduction to this process, the risk management plan is the real purpose of this process. In fact, it is the process's sole output.

The risk management plan is a roadmap to the other five risk management processes. It defines what level of risk will be considered tolerable for the project, how risk will be managed, who will be responsible for risk activities, the amounts of time and cost that will be allotted to risk activities, and how risk findings will be communicated.

Another important part of the risk management plan is a description of how risks will be categorized. This will be a significant help in the subsequent risk processes. One tool for creating consistent risk categories is the risk breakdown structure (RBS). Because of the RBS's introduction and expanded treatment in this edition of the PMBOK Guide, you should expect to see it on the exam.

The RBS, like its cousin the WBS, is a graphical, hierarchical decomposition used to facilitate understanding and organization. In this case, however, we are breaking down the categories of risks and not the work. One important thing to note with the RBS is that we are not breaking down the actual risks (they won't be known until we perform the Risk Identification process). Instead, we are breaking down the categories of risks that we will evaluate.

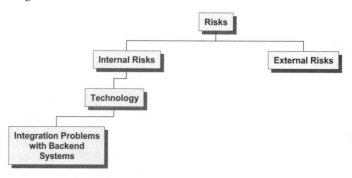

Risk Mgt Planning

Risk Identification

What it is:

Risk Identification is a planning process that evaluates the project to identify which risks could impact the project and to understand the nature of these risks.

There is a single output from this process, and that should help you understand it better. The output is the risk register, which is a list of all risks, their causes, and any possible responses to those risks that can be identified at this point in the project.

Be aware that Risk Identification, like many processes discussed in this book, is often performed multiple times on the project. This may be especially true for Risk Identification, since your understanding of risk, and the nature of the risks themselves, will change and evolve as the project progresses.

Why it is important:

Risk Identification builds the risk register, which is needed before the remaining four risk processes (Qualitative Risk Analysis, Quantitative Risk Analysis, Risk Response Planning, and Risk Monitoring and Control) may be performed. This list of risks will drive the planning processes.

When it is performed:

Although Risk Identification is typically performed early on the project, risks change over time, and new risks arise. It may be necessary to perform this process multiple times throughout the project.

How it works:

Inputs

Enterprise Environmental Factors — See Chapter 2, Common Inputs

Organizational Process Assets — See Chapter 2, Common Inputs

Project Scope Statement — See Scope Definition - Outputs

Risk Management Plan — See Risk Management Planning, Outputs

Project Management Plan — See Chapter 2, Common Inputs

Tools

Documentation Reviews

A documentation review is a review of all project documentation that exists to date. The documentation is reviewed for completeness, correctness, and consistency. For instance, if the plan appears sketchy or quickly thrown together, that could identify a significant risk - especially if the project were of high importance.

Information Gathering Techniques

There are numerous techniques for gathering information to create the risk register. The techniques most commonly discussed in the context of risk are: brainstorming, Delphi technique, expert interviews, root cause identification, and SWOT analysis.

SWOT analysis is particularly useful since it is a tool used to measure each risk's strengths (S), weaknesses (W), opportunities (O), and threats (T). Each risk is plotted, and the quadrant where the weakness (usually internal) and threats (usually external) are highest, and the quadrant where strengths (again, usually internal), and opportunities (usually external) are highest will represent the highest risks on the project.

SWOT analysis can give you another perspective on risk that will often help you identify your most significant project risk factors.

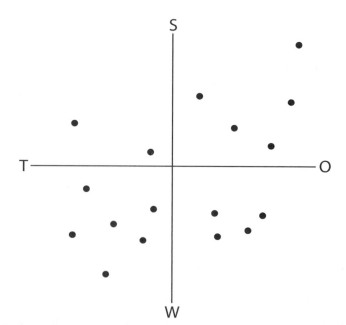

Illustration of one type of SWOT analysis where each dot represents a specific risk

Risk Identification

Checklist Analysis

Checklist analysis uses a Risk Breakdown Structure (RBS), either from this project or from a previous project, to check off items and ensure that all significant risks or categories are being evaluated. Although it may not be exhaustive, this tool provides structure to the Risk Identification process.

Assumptions Analysis

Assumptions should not only be documented; they should be analyzed and challenged if necessary.

Diagramming Techniques

Ishikawa diagrams, also called cause-and-effect diagrams and fishbone diagrams, are one way to show how potential causes can lead to risks.

Another diagramming method used to identify risks is influence diagrams. This category shows how one set of factors may influence another. For instance, late arrival of materials may not be a significant risk by itself, but it may influence other factors, such as triggering overtime work, or causing quality problems later on in the project due to inadequate time to properly perform the work.

Finally, flow charts are useful in identifying risks. Flow charts are graphical representations of complex process flows. They are especially useful because they can break down something very complex into an understandable diagram.

Outputs

Risk Register

As stated earlier, the risk register provides a list of all identified risks on the project, what the possible reactions to this risk are, what the root causes are, and what categories the risks fall into. It is also common to update the RBS with the more specific information as the following example illustrates.

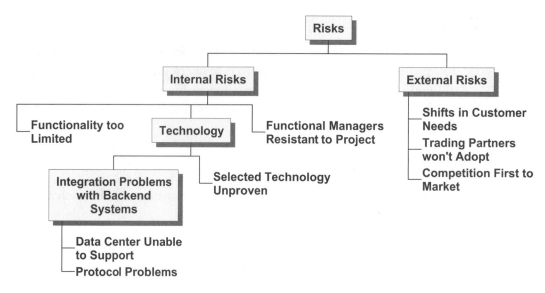

A more complete RBS, including identified risks

The risk register is an essential input into the remaining risk management processes and may be updated throughout the life of the project.

Risk ID	Risk	Responses	Root Cause	Categories
R001	Threat of being hacked	Firewall; intrusion detection software	Poorly designed security; Outdated technology	Security

Fragment of a Risk Register

Risk Identification

Qualitative Risk Analysis

What it is:

The process of Qualitative Risk Analysis is usually done rapidly on the project in order to determine which risks are the highest priority on the project.

It takes each risk from the risk register and works to analyze its probability of occurring and impact to the project if it did occur. By using the probability and impact matrix (PIM), a prioritization and ranking can be created, which is updated on the risk register.

Why it is important:

This process helps you rank and prioritize the risks so that you can put the right emphasis on the right risks. It helps to ensure that time and resources are spent in the right risk areas.

When it is performed:

Qualitative risk analysis, like many other risk processes, is usually performed more than once on a project. The reason for this is twofold:

1. Qualitative risk analysis can usually be performed fairly quickly relative to other planning processes.
2. It is normal for risks and their underlying characteristics to change over the life of the project, making it important to revisit often.

How it works:

Inputs

Risk Management Plan

The risk management plan should define the overall approach to risk on the project, including how much risk is acceptable and who will be responsible for carrying out the analysis of the risks.

Risk Register

The risk register specifies each risk to be analyzed as part of this process.

Organizational Process Assets — See Chapter 2, Common Inputs

Project Scope Statement — See Chapter 5, Scope Definition, Outputs

Tools

The next two tools, because of their similarities, will be discussed together. Although they are different, it is highly unlikely you would be called upon to differentiate between them for the exam.

Risk Probability and Impact Assessment / Probability and Impact Matrix

When evaluating risks to determine what the highest priorities should be, the two tools and techniques mentioned above can assist you. The way they are used is that each risk in the risk register is evaluated for its likelihood of occurring and its potential impact on the project. Each of these two values is given a ranking (such as low, medium, high, or 1 through 10) and are multiplied together to get a risk score. This resulting score is used to set the priorities.

Risk Data Quality Assessment

The data used should be objectively evaluated to determine whether or not it is accurate and of acceptable quality. For instance, if you were evaluating weather risk for a construction project, you would need to evaluate the quality of the weather data you were using.

Risk Categorization

Categorizing the detailed risks can help you build a better big-picture of the risks. This may help you understand which parts of the project have the highest degree of uncertainty.

Risk Urgency Assessment

Urgent risks are those that cannot wait. As you are evaluating the risks, it is important to determine which risks are the most urgent, requiring immediate attention. For instance, if you determined that a building's structural support may be inadequate, that would require immediate attention, while other risks, such as future weather threats, although equally important, might be less urgent.

Outputs

Risk Register Updates

The risk register, developed earlier in the Risk Identification process, contains a list of all the risks. Now this register is further completed, including the priority of the risks, the urgency of the risks, the categorization of the risks, and any trends that were noticed while performing this process.

Qualitative Risk Analysis

Quantitative Risk Analysis

What it is:

This process is easy to confuse with the previously covered Qualitative Risk Analysis, and in reality the processes have quite a lot in common; however, Quantitative Risk Analysis seeks to assign a projected value to (quantify) the risks that have been ranked by Qualitative Risk Analysis. This likely value is typically specified in terms of cost or time.

Why it is important:

Quantitative Risk Analysis updates the risk register, and this information will be used by the subsequent two processes (Risk Response Planning and Risk Monitoring and Control). Without performing this process, the information about the identified risk is less complete and less useful.

When it is performed:

Quantitative Risk Analysis relies on the prioritized list of risks from the Qualitative Risk Analysis process. Therefore, it is usually performed right after Qualitative Risk Analysis; however, in some cases they may be performed at the same time.

How it works:

Inputs

Organizational Process Assets — See Chapter 2, Common Inputs

Project Scope Statement — See Scope Definition, Outputs

Risk Management Plan — See Risk Management Planning, Outputs

Risk Register — See Risk Identification, Outputs

Project Management Plan — See Chapter 2, Common Inputs

Tools

Data Gathering and Representation Techniques

Interviewing

Interviewing uses a structured interview to ask experts about the likelihood and impact of identified risks. After interviewing several experts, for instance, the project manager might create pessimistic, optimistic, and realistic values associated with each risk.

Expert Judgment

People with expertise in the areas of risk that you are evaluating are one of the richest sources of data gathering. Asking experts to review your data and your methodology can be very useful.

Quantitative Risk Analysis and Modeling Techniques

Sensitivity Analysis

Sensitivity analysis is used to analyze your project and determine how sensitive it is to risk. In other words, you are analyzing whether the occurrence of a particular negative risk event would ruin the project, or merely be an inconvenience.

Tornado Diagrams

Tornado diagrams, named for the funnel shape of their bars, are one way to analyze project sensitivity to cost or other factors.

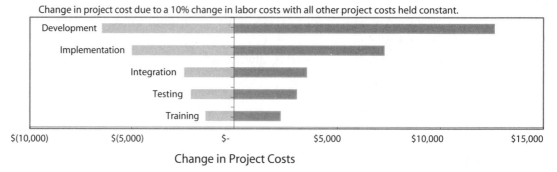

Change in project cost due to a 10% change in labor costs with all other project costs held constant.

Change in Project Costs

A tornado diagram, used to depict risks

The tornado diagram above depicts the effects of a 10% change in labor costs on the project. If labor costs increase by 10% and all other costs hold steady, development will be affected the most. Specifically, if the costs rise by 10%, then the development costs will rise by approximately $13,000. If the labor costs fall by 10%, development costs will fall by approximately $7,000. This shows how sensitive each analyzed area of the project is to risk (in this case, the risk of a cost increase).

A tornado diagram ranks the bars from greatest to least on the project so that the chart takes on a tornado-like shape.

Expected Monetary Value Analysis

Expected monetary value analysis takes uncertain events and calculates a most likely monetary value (i.e. dollar amount). It is typically calculated by using decision trees, covered next.

Quantitative Risk Analysis

Decision Tree Analysis

Decision trees are used to show probability and arrive at a dollar amount associated with each risk.

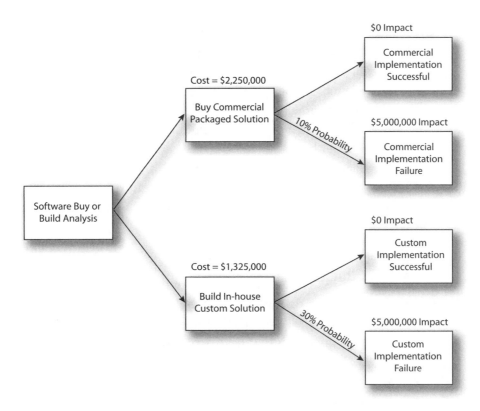

The numbers for this decision tree work out as follows:

	Initial Cost	Risk cost	Probability	Total
Commercial Package	$2,250,000	$5,000,000	10%	$2,750,000
Custom Software	$1,325,000	$5,000,000	30%	$2,825,000

*The totals above were calculated by first multiplying the risk cost by the probability and then adding it to the initial cost. e.g. $5,000,000 * 10% = $500,000. $2,250,000 + $500,000 = $2,750,000.*

In the preceding example, the analysis shows that the custom software has a higher overall cost due to the higher risk. Decision trees can get very complex as they grow larger, but this method is a good overall tool to quantify the outcome of various options.

Quantitative Risk Analysis

Modeling and Simulation

There are almost as many types of simulation as there are projects; however, one technique for simulating the schedule is Monte Carlo analysis.

This is a favorite topic on the exam. Monte Carlo analysis, also discussed in Chapter 6 – Time Management, is a tool that takes details and assembles a big picture. Performed by computer, Monte Carlo analysis throws large numbers of scenarios at the schedule to see the impact of certain risk events. This technique will show you what is not always evident by simply looking at the schedule. It will often identify tasks that may not appear inherently high risk, but in the event they are delayed, the whole project may be adversely affected.

Outputs

Risk Register Updates

The risk register is updated with the probabilities associated with each identified risk and the probability of meeting the project's cost and time projections. Additionally, the priorities of the risks should be updated, and any trends that have been observed should be noted.

Do not forget that risk may be beneficial! As an example, when you purchase a lottery ticket, you are running the risk that you will win money, and that risk can be quantified. If you are constructing a building, you would plan for a certain amount of bad weather to impact the construction schedule; however, you run the risk that the weather will be worse than anticipated as well as the risk that the weather will be better than anticipated. This usage of the word risk is counter-intuitive to many people but it is correct within the domain of project management, because *the risk is in the uncertainty, not just in the outcome.*

Prioritized List of Quantified Risks

Lists of risk should be prioritized by the numbers in this process. For instance, based on the expected value (probability x $ impact), the following 4 risks are ranked in the table. The rankings would show you how to manage these risks.

Risk	Probability	Impact	Expected Value
Risk B	25%	$1,750,000.00	$ 437,500.00
Risk C	50%	$ 600,000.00	$ 300,000.00
Risk D	80%	$ 200,000.00	$ 160,000.00
Risk A	13%	$ 152,200.00	$ 19,786.00

Quantitative Risk Analysis

Risk Response Planning

What it is:

Earlier, in the process of Risk Management Planning, we created a general approach to risk (the risk management plan). Then, in Risk Identification, we created a list of risks and started our risk register. Then we qualitatively and quantitatively analyzed the risks, and now we are ready to create a detailed plan for managing the risk. That is precisely what Risk Response Planning does; it creates a plan for how each risk will be handled.

Remember that risk can be a positive or negative event (e.g. there is a risk that the project will finish late, but there is also a risk that it will finish early). Therefore, careful consideration must be given to each risk, whether the impact of that risk is positive or negative.

Why it is important:

Up to this point, all we have done is identify and analyze the risks, but now that the analysis is complete, we need to create a specific plan. The resulting plan is actionable, meaning that it assigns specific tasks and responsibilities to specific team members.

When it is performed:

One of the helpful things about the risk management processes is that the processes are typically conducted in the order that they are presented in this book. This means that you begin with Risk Management Planning, continue with Risk Identification, proceed with Qualitative Risk Analysis, followed by Quantitative Risk Analysis, and then by this process, Risk Response Planning.

How it works:

Inputs

Risk Management Plan — See Risk Management Planning, Outputs

Risk Register — See Risk Identification, Outputs

Tools and Techniques

You will almost certainly see exam questions related to the risk responses. Be sure you can identify different responses based on behaviors described in the test questions.

Strategies for Negative Risks or Threats

Avoid

Avoidance is a very appropriate tool for working with undesirable risk in many circumstances. For instance, a software project may choose to avoid the risk associated with using a particular piece of cutting edge technology in favor of using a slower but more reliable technology.

Transfer

To transfer a risk to another party is to make it their responsibility. Contractual agreements and insurance are common ways to transfer risks.

Mitigate

Mitigating a risk simply means to make it less. For instance, if you were concerned about the risk of weather damage to a construction project, you might choose to construct the building outside of the rainy season.

Strategies for Positive Risks or Opportunities

As is stressed throughout this chapter, risks can be positive or negative, and where positive risks are concerned, the project manager wants to take steps to make them more likely. The following are specific strategies taken to capitalize on the positive risks.

Exploit

The definition for risk is uncertainty. Where the strategy of exploitation is concerned, you are trying to remove any uncertainty. For instance, if a positive risk of finishing the project early is identified, then adding enough people to ensure that the project is completed early would be an example of exploiting the risk.

Share

In order to share a positive risk, the project seeks to improve their chances of the risk occurring by working with another party. For instance, if a defense contractor identifies a positive risk of getting a large order, they may determine that sharing that risk by partnering with another defense firm, or even a competitor, would be an acceptable strategy.

Enhance

Enhancing a positive risk first requires that you understand the underlying cause(s) of the risk. By working to influence the underlying risk triggers, you can increase the likelihood of the risk occurring.

Risk Response Planning

Key Fact

Strategies for Both Threats and Opportunities

Acceptance

Acceptance is often a perfectly reasonable strategy for dealing with risk, whether positive or negative. When accepting a risk you are simply acknowledging that the best strategy may not be to avoid, transfer, mitigate, share, or enhance it. Instead, the best strategy may be simply to accept it and continue with the project. Many people miss questions on the exam related to this, because they don't have the mindset that acceptance may be the best strategy if the cost or impact of the other strategies is too great.

Contingent Response Strategy

A contingent response strategy is one where the project team may make one decision related to risk, but make that decision contingent upon certain conditions. For example, a project team may decide to mitigate a technology risk by hiring an outside firm with expertise in that technology, but that decision might be contingent upon the outside firm meeting intermediate milestones related to that risk.

Outputs

Risk Register Updates

Now that a specific plan has been created for each risk in the risk register, the register should be updated to reflect this new information.

Project Management Plan Updates — See Chapter 2, Common Inputs

Risk-Related Contractual Agreements

One of the tools for this process is to transfer the risk to another party. This tool can often result in contractual agreements. For instance, a company that has little experience in mission-critical software development may contract out that part of the project, but risk-related contractual agreements would typically accompany this decision. In this example, it might be appropriate to specify cost, time, and performance targets for the subcontracting software company to meet in order to receive full payment.

Risk Monitoring and Control

What it is:

At this point, you should have detected a pattern with the knowledge areas. All of them have a monitoring and controlling process that looks back over the plans and any execution that has taken place and compares them. In these monitoring and controlling processes, you are asking questions such as, "Did we plan properly?" "Did the results come out the way we anticipated?" "If the results did not match the plan, should we take corrective action by modifying the plan or changing the way we are executing?" "Are there lessons learned that we need to feed into future projects?"

Why it is important:

Plans have to be reassessed and reevaluated. Where risk is concerned, we've done quite a bit of planning, identifying, analyzing, and predicting, but the process of Risk Monitoring and Control takes a look back to evaluate how all of that planning is lining up with reality.

When it is performed:

Risk Monitoring and Control is a process that is performed almost continually throughout the project. That is not to say that you do these activities without stopping or that someone is assigned full time, but rather that monitoring and controlling the risk is an ongoing concern.

How it works:

Inputs

Risk Management Plan — See Risk Management Planning, Outputs

Risk Register — See Risk Identification, Outputs

Approved Change Requests — See Chapter 2, Common Inputs

Work Performance Information

Work performance information is used as an input here since monitoring and controlling processes compare the plan to the results. The plan is brought in as an input above, and the work performance information provides information on the results. For instance, the status of a deliverable provides helpful information related to schedule risk, cost risk, or other areas of concern.

Performance Reports

The performance reports do not focus so much on what has been done as they do on how it was done. For instance, whereas the work performance information provides information on the status of deliverables, the performance reports focus on cost, time, and quality performance. Where the performance reports are concerned, the actual results are compared against the baselines to show how the project is performing against the plan.

Tools

 Risk Reassessment

As you perform a project, your information about risks, and even the very nature of the risks, change. You should reassess this information as often as necessary in order to make sure that the risk needs of the project are current and accurate. Note that a constant reassessment may not be required by all projects. Some projects may not need to reassess their risk information at all, while others may need more frequent updates.

 Risk Audits

The important thing to know about risk audits is that they are focused on overall risk management. In other words, they are more about the top-down process than they are about individual risks. Periodic risk audits evaluate how the risk management plan and the risk response plan are working as the project progresses and also whether the risks which were identified and prioritized are actually occurring.

 Variance and Trend Analysis

Variance analysis focuses on the difference between what was planned and what was executed. Trend analysis shows how performance is trending. The reason trend analysis is important is that a one-time snapshot of cost may not cause concern, but a trend showing worsening cost performance may indicate that things are steadily worsening and may indicate that a problem is imminent.

Technical Performance Measurement

Performance can take on many flavors. In this case, technical performance measurement focuses on functionality, looking at how the project has met its goals for delivering the scope over time.

Risk Monitoring/Control

Reserve Analysis

The project's reserve (also called contingency) can apply to schedule, time or cost. Periodically, the project's reserve, whether cost or time, should be evaluated to ensure that it is sufficient to address the amount of risk the project expects to encounter.

Status Meetings

This particular technique is not necessarily suggesting that you have specially called status meetings related to risk. Instead, it is suggesting that you create a project culture where bringing up items related to risk is always acceptable and risk is discussed regularly.

Outputs

Risk Register Updates

New risk information, whether it is changes to your risk estimates or actual numbers (such as costs related to weather damage) should be regularly updated in the risk register.

Requested Changes

When risk events occur, change requests to the project are a normal outcome. In addition, even when the events do not occur, the project may be changed as a result of new risk-related information gathered during this process.

Recommended Corrective Actions

Corrective action is one of the most important concepts for the exam. It is anything done to bring future results in line with the plan, and in this case, corrective action to the project could include any actions taken to ensure that the future project results and the plan were in alignment. That could mean changing the plan, or it could mean changing the way the plan is executed or even changing things about the environment. The most important thing to keep in mind is that whatever changes are affected, they are intended to help your risk plans and the future line up. These recommendations are typically funneled in through the integrated change control system.

Recommended Preventive Actions

Whereas corrective action (above) is about making sure a problem does not reoccur, preventive action is about making sure a problem never occurs.

Organizational Process Assets Updates

All of the risk plans and information related to them, including analysis and corrective actions, can be archived for use on future projects. Over time, these plans become an asset to assist in future project planning and development.

Project Management Plan Updates

Any changes that are made to the project should be updated in the project management plan.

Risk Monitoring/Control

Risk Management Questions

1. You are managing the construction of a data center, but the location is in an area highly prone to earthquakes. In order to deal with this risk, you have chosen a type of building and foundation that is particularly earthquake resistant. This is an example of:

   A. Risk transfer.

   B. Risk avoidance.

   C. Risk mitigation.

   D. Risk acceptance.

2. You are evaluating the risk by trying to produce a risk score for each risk. This is an example of which tool?

   A. Monte Carlo analysis.

   B. Probability impact matrix.

   C. RACI Chart.

   D. Cause and effect diagrams.

3. As part of your project, you have identified a significant risk of cost overrun on a software component that is integral to the product. Which represents the BEST strategy in dealing with this risk?

   A. Outsource the software development.

   B. Insure the cost.

   C. Double the estimate.

   D. Eliminate the need for this component.

4. Planning meetings and analysis are used in which process?

   A. As part of Risk Monitoring and Control.

   B. As part of Quantitative Risk Analysis.

   C. As part of Risk Response Planning.

   D. As part of Risk Management Planning.

5. Refer to the diagram below. What is the expected value of Result A?

   A. $200,000.
   B. $100,000.
   C. $50,000.
   D. $25,000.

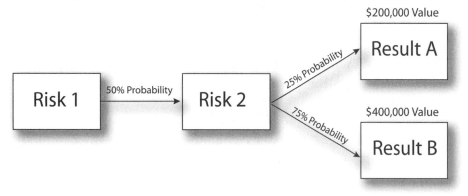

6. Refer to the diagram from the previous question. What risk management tool is employed in this diagram?

   A. Earned value management.

   B. Sensitivity analysis.

   C. Decision tree analysis.

   D. Flowcharting.

7. Marie is meeting with her project team to evaluate each identified risk and try to assign an estimated dollar amount or time impact estimate to it. Which process is her team performing?

   A. Quantitative Risk Analysis.

   B. Qualitative Risk Analysis.

   C. Risk Response Planning.

   D. Risk Monitoring and Control.

8. If a project manager is recommending that immediate corrective action be taken, which process is he involved in?

    A. Qualitative Risk Analysis.

    B. Risk Management Planning.

    C. Risk Identification.

    D. Risk Monitoring and Control.

9. What is the BEST source of information about potential risk on your project?

    A. Computer risk analysis.

    B. Interviews with team members from other projects.

    C. Historical records from similar projects.

    D. Your own experience in this industry.

10. You have just finished a thorough Monte Carlo analysis for your project. Which of the following would the analysis MOST likely identify?

    A. Divergent paths causing risk.

    B. Points of schedule risk.

    C. Points of schedule conflict that lead to risk.

    D. Gaps in the project path that could create risk.

11. Your company is beginning a new building project and has assigned you the role of project manager. During the first few meetings with stakeholders you become aware of several risks that are of concern to the project sponsor. The topic of risk management, however, has yet to be addressed. What is the first thing you should do to address the project risks?

    A. Develop a risk management plan.

    B. Identify project risks.

    C. Plan responses to project risks.

    D. Determine how risks will be controlled.

12.   **Risk Management Planning is:**

   A.   A process of identifying potential risks for a project.

   B.   Deciding how risk management activities will be structured and performed.

   C.   Assessing the impact and likelihood of project risks.

   D.   Numerical analysis of the probability of project risks.

13.   **Which of the following is an output of Risk Identification?**

   A.   Risk register.

   B.   Probabilistic analysis.

   C.   Risk-related contractual agreements.

   D.   Recommended cash reserves.

14.   **Which of the following would NOT be a strategy for dealing with negative risk?**

   A.   Avoid.

   B.   Transfer.

   C.   Share.

   D.   Mitigate.

15.   **A risk probability and impact assessment is used in:**

   A.   Risk Identification.

   B.   Qualitative Risk Analysis.

   C.   Quantitative Risk Analysis.

   D.   Risk Response Planning.

Answers to Risk Management Questions

1.   C. The best answer here is risk mitigation since you are taking steps to lessen the risk. 'A' is incorrect because you are not transferring the risk to anyone else. 'B' is incorrect because you would need to relocate in order to completely avoid the risk of earthquake. 'D' is incorrect because you are not merely accepting the risk – you are taking steps to make it less severe.

2.   B. The probability impact matrix (PIM) derives a risk score by multiplying the probability of the risk by its impact (both of these numbers are estimated). This resulting risk score may be used to help prioritize the risk register.

3.   A. Outsourcing the software development could allow you to cap the cost. 'B' is not a good choice because costs for development such as this cannot be insured in a cost-effective manner. 'C' is not correct because doubling the estimate does not deal with the root of the problem. It only arbitrarily changes the estimate. 'D' is incorrect because you cannot simply eliminate every high risk component in the real world.

4.   D. Planning meetings and analysis are a tool of the process of Risk Management Planning.

5.   D. The way this problem is solved is by multiplying out the probabilities times the value. In this case, it the 50% probability of Risk 1 X the 25% probability of Risk 2 X the $200,000 value of result A. .5 X .25 * 200,000 = $25,000.

6.   C. This is an example of decision tree analysis.

7.   A. You should have seen the fact that Marie's team was quantifying the risks by seeking to assign a dollar or time estimate to them, and Quantitative Risk Analysis is the process that does this.

8.   D. Recommended corrective action is the result of monitoring and controlling processes, and the only monitoring and controlling process in the choices was Risk Monitoring and Control.

9. C. Historical records from similar projects would provide you with the best source of information on potential risks. 'A', 'B', and 'D' are all good inputs or tools, but they would not be as pertinent or helpful as the records from other similar projects. Historical information gets brought into your planning processes as an organizational process asset.

10. B. One of the things Monte Carlo analysis would show you is where schedule risk exists on the project. 'A' is incorrect, because it is typically convergent and not divergent tasks that create schedule risk. 'C' is incorrect because it is not looking for schedule conflicts – those would be corrected in Schedule Development. 'D' is incorrect because gaps in the project path do not, by themselves, cause risk.

11. A. You should develop the risk management plan. A risk management plan will outline how all risk planning activities and decisions will be approached. Methods of identification, qualification, quantification, response planning, and control will all follow the development of the risk management plan.

12. B. Risk management planning is not planning for actual risks (which include choices 'A', 'C', and 'D'); it is the PROCESS of deciding how all risk planning activities and decisions will be approached. It is the plan for how to plan.

13. A. The risk register is the only output of Risk Identification, and it is updated in Qualitative Risk Analysis, Quantitative Risk Analysis, Risk Response Planning, and Risk Monitoring and Control.

14. C. There are three identified strategies for dealing with negative risks. They are: mitigate, transfer, and avoid. The reason that 'C' was incorrect is that share is a strategy for managing a positive risk or opportunity.

15. B. The hardest part about risk is keeping the various processes straight. Since the outputs are similar (for the most part), focus more of your study on the processes themselves and their tools. In this question, the tool of risk probability and impact assessment is a tool of Qualitative Risk Analysis.

Chapter 11

Procurement Management

Difficulty	Memorization	Exam Importance
High	Medium	Medium

Procurement management is the set of processes performed to obtain goods, services, or scope from outside the organization.

Procurement management can be a very challenging knowledge area on the exam. One reason it can be so difficult is that relatively few people have formal procurement training in their background.

Philosophy

PMI's procurement management approach is steeped in formal government procurement practices. In fact, many of the processes, tools, techniques, and outputs found here are near duplicates of those used by many government and military institutions in the United States.

The overarching philosophy of procurement management is that it should be formal. Many people's practical experience may differ from this rigid approach, but it is necessary to understand it and to be able to apply PMI's philosophy on the exam.

Importance

Several questions on the exam will be drawn from procurement management. If formal procurement is new to you, this material is especially important.

There are not any formulas to learn or complex techniques to apply; however, there is a significant amount of material presented in this chapter.

The processes of Project Procurement Management with their *primary* outputs

Procurement Management

Plan Purchases and Acquisitions
Procurement Mgt Plan
Contract S.O.W.

Plan Contracting
Procurement Docs
Evaluation Criteria

Request Seller Responses
Qualified Sellers List

Select Sellers
Contract
Contract Mgt. Plan

Contract Administration
Risk Register Updates
Contract Agreements

Contract Closure
Risk Register Updates
Requested Changes

Preparation

As mentioned earlier, it would be wise to take special care in this section if you do not have a background in formal procurement activities.

Keep in mind as you approach this material that the PMBOK was not written to be memorized. It was written to be practiced and applied. For this chapter in particular, understanding is more important than memorizing.

In this chapter, key terms, concepts, and the processes and their components are provided.

PMI's procurement management processes are quite involved. Test takers would do well to read this chapter carefully and then read Chapter 12, Project Procurement Management of the 3rd Edition PMBOK Guide.

Procurement Processes

There are six processes in procurement management, tying with risk management for the most processes of any knowledge area on the exam. These processes are displayed in the figure at the beginning of the chapter and summarized in the tables below.

Process Group	Procurement Management Process
Initiating	(none)
Planning	Plan Purchases and Acquisitions, Plan Contracting
Executing	Request Seller Responses, Select Sellers
Monitoring & Controlling	Contract Administration
Closing	Contract Closure

Process	Key Outputs
Plan Purchases and Acquisitions	Procurement Mgt. Plan, Contract S.O.W.
Plan Contracting	Procurement Documents, Eval. Criteria
Request Seller Responses	Proposals
Select Sellers	Selected Sellers, Contract, Contract Mgt. Plan
Contract Administration	Contract Documentation, Updates
Contract Closure	Closed Contracts

Procurement Roles

In procurement management, there are two primary roles defined, and the project manager could play either of these roles. In fact, it is not uncommon for project managers to play both roles on the same project. The roles are:

Buyer

The organization or party purchasing (procuring) the goods or services from the seller.

Seller

The organization or party providing or delivering the goods or services to the buyer.

Plan Purchases and Acquisitions

What it is:

> This process involves looking at the project and determining which components or services of the project will be made or performed internally and which will be "procured" from an external source. After that decision is made, the project manager must determine the appropriate type of contracts to be used on the project.

Why it is important:

> Currently best practices in the field of project management favor buying externally vs. building internally, all other things being equal; however, there are numerous factors that should go into your decision on whether to "make or buy."

> Carefully planning what to procure, and how to go about the processes of procurement, will ensure that right things are procured in the right way.

When it is performed:

> Because a project may have multiple subcontractors, potentially in every phase of the project, any of the procurement processes could be performed repeatedly and at any time throughout the project.

How it works:

Inputs

Organizational Process Assets — See Chapter 2, Common Inputs

Project Management Plan — See Chapter 2, Common Inputs

Enterprise Environmental Factors

> There may be factors at work in an organization that have a strong influence on procurement. For instance, an organization may have a strong culture of "build internally vs. buy" or they could have a strong culture of buying from a few trusted sellers. All of this should be factored in when making procurement decisions.

Project Scope Statement

The project scope statement defines the scope of the project. This information will be useful to review when considering what components of the scope should be procured (i.e. performed by groups outside the organization).

Work Breakdown Structure

The WBS is an organization of all of the deliverables on the project. Oftentimes when reviewing the WBS, an entire segment that may be "broken off" and procured becomes apparent.

WBS Dictionary

The WBS dictionary always accompanies the WBS. It provides expanded information on each node of the WBS.

Tools

Make-or-Buy Analysis

Make-or-buy analysis can be difficult to sum up succinctly. The analysis looks at all of the factors that could sway the decision toward making internally or buying externally, including risk factors, cost, releasing proprietary information, and a host of other decision points.

When using this tool, the project must often look past itself. For instance, writing a software component may not make as much sense as procuring it externally where only the project is concerned; however, if the performing organization has an interest in developing the capability to build that kind of software, it may make sense for the project to make vs. buy.

Expert Judgment

Where procurement planning is concerned, expert judgment can be of tremendous value. There will often be scope considerations, technical considerations, legal, cost, and schedule considerations, and bringing in people with expertise in this area can help the project team make the best decisions.

| 🔑 Key Fact | *Contract Type* |

When procuring goods or services, the type of contract that governs the deal can make a significant difference in who bears the risk. There are three categories of contracts you must know for the test. They are listed below with information on each one:

Fixed Price Contracts (also known as Lump Sum Contracts)

Fixed price contracts are the easiest ones to understand. There is generally a single fee, although payment terms may be specified so that the cost is not necessarily a lump sum payable at the end.

This type of contract is very popular when the scope of work is thoroughly defined and completely known. Two types of fixed price contracts are:

Fixed Price Incentive Fee

The price is fixed, with an incentive fee for meeting a target specified in the contract (such as finishing the work ahead of schedule).

Fixed Price Economic Price Adjustment

This type of contract is popular in cases where fluctuations in the exchange rate or interest rate may impact the project. In this case, an economic stipulation may be included to protect the seller or the buyer. The economic stipulation may be based on the interest rate, the consumer price index, cost of living adjustments, currency exchange rates, or other indices.

Cost Reimbursable Contracts

There are two common types of cost reimbursable contracts:

Cost Plus Fixed Fee

The seller passes the cost back to the buyer and receives an additional fixed fee upon completion of the project.

Cost Plus Incentive Fee

The seller passes the cost back to the buyer and gets an incentive fee for meeting a target (usually tied back to keeping costs low) specified in the contract.

Time and Materials Contracts

In a time and materials contract, the seller charges for time plus the cost of any materials needed to complete the work.

Type of Contract	Who Bears the Risk	Explanation
Fixed Price	Seller	Since the price is fixed, cost overruns may not be passed on to the buyer and must be borne by the seller.
Cost Plus Fixed Fee	Buyer	Since all costs must be reimbursed to the seller, the buyer bears the risk of cost overruns.
Cost Plus Incentive Fee	Buyer and Seller	The buyer bears most of the risk here, but the incentive fee for the seller motivates that seller to keep costs down.
Time and Materials	Buyer	The buyer pays the seller for all time and materials the seller applies to the project. The buyer bears the most risk of cost overruns.

Point of Total Assumption

Key Fact

Because there are numerous types of contracts where the risk is shared to one degree or another, it is important to be able to calculate how risk is allocated between the buyer and seller. One consideration, particularly when using Fixed Price Incentive Fee contracts is the Point of Total Assumption.

The Point of Total Assumption (PTA) is the point in the contract where a subcontractor assumes responsibility for all additional costs. This concept can be challenging to understand at first, so to help with this, consider a situation where company ABC is subcontracting out the installation of industrial shelving to company XYZ for an estimated $75,000. The selected contract is cost plus fixed price, so ABC pushes for a cap (called a cost ceiling) to protect them from serious cost overruns. The terms of the contract are that XYZ's target cost is $71,000, the target price to ABC is $75,000 and XYZ's ceiling price to ABC is $84,000; however, for every dollar over the target price, the share ratio is 3:1. This means that ABC (the buyer) will pay $0.75, while XYZ (the seller) will have to pay $0.25 of every dollar overrun. Knowing this information, it is fairly simple to calculate the PTA. The formula is:

Target cost + (ceiling price – target price) ÷ ABC's % share of cost overrun.

In this case, it would be $71,000 + ($84,000 - $75,000) ÷ .75, which simplifies to $71,000 + $12,000 = $83,000.

Plan Purchases/Acquisitions

In other words, at the point the contract reaches $83,000, the subcontractor (XYZ) would assume the total burden of cost overrun. The ceiling price is still $84,000, but XYZ is bearing 100% of the cost overrun burden above $83,000 (the PTA). The PTA is important, because it helps identify the point in the contract where the seller has the most motivation to bring things to completion.

Outputs

Procurement Management Plan

The procurement management plan is an important output of the Plan Purchases and Acquisitions process. It defines how all of the other procurement management processes will be carried out. This includes defining what will be procured on the project, how a seller will be selected, what types of contracts will be used, how risk will be managed, and how sellers will be managed, including how their performance will be measured.

Contract Statement of Work

Many people find this document confusing when first approaching it, but it is highly important for the exam! If you recall the project scope statement, produced as part of the Scope Definition process, then you will know that the project's scope has been defined at this point. The statement of work is not merely a replication of what we did in Scope Definition. Instead, the contract statement of work is important because it helps explain a section of the scope to potential sellers in enough detail so that they can decide whether they want to (or are qualified to) pursue the work in question.

One key point to understand about the contract statement of work is that it is not the entire project's statement of work. Instead, it only defines the scope that the potential seller would need to understand to complete their part of the sub-project.

Make-or-Buy Decisions

During this process, the project team performed make-or-buy analysis as a tool, and now it is time to act upon the data gathered. The decisions should be made and documented, and enough information to justify why these decisions were made should be included.

Requested Changes

Sometimes changes need to be made to the project in order to facilitate procurement. For instance, a software application may be redesigned in order to allow a subcontractor to use their own database and keep their work and data separate from that of the core team. These requested changes should be channeled back through Integrated Change Control to evaluate their impact on the rest of the project.

Plan Contracting

What it is:

Now that the initial (and somewhat high-level) procurement planning has taken place, it is time to create the detailed documents, such as the request for proposal (RFP), that will allow the sub-project to be bid out and managed.

Why it is important:

The Plan Contracting process is important because it provides the definition and details needed to conduct the next few procurement processes. These documents allow potential sellers to know exactly what is expected of them in terms of the work to be done, how it is to be done, cost, time, and quality expectations, etc.

When it is performed:

This process, like all of the procurement management processes, may be performed more than once on a project. For instance, if you planned to contract out five components of the project, you would likely perform this process five times.

How it works:

Inputs

Procurement Management Plan — See Plan Purchases and Acquisitions, Outputs

Contract Statement of Work — See Plan Purchases and Acquisitions, Outputs

Make-or-Buy Decisions — See Plan Purchases and Acquisitions, Outputs

Project Management Plan — See Chapter 2, Common Inputs

Tools

Standard Forms

Keep in mind that the purpose of this process is to create the procurement documents such as the RFP (see outputs below for more information on the documents produced). When an RFP is created, it is generally unheard of to start with a blank sheet of paper. Instead, it is more common to begin with a standard template or form that provides standard language or at the very least a checklist of items to consider.

Expert Judgment

In the area of creating procurement documents, very few project managers have all of the expertise needed to create an RFP or any of the other documents needed to support solicitation.

Outputs

Procurement Documents

The procurement documents should be produced by the buyer. They may be called several things, including proposals, bids, and similar names. These documents may be general or detailed, depending on the need. For instance, if you were a manufacturing company, and your request for proposal (RFP) was related to computer networking, you may choose to keep the proposal fairly general so that your potential sellers could provide specifics that were in their areas of expertise. If, however, you were an automaker and wanted to procure the braking assembly as part of a new automobile, the RFP for that would likely be highly specific and detailed.

If the item being procured is not within the buyer's area of expertise, the buyer may want to ensure that the procurement documents allow for enough flexibility to get creative responses from the sellers.

These procurement documents are invitations and requests for potential sellers to evaluate the work and prepare a proposal.

Evaluation Criteria

Before taking the CAPM Exam, make sure you understand that evaluation criteria are created by the buyer at the same time as the procurement documents. In other words, at the same time you assemble the procurement documentation, you decide how you will select the winning bid. It is not always mandatory that the evaluation criteria be objective, or even that you reveal it to the potential sellers. For instance, you might wish to select a winning bid based on their ability to work well with your team (note that this could be illegal on some public-sector projects, and rules regarding evaluation criteria will differ among organizations and industries).

Contract Statement of Work updates

The easiest way to think about this is that the contract statement of work is the general document, and the procurement documents provide the specifics. As you are documenting the details out in the RFP (or similar procurement document), it is normal that you may want to make some changes to the more general contract statement of work.

Request Seller Responses

What it is:

This is a somewhat unusual process in that most of the work here is being performed by the potential sellers. Request Seller Responses is the process concerned with distributing the procurement documents out to the potential sellers and having them respond with how they would perform the work and their qualifications to perform the work.

Why it is important:

One result of this process is that you get proposals from your customers, paving the way for you to select the best one(s) for your project.

When it is performed:

In a project where goods or services are being procured, this process may be performed one or multiple times. While there is no prescribed timeframe for when it is performed, it will always come after the Plan Contracting process.

How it works:

Inputs

Organizational Process Assets — See Chapter 2, Common Inputs

Procurement Management Plan — See Plan Purchases and Acquisitions, Outputs

Procurement Documents — See Plan Contracting, Outputs

Tools

Bidder Conferences

The important point regarding bidder conferences is that all interested potential sellers are given the procurement documents (typically in advance of the conference) and are allowed to ask questions. Using this type of meeting, all bidders are kept on a level playing field, and none has more or less access to people or information than the others.

Advertising

Oftentimes bids must be advertised, either in order to ensure that an adequate number of qualified sellers know about the bid or to meet legal requirements. For instance, some governments require that certain bids be advertised to the public. These ads may be distributed through public means, such as periodicals or the Internet, or they may be advertised only to the qualified sellers list.

Develop Qualified Sellers List

If the performing organization requires that sellers be on a list of qualified sellers, then the list should be used. If the buyer's organization has no such list, then one may be developed for the purpose of the project.

Outputs

Qualified Sellers List

As mentioned above, a qualified sellers list may be developed for this project if one does not already exist.

Procurement Document Package

This is the formal package of documents that includes the packaging of procurement documents created earlier (e.g. Request for Proposal, Invitation for Bid, or Request for Quotation). These are distributed to the potential sellers.

Proposals

The proposal is the answer to the procurement document package described above. It is prepared by the seller and includes whatever information was requested by the buyer. Typically, the seller's qualifications are included, along with how they would deliver the goods or services, the price, their projected performance, and any helpful technical details that would assist the buyer in deciding to use the seller. These proposals are often followed up by interviews with the buyer which allow the buyer and seller to explore the potential seller's proposal in greater detail.

Select Sellers

What it is:

Most of the processes in the 3rd Edition PMBOK Guide do exactly what they sound like. In this case, the process of Select Sellers does just that. It picks a seller who will be awarded a contract.

Why it is important:

This one gets the ball rolling with procurement. So far you have planned what you want to procure, written an RFP, issued it to potential sellers and held your bidders conferences, and you have received proposals from your potential sellers. Now you are going to select one of those proposals and issue a contract. You know, however, that real life isn't that simple, and this can be a very tricky area on the CAPM Exam as well.

When it is performed :

To state the obvious, this process is performed when you are ready to select a seller. This means that it will occur after Plan Purchases and Acquisitions, Plan Contracting, and Request Seller Proposals.

Like the other procurement processes, Select Sellers is performed as needed. It may be performed multiple times if there were multiple contracts, or it would not be performed at all if the project is not procuring anything.

How it works:

Inputs

Organizational Process Assets — *See Chapter 2, Common Inputs*

Procurement Management Plan — *See Plan Purchases and Acquisitions, Outputs*

Evaluation Criteria — *See Plan Contracting, Outputs*

Procurement Document Package — *See Request Seller Responses, Outputs*

Proposals — See Request Seller Responses, Outputs

Qualified Sellers List — See Request Seller Responses, Outputs

Project Management Plan — See Chapter 2, Common Inputs

Tools

Weighting System

When the buyer receives proposals from the seller, there needs to be some way to rank and quantify the information. The reason for this is to be as objective as possible.

For instance, if you specified in your procurement documents that you wanted networking experience, then you need some way to rank your potential seller responses based on their networking experiences. You may do this by assigning a 1 through 10 ranking or some other scale.

Following this procedure for all key information in the procurement process will help make seller selection easier.

Independent Estimates

The buyer may go and commission independent estimates to validate the proposals and bids received from the potential sellers. For example, the buyer may go out and ask an independent group to prepare an estimate so that they have an objective source of information. These independent estimates are often referred to as "should-cost" estimates.

Screening System

Screening systems set the bar at a certain level so that they can filter out certain non-qualified sellers. For instance, a buyer may require that all sellers be ISO-9002 certified in order to submit a bid. A screening system is put into place to allow only the bids of ISO-9002 certified companies through.

Contract Negotiations

Negotiations between the buyer and the potential seller are performed with the goal of reaching mutual agreement on the contractual terms and conditions.

Where the exam is concerned, the goal of negotiations is to reach a win-win scenario between the buyer and seller. When the buyer exerts too much pressure on the seller or negotiates an untenable deal, this can backfire on both of them in the long run.

Keep in mind that the project manager may or may not be the person who conducts these negotiations, as this can be a highly specialized area. On large and complex contracts, professional negotiators are the norm.

Seller Rating Systems

An organization may keep a grading system on the past performance of sellers. For example, a company may keep records on how well a seller previously did, and this can be used as a rating system that may be used as part of future seller selection.

Expert Judgment

In the area of selecting a seller, the buyer can use expert judgment to evaluate the bids and proposals.

Proposal Evaluation Techniques

There is no one way to evaluate proposals. In reality, there are as many techniques as there are buyers. This tool is essentially a combination of the other tools in the Select Seller process, used to evaluate the seller's bid or proposal.

Outputs

Selected Sellers

The RFP has been generated, the sellers have submitted their proposals, the negotiations have taken place, and now a seller is selected to provide goods or services on the project.

Contract

The contract is a formal document governing the relationship between the buyer and seller. Contracts are legal documents with highly specialized and technical language and should be written and changed only by people specializing in that field (e.g. the contracting officer, procurement office, lawyer, legal counsel). The project manager should not attempt to write, negotiate, or change the contract on his own.

The contract describes the work to be performed and perhaps the way in which that work will be performed (e.g., location, work conditions). It may specify who will do the work, when and how the seller will be paid, and delivery terms.

In reality, there is very little that the contract cannot specify in one way or another, so long as the terms and conditions are legal and they are mutually agreed upon by buyer and seller. Several other legal factors may come into play depending on the country that governs the contract, legal consideration, and other technical legal matters that are out of scope of this discussion.

An important component to include with the contract is how disputes (also called claims) will be resolved. This includes the process of dispute resolution, the parties who will be involved, and where the dispute resolution will take place.

Contract Management Plan

This component of the project management plan describes how the contract will be managed and how changes to the contract will be managed.

There may be more than one contract management plan on a project if there is more than one contract on the project.

Resource Availability

As resources and their availability are modified as a result of the contract, they should be updated. For instance, if a contract specifies that a team will work on site or that a piece of equipment will be available for a range of dates, these terms need to be documented, and appropriate resource calendars should be updated.

Procurement Management Plan Updates — See Plan Purchases and Acquisitions, Outputs

Requested Changes — See Chapter 2, Common Outputs

Select Sellers

Contract Administration

What it is:

In a nutshell, Contract Administration is the process where the buyer and seller review the contract and the work results to ensure that the results match the contract. This typically includes a review of:

- Were the goods or services delivered?
- Were the goods or services delivered on time?
- Were the right amounts invoiced or paid for the goods or services?
- Were any additional conditions of the contract met?

The process of Contract Administration is a process performed by the buyer and the seller, and because of the ramifications of any issues here, the project managers from both the buyer and seller should use whatever resources are necessary to ensure that all of these ramifications are fully understood.

Why it is important:

When looking at this from a project management perspective, the contract may be viewed as a plan (albeit a very specialized and binding type of plan). The process of Contract Administration ensures that the results of the project match this plan and that all conditions of the contract are met.

When it is performed:

Contract Administration, like the other procurement management processes, may be performed throughout the project if goods or services are being procured.

It typically occurs for a given contract at predefined intervals, but may also be performed as requested or needed.

Contract Administration

How it works:

Inputs

Contract — See Select Sellers, Outputs

Contract Management Plan — See Select Sellers, Outputs

Selected Sellers — See Select Sellers, Outputs

Performance Reports — See Performance Reporting, Outputs

Approved Change Requests — See Chapter 2, Common Inputs

Work Performance Information — See Direct and Manage Project Execution, Outputs

Tools

Contract Change Control System

The contract change control system is a component of the integrated change control system, and you will likely have a separate one for each contract. It was defined in the Select Sellers process. This system describes the procedures for how the contract may be changed, and it would typically include the people and the steps that need to be taken.

Buyer-Conducted Performance Review

This is a periodic review, initiated by the buyer but including the seller, where the seller's progress is measured against the contract and any other applicable plans. The seller is shown any areas where they are compliant as well as any areas where performance is a problem.

Inspections and Audits

This tool focuses on the product itself and its conformance to specifications. One important difference between this and the previous tool is that although inspections and audits do not seek to measure the seller's performance (i.e. how quickly or cost-effectively they are delivering the results), the buyer may use them to help the seller find problems in the way they are delivering the work results.

Contract Administration

Performance Reporting

Performance reporting is an excellent tool to help measure the seller's performance against the plan. This may include such items as earned value, the cost performance and schedule performance indices, and trend analysis. Oftentimes there are contract conditions tied to performance (e.g. seller must deliver at least 50% of the quantity of motors within 30 days of executing this contract).

Payment System

A payment system helps ensure that invoices and payments match up and that the right amount is being invoiced for the right deliverables at the right time. Additionally, payment systems will help avoid duplicate payments (or invoices if you are the seller). This tool can be of particular importance when payments are specified in the contract.

Claims Administration

Claims are basically disagreements. They may be about scope, the impact of a change, or the interpretation of some piece of the contract. The essential (legally binding) elements of the process for claims administration are defined in the contract itself, but there may be additional components in the contract management plan.

The most important thing about claims administration is to understand that they must be managed and ultimately resolved and that the process for doing so should be defined in advance of the claim.

Records Management System

The project manager uses the records management system to keep track of all communication that would be relevant to the contract.

Information Technology

Contract administration can be administratively burdensome, especially where larger contracts are concerned, and information technology can be used as a tool to help manage the large stream of information.

Contract Administration

Outputs

Contract Documentation

In short, contract documentation includes everything relevant to the contract, and it is kept by the buyer and the seller (although they would certainly keep separate documentation as well).

Items such as supporting detail on deliverables and performance should be kept, as well as financial records. Also, any changes from the original contract should be included in the contract documentation.

Organizational Process Assets Updates

There are many items that come out of contract administration that may be assets, but one of the most common ones to be updated as part of this process is the information on the seller's performance during the project. This could assist future projects in deciding whether to use this seller in the future.

Requested Changes — See Chapter 2, Common Outputs

Recommended Corrective Action — See Chapter 2, Common Outputs

Project Management Plan Updates — See Chapter 2, Common Outputs

Contract Closure

What it is:

Contract Closure is the process where the contract is completed by the buyer and seller. Ideally, the contract is terminated amicably with the seller delivering all of the contracted items and the buyer making all payments on time, but it isn't always done that way. For instance, the buyer may consider a seller to be in default and cancel the contract, or a buyer and seller may mutually agree to terminate the contract for any reason.

Why it is important:

Every contract must be closed. Contracts inadvertently left open potentially put both the buyer and seller at risk. This process is tightly linked to the Close Project process in integration management as it contributes to the closure of the entire project.

When it is performed:

This process is performed at the end of each contract, whether or not that end is successful. When the contract is completed or terminated for any reason, this process is performed.

How it works:

Inputs

Procurement Management Plan — See Plan Purchases and Acquisitions, Outputs

Contract Management Plan — See Select Sellers, Outputs

Contract Documentation — See Contract Administration, Outputs

Contract Closure Procedure

The procedures for closing the contract are typically specified in the contract and the contract management plan.

Tools

Procurement Audits

The point of a procurement audit is to capture lessons learned from a contracting perspective.

Records Management System

Contract documentation should always be archived for future reference. Many organizations have records management systems to facilitate the storing, archiving, and retrieval of records like this.

Outputs

Closed Contracts

The closed contracts are the essential outputs from Contract Closure.

Organizational Process Assets Updates

In addition to any other assets that may need updating, the lessons learned captured in this process (during the procurement audit) are formally documented here.

Procurement Management Questions

1.   The contract type that represents the highest risk to the seller is:

   A.   Fixed price plus incentive.

   B.   Cost reimbursable.

   C.   Fixed price.

   D.   Cost reimbursable plus incentive.

2.   You have been tasked with managing the seller responses to a request for proposal issued by your company. The seller responses were numerous, and now you have been asked to rank the proposals from highest to lowest in terms of their response. What are you going to use as a means to rank the sellers?

   A.   Evaluation criteria.

   B.   Request for quotation.

   C.   Seller response guidelines.

   D.   Seller selection matrix.

3.   Make or buy analysis is a tool used in which process?

   A.   Plan Purchases and Acquisitions.

   B.   Request Seller Responses.

   C.   Plan Contracting.

   D.   Procurement Analysis.

4.   Which of the following represents the right sequence of processes?

   A.   Plan Contracting, Plan Purchases and Acquisitions, Request Seller Responses, Select Sellers, Contract Administration.

   B.   Plan Contracting, Plan Purchases and Acquisitions, Select Sellers, Request Seller Responses, Contract Administration.

   C.   Plan Purchases and Acquisitions, Plan Contracting, Contract Administration, Request Seller Responses, Select Sellers.

   D.   Plan Purchases and Acquisitions, Plan Contracting, Request Seller Responses, Select Sellers, Contract Administration.

5.   You are managing a large software project when the need for a new series of database tables is discovered. The need was previously unplanned, and your organization's staff is 100% utilized, so you decide to go outside the company and procure this piece of work. When you meet with prospective sellers, you realize that the scope of work is not completely defined, but everyone agrees that the project is relatively small, and your need is urgent. Which type of contract makes the MOST sense?

   A.   Fixed price.

   B.   Time and materials.

   C.   Open ended.

   D.   Cost plus incentive fee.

6.   Your project plan calls for you to go through procurement in order to buy a specialty motor for an industrial robot. Because of patent issues, this motor is only available from one supplier that is across the country. After investigation, you believe that you could procure the motor from this company for a price that is within your budget. What is your BEST course of action?

   A.   Revisit the design and alter the specification to allow for a comparable motor.

   B.   Procure the motor from this source even though they are the sole source.

   C.   See if the component may be produced in another country, avoiding your country's patent issues.

   D.   Take the product out of the procurement management process.

7.   You have a supplier that is supplying parts to you under contract. The terms and conditions give you the right to change some aspects of the contract at any time, and you need to significantly lower the quantities due to a change in project scope. How should you notify the supplier?

   A.   Take them to lunch and explain the situation gently to preserve the relationship.

   B.   Have your attorney call their attorney.

   C.   Communicate with the supplier via e-mail.

   D.   Send them a formal, written notice that the contract has been changed.

8. Your project has been terminated immediately due to a cancellation by the customer. What action should you take FIRST?

    A. Call a meeting with the customer.

    B. Enter contract closure.

    C. Ask your team leads for a final status report.

    D. Verify this change against the procurement management plan.

9. You are evaluating proposals from prospective sellers. What process are you involved in?

    A. Plan Contracting.

    B. Request Seller Responses.

    C. Select Sellers.

    D. Contract Administration.

10. Your project scope calls for a piece of software that will control a valve in a pressurized pipeline. Your company has some experience with this type of software, but resources are tight, and it is not part of your company's core competency. You are considering involving other sellers but want to decide whether it is a better decision to produce this within your company or source it externally. What activity are you performing?

    A. Source selection.

    B. Make or buy analysis.

    C. Rational project procurement.

    D. Source evaluation.

11. Your organization is holding a bidders conference to discuss the project with prospective sellers, and a trusted seller you have worked with many times in the past has asked if they can meet with the project manager the day before the conference to cover some questions they do not wish to ask in front of other sellers. Should your organization meet with the seller?

     A. Yes, the more that prospective sellers know about the project, the better.

     B. Yes, they are your primary seller, and past history should be factored in.

     C. No, prospective suppliers should be kept on equal footing.

     D. No, that would represent an illegal activity.

12. The most important thing to focus on in contract negotiations is:

     A. To negotiate the best price possible for your project.

     B. To maintain the integrity of the scope.

     C. To negotiate a deal that both parties are comfortable with.

     D. To make sure legal counsel or the contract administrator has approved your negotiating points.

13. If a project manager was performing Contract Administration, which of the following duties might he be performing?

     A. Approving seller invoices.

     B. Negotiating the contract.

     C. Closing the contract.

     D. Weighing seller responses.

14. Who generally bears the risk in a time and materials contract?

     A. The buyer.

     B. The seller.

     C. The buyer early in the project and the seller later on.

     D. It depends on the materials used.

15. Your company is outsourcing a project in an area where it has little experience. The procurement documents should be:

    A.   Completely rigid to ensure no deviation from sellers.

    B.   Flexible enough to encourage creativity in seller responses.

    C.   Informal.

    D.   Reviewed by senior management.

Answers to Procurement Management Questions

1. C. This question was easier than it may have first appeared to be. Fixed price is the highest risk to the seller since the seller must bear the risk of any cost overruns. Choice 'B' would provide the highest risk to the buyer.

2. A. The evaluation criteria will provide the guidelines by which you can evaluate and rank responses. The RFQ would not necessarily help you pick the seller, as it is their proposal that is of interest. 'C' and 'D' were terms that were made up for this question.

3. A. Make or buy analysis is a tool used during the Plan Purchases and Acquisitions process, where you are deciding which deliverables should be procured and what should be created internally. 'D' is not a real process, and 'B' and 'C' are incorrect, because by the time you plan contracting or request responses from sellers, you need to already know what you are going to make and what you are going to buy.

4. D. Plan Purchases and Acquisitions, Plan Contracting, Request Seller Responses, Select Sellers, Contract Administration. A partial explanation that may help you understand why this sequence is correct and the others are not is that the outputs earlier processes are used as inputs into one or more subsequent processes. In this case, Plan Purchases and Acquisitions produces the Procurement Management Plan, which becomes an input into Plan Contracting. Plan Contracting produces the procurement documents, which are an input into Request Seller Responses. Request Seller Responses produces the procurement document package, which is used as an input into Select Sellers. Select Sellers produces the contract, which is an input into Contract Administration. This should help you understand why the processes must take place (at least initially) in this order.

5. B. Time and Materials. Choice 'A' is incorrect because the scope is not defined enough to establish a fair fixed price. Choice 'C' is a made up type of contract. Choice 'D' would not make sense in this case since the seller's costs are not abundantly clear, and this type of contract would create too much risk.

6. B. This one may trick some who think that it is wrong to use a sole source. In many cases it is the only choice. 'A' would not be good since the design has nothing to do with this. 'C' is not necessary in this case, since the issue is not a legal issue. Choice 'D' would be completely invalid since the item is still being procured outside of your organization.

7. D. Choices 'A' and 'B' are verbal. Contract changes should always be made in writing! 'C' is written, but e-mail is not the proper forum for making important contractual changes.

8. B. There are plenty of questions on the CAPM Exam that defy common sense. This one asks for your FIRST action, and the most appropriate action is to enter Contract Closure. Choices 'A' and 'C' may be appropriate at some point, but if a project is terminated, Contract Closure needs to be performed.

9. C. If you are evaluating seller responses, you are performing the process of Select Sellers. The seller proposals are brought into this process, and they are screened, weighted, rated, and evaluated against the criteria.

10. B. Make or buy analysis is the process where an organization decides whether it should produce the product internally or outsource it. This is done as part of the Plan Purchases and Acquisitions process.

11. C. If you are involved in formal procurement, you should make every effort to keep sellers on equal footing. If one seller is provided with an advantage, it negates much of the value of the procurement process.

12. C. The most important point is to create a deal that everyone feels good about. 'A' sounds like a good choice, but it is incorrect, since the best possible price might not be fair to your seller, and that could create a bad scenario for the project in the future. 'B' is important, but that is not the primary focus of negotiations. 'D' may or may not be necessary, depending on the situation.

13. A. One of the activities in Contract Administration is to pay seller invoices or generate invoices if you are the seller. Make sure to learn the primary process inputs, tools, techniques, and outputs for the processes.

14. A. In a time and materials contract, the buyer has to pay the seller for all time and materials, and often times it involves an incomplete scope definition. Therefore, the buyer is the one most at risk.

15.   B. In this scenario, you want sellers to respond with their own ideas. Procurement documents should be rigid enough to get responses to the same scope of work, and flexible enough to allow sellers to interject their own good ideas and creativity. Many people incorrectly choose 'A' because they assume that a rigid approach is almost always correct, but in this example, you do not have sufficient experience to rigidly manage the process, and you want your sellers to give you some guidance in their proposals. 'C' was clearly incorrect, as procurement is something that should be done formally. 'D' is incorrect because senior management has many functions in an organization, but they would not be expected to review procurement documents.

How To Pass The CAPM

Difficulty	Memorization	Exam Importance	Corresponding PMBOK Chapter
Low	Low	High	Not covered in PMBOK

Passing the CAPM on your first try has nothing to do with good luck. It is all about preparation and strategy. While the other chapters in this book are all about the preparation, this chapter focuses on the test strategy itself. The following are techniques on how you can be sure to avoid careless mistakes during your exam.

Reading the Questions

The CAPM has developed a reputation for having questions every bit as difficult as the PMP exam, so a critical step to passing is to read and understand each question. Questions on the exam may be long and have many twists and turns. They are often full of irrelevant information thrown in intentionally to distract you from the relevant facts. Those who pass the CAPM know to read the questions carefully. Many times the only relevant information is contained at the very the end. Consider the following example:

Q: Mark has a project where task A is dependent on the start and has a duration of 3. Task B is dependent on start and has a duration of 5. Task C is dependent on A and has a duration of 4. Task D is dependent on B and has a duration of 6, and the finish is dependent on tasks C and D. Mark is using his project network diagram to help create a schedule. The schedule for the project is usually created during which process?

    A. Cost Estimating.
    B. Cost Budgeting.
    C. Schedule Control.
    D. Schedule Development.

Questions like the one above are not uncommon on the CAPM Exam. If you froze up or took the time to try and diagram out the scenario, you would have wasted valuable time, when the question was only asking you to pick the process (the answer is 'D').

On lengthy questions, the best practice is to quickly skip down to the last sentence for a clue as to what the question is asking. Then read the entire question thoroughly. Most of them have a very short final sentence that will summarize the actual question. Make sure, however, to read the entire question at least once! Don't simply rely on the last sentence.

Just as important as carefully reading the questions is reading each of the four answers. You should never stop reading the answers as soon as you find one you like. Instead, always read all four answers before making your selection.

A Guessing Strategy

By simply reading the material in this book, you will immediately know how to answer many of the questions on the exam. For many others, you will have an instinctive guess. If you have studied the other chapters, you should trust that instinct. It is not there by chance. Your instinct was created by exposing yourself to this material in different ways. Your mind will begin to gravitate toward the right answer even if you are not explicitly aware of it.

Guessing on the CAPM does not have to be left purely to chance. If you do not know the answer immediately, begin by eliminating wrong answers, or ones you suspect are wrong. Let's take a fairly difficult question as an example:

Q: **Organizational Process Assets are used as an input to all of the following processes EXCEPT:**

      A. Activity Definition.
      B. Create Project Charter.
      C. Direct and Manage Project Execution.
      D. Quantitative Risk Analysis.

Unless you have memorized all of the inputs to all of the processes (the PMBOK Guide lists over 592 inputs, tools, and outputs), you are going to have to guess at this one. However, if you throw up your hands and pick one, you only have a 25% chance of getting it right. Instead, you should think about what is being asked. Organizational process assets are used as an input to processes all over the PMBOK Guide, so that doesn't offer help, but when you stop to consider that it is used primarily in planning processes, suddenly the picture becomes a little clearer. Now you can see that 'A' and 'B' are probably not the right answer. Both of these would be a good fit for historical information, which is an organizational process asset. Now you have a 50% chance of guessing between 'C' and 'D'. Look at them more carefully and ask yourself where would historical information most likely be used an input? Quantitative risk analysis is a good guess, since you might use past results (an organizational process asset) to help you analyze and quantify risk. So now, you are left with choice 'C', Direct and Manage Project Execution, as the one that looks least likely to have an organizational process asset as an input. It may be a guess, but it is a very educated one.

The method here is simply to think about each answer and eliminate ones that are obviously wrong. Even if you only knock off one wrong answer, you have significantly increased your odds of choosing the right one. You will find that most times you can knock off at least two, evening your chances of answering the question correctly.

Spotting Tricks and Traps

The CAPM does have trick questions. They are designed specifically to catch people who are coming in with little formal process experience, those who have thumbed through the PMBOK a few times and are now going to take the exam. These people try to rely on their work experience, which often does not line up with PMI's prescribed method for doing things. As a result, they typically don't even come close to passing the exam.

At times, however, these trick questions can also fool a seasoned pro! Listed below are some techniques you can use so that you will not fall into these traps.

Follow the Process

This is always the right answer. There will be questions on your exam that give you "common sense" scenarios that will give you a seemingly innocent way to skip the formal process and save time, or perhaps avoid some conflict by not following procedure. This is almost certainly a trap. The right answer is to follow PMI's process! Do not give in to pressure from irate customers, stakeholders, or even your boss to do otherwise.

Don't Take the Easy Way Out

There will often be choices that allow you to postpone a difficult decision, dodge a thorny issue, or ignore a problem. This is almost never the right thing to do for questions on the exam.

Act Directly and Say What You Mean

In PMI's world, project managers communicate directly. They do not dance around the issue, gossip, or imply things, and they do not communicate through a third party. If they have bad news to tell the customer, they go to the customer and tell them the facts – and the sooner, the better. If they have a problem with a team member, they confront the person, usually directly, although at times it may be appropriate to get the team member's functional manager involved.

Study the Roles

By the time you take the exam, you should be confident about the roles of stakeholders, sponsors, customers, team members, functional managers, the project office, and most importantly, the project manager (plus the other roles that are discussed in Chapter 2 – Foundational Terms and Concepts). Expect several "who should perform this activity" type questions. If you have absolutely no clue, guessing the "project manager" is a good idea.

Additionally, understand the difference between the different types of organizations (projectized, matrix, and functional). Most of your questions will pertain to matrix organizations, so focus your study on that one.

Project Manager's Role

Expanding on the previous point, project managers are the ones who make decisions and carry them out. They have the final decision on most points, can spend budget, can change schedules, and can approve or refuse scope. For the test, assume that the project manager is large and in charge!

Another attribute of project managers is that they are proactive in their approach to managing tasks and information. They do not wait for changes to occur. Instead, they are actively influencing the factors that contribute to change. Instead of waiting for information to come to them, they are actively communicating and making certain they have accurate and up-to-date information.

Don't Get Stuck

You should expect to find a few questions on the exam that you do not know how to answer. You will look at it and see 4 correct answers, making it impossible to pick just 1. In this case, do not agonize. Even using every good technique, you will still have to make an educated guess at some questions. Some test takers can get quite upset at this, and it can undermine their confidence. If a question stumps you, simply mark it for review and move on. Never spend 15 minutes staring at a single question unless you have already answered all the others. One question is only worth one a fraction of a percent on the exam, so if you do not know the answer, do not obsess over it.

You may even discover that a block of questions seem especially difficult to you. This experience can be discouraging and may cause your confidence to waver. Don't be alarmed if you happen upon several difficult questions in a row. Keep marking them for review and keep moving, until you come to more familiar ground. You may find that questions later in the test will offer you hints or jog your memory, helping you with those you initially found difficult.

Exam Time Management

You will have a few minutes at the beginning to go through a tutorial. You probably won't find much value in the actual tutorial; however, you absolutely should take it. After going through it, you will be given a chance to wait before taking the test. Use that time to write down essential formulas and processes on your scratch paper.

Scratch Paper

You will be given five sheets of blank paper when you walk into the exam. You may not carry your own paper into the test. When you sit down to begin the exam, you should write down a few key things. Regardless of how well you know this material, at a minimum, write the following on your first sheet of scratch paper.

1. Earned Value formulas (EV, PV, AC, CPI, CPI^C, SPI, CV, SV, BAC, EAC, ETC) from Chapter 7. You will probably need to refer to these several times during the exam, and it will save time and improve your accuracy if you have written them out.
2. The time management formulas for the three point estimates and standard deviation.
3. The communication channels formulas described in Chapter 10.

Even if you are tempted to skip this step, don't! When you come to a lengthy and confusing question that requires you to calculate several different values, you will be glad that you already have your formulas written down for review. This will free your mind to concentrate on the specific question rather than on recalling a formula.

Budgeting Your Time

Going into the exam, you may be fast or you may be a slower test taker. Everyone should walk into the exam with a strategy for managing their time, based on their own pace. Do not underestimate how hard it is to sit for a 150 question, 3 hour exam. The test-taking process is strenuous and mentally and physically taxing.

If you have a test time management strategy that has served you well in the past, you should use that. If not, here is a generic strategy that many people have used "as is" to take and pass the CAPM.

1. Sit for the tutorial and download your information to your scratch paper.
2. When the exam begins, take the first 75 questions, pacing yourself to take approximately 45 minutes.
3. Take your first break. Spend 5 minutes stretching and get a bite of food from your locker.
4. Take the next 75 questions, again pacing yourself to take 45 to 50 minutes.
5. Take your 2nd break. Spend approximately 10 minutes, go to the bathroom, and get a snack.
6. At this point, you should be at about two hours into the test or less.
7. Perform a review of the first 75 questions. Pace yourself to finish this in about 25 minutes.
8. Take a short 5 minute stretch break if needed.
9. Review last 75 questions and any other ones in your remaining time.

Managing Your Review

When you make a review pass through the exam, you will come across questions that you missed the first time but that are apparent when you look at them again. This is normal, and you should not hesitate to change any answers that you can see you missed. Many people change as many as 10% of the answers on their review. If you catch yourself changing more than that, be careful! You may be second guessing yourself and actually do more harm than good.

When you go through your review pass on the exam, do not take the whole test over again. Instead, employ three rapid fire steps:

1. Did you read the question correctly the first time?
2. Did your selected answer match what was being asked?
3. Perform a complete check of your math where applicable.

Managing Anxiety

Finally, if test-taking has always been a fear-inducing activity for you, there is one simple strategy that may help you manage the physical symptoms of anxiety so that your thinking and memory are not impaired: Take a deep breath. This may sound like obvious advice, but it is based on sound research. Studies in the field of stress management have shown that feelings of anxiety (the "fight or flight" response") are linked with elevated levels of adrenaline and certain brain chemicals. One way to help bring your brain chemistry back into balance is to draw a deep breath, hold it for about six seconds, and slowly release it. Repeat this breathing pattern whenever you begin to feel panicky over particular questions. It will help to slow your heart rate and clear your mind for greater concentration on the task at hand.

Another thing to remember is that many people who take the exam do not pass – especially on their first attempt. While no one wants to fail the test, you can turn around immediately and apply to take it again (at a reduced rate). You can take the exam up to three times in a year starting with the time you receive your letter of eligibility from PMI.

If you do have to take the exam again, use it as a learning experience. You will have a much higher chance for success on your next attempt, and you will have your score sheet that gives you a breakdown of where you need to study. As the inspired Jerome Kern once penned to music, "Take a deep breath; pick yourself up; dust yourself off; start all over again."

Final Exam

Difficulty	Memorization	Exam Importance	Corresponding PMBOK Chapter
Low	Low	High	Not covered in PMBOK

Instructions

This simulated CAPM Exam may be used in several ways. If you take it as a final, you will get a very good idea how you would do if you walked right in to take the CAPM Exam. In that way, it can be a very good readiness indicator.

Perhaps the best way to use this exam is to take it again and again, reviewing the answers that go with each question. The answers and explanations will give you insight into the formation of each question and the thought process you should follow to answer it.

Prior to taking the CAPM, the best strategy is to take this exam repeatedly, reviewing the answers, until you can make a score of 90% or better.

If you are taking this as a final exam, you have 3 hours (180 minutes) to complete the following 150 questions, including any breaks you may take.

Each question has only one best answer. Mark the one best answer on your answer sheet by filling in the circle next to A, B, C, or D.

On the actual CAPM Exam, only 135 of the 150 questions will be graded, but you do not know which questions count and which do not. A passing score is on the CAPM Exam is 88 out of 135, which is 65%. For this practice final, you need to correctly answer at least 98 out of the 150 possible questions in order to pass.

1. During testing, multiple defects were identified in a product. The project manager overseeing this product's development can best use which tool to help prioritize the problems?

    A. Pareto diagram.
    B. Control chart.
    C. Variance analysis.
    D. Order of magnitude estimate.

2. You are the manager of an aircraft design project. A significant portion of this aircraft will be designed by a subcontracting firm. How will this affect your communications management plan?

    A. More formal verbal communication will be required.
    B. Performance reports will be more detailed.
    C. More formal written communication will be required.
    D. Official communication channels will significantly increase.

3. What officially creates the project?

    A. The project initiation document.
    B. The kickoff meeting.
    C. The project charter.
    D. The statement of work.

4. The Delphi technique is a way to:

    A. Analyze performance.
    B. Gather expert opinion.
    C. Resolve conflict.
    D. Estimate durations.

5. The work authorization system makes sure that:

    A. All the work and only the work gets performed.
    B. Work gets performed in right order and at the right time.
    C. Work is done completely and correctly.
    D. Functional managers are allowed complete control over who is assigned and when.

6. Your team is hard at work on their assigned project tasks when one team member discovers a risk that was not identified during risk planning. What is the FIRST thing to do?

   A. Halt work on the project.
   B. Update the risk management plan.
   C. Look for ways to mitigate the risk.
   D. Assess the risk.

7. The activity duration estimates should be developed by:

   A. The person or team doing the work.
   B. The project manager.
   C. Senior management.
   D. The customer.

8. The project plan should be all of the following EXCEPT:

   A. A formal document.
   B. Distributed to stakeholders in accordance with the communications management plan.
   C. Approved by all project stakeholders.
   D. Used to manage project execution.

9. You have been asked to take charge of project planning for a new project, but you have very little experience in managing projects. What will be the best source of help for you?

   A. Your education.
   B. Your on-the-job training.
   C. Historical information.
   D. Your functional manager.

10. The majority of the project budget is expended on:

    A. Project plan development.
    B. Project plan execution.
    C. Integrated change control.
    D. Project communication.

11.   Corrective action is:

A.   Fixing past anomalies.
B.   Anything done to bring the project's future performance in line
        with the project management plan.
C.   The responsibility of the change control board.
D.   An output of project plan execution.

12.   Outputs of Direct and Manage Project Execution include:

A.   Deliverables and performance reports.
B.   Deliverables and corrective action.
C.   Deliverables and work performance information.
D.   Performance reports and requested changes.

13.   Your original plan was to construct a building with six stories, with
        each story costing $150,000. This was to be completed in four months;
        however, the project has not gone as planned. Two months into the
        project, earned value is $400,000. What is the budgeted at completion?

A.   450,000
B.   600,000
C.   800,000
D.   900,000

14.   Project integration is primarily the responsibility of:

A. The project team.
B. The project manager.
C. Senior management.
D. The project sponsor.

15.   One of your team members has discovered a way to add an extra
        deliverable to the project that will have minimal impact on the project
        schedule and cost. The project cost performance index is 1.3 and the
        schedule performance index is 1.5. The functionality was not included
        in the scope. How should you proceed?

A.   Conform to the project scope and do not add the deliverable.
B.   Deliver the extra work to the customer since it will not increase
        their costs.
C.   Reject the deliverable because you are behind schedule.
D.   Ask senior management for a decision.

16. If a project manager is unsure who has the authority to approve changes in project scope, she should consult:

    A. The customer.
    B. The scope statement.
    C. The sponsor.
    D. The scope management plan.

17. An end user has just requested a minor change to the project that will not impact the project schedule. How should you, the project manager, respond?

    A. Authorize the change quickly to ensure that the schedule can truly remain unaffected.
    B. Deny the change to help prevent scope creep.
    C. Evaluate the impact of the change on the other project constraints.
    D. Submit the change request to the customer for approval.

18. Which of the following tools is NOT used in initiating a project?

    A. Project selection methods.
    B. Project management methodology
    C. Expert judgment.
    D. Earned value analysis.

19. In which group of processes should the project manager be assigned his or her role in the project?

    A. Initiating.
    B. Planning.
    C. Executing.
    D. Controlling.

20. A project charter should always include:

    A. Historical information.
    B. The business need underlying the project.
    C. A detailed budget.
    D. The scope management plan.

21. Your project team has just received the sponsor's approval for the scope statement. What is the NEXT step that needs to be taken?

    A. Develop the product description.
    B. Create a work breakdown structure.
    C. Hold the kickoff meeting.
    D. Create the network diagram.

22. Which of the following is NOT an input into Scope Definition?

    A. Accepted deliverables.
    B. Organizational process assets.
    C. Project charter.
    D. Preliminary project scope statement.

23. The key function of the project manager's job in project integration is:

    A. Minimizing conflict to promote team unity.
    B. Making key decisions about resource allocation.
    C. Communicating with people of various backgrounds.
    D. Problem-solving and decision-making between project subsystems.

24. In which of the following documents could the sponsor find work package descriptions?

    A. The work breakdown structure dictionary.
    B. The project charter.
    C. The scope management plan.
    D. The project scope statement.

25. The process in which project deliverables are reviewed and accepted is called:

    A. Scope planning.
    B. Scope verification.
    C. Initiation.
    D. Scope change control.

26.   A statement of work is:

    A.   A type of contract.

    B.   A description of the project's product.

    C.   Necessary for every project.

    D.   A description of the part of a product to be obtained from an outside vendor.

27.   A commercial real-estate developer is planning to build a new office complex. He contracts with a construction firm to build one of the buildings for the actual cost of providing the materials and services plus a fixed fee for profit. What type of contract does this scenario represent?

    A.   Independent vendor.

    B.   Fixed price.

    C.   Cost-reimbursable.

    D.   Time and materials.

28.   Which of the following is NOT a purpose that Create WBS serves?

    A.   To increase the accuracy of estimates.

    B.   To help facilitate roles and responsibilities.

    C.   To document the relationship between the product and the business need.

    D.   To define a baseline for project performance.

29.   You are assigned to replace a project manager on a large software project for a telecommunications company in the middle of executing the work. Portions of the software are being supplied by subcontractors working at your company's offices. You would like to know what performance metrics are going to be tracked for these contract workers. Where could you find such information?

    A.   The project charter.

    B.   The procurement management plan.

    C.   The work breakdown structure.

    D.   The organizational chart.

30.   Which of the following is NOT a type of contract?

    A.   Cost-revisable.
    B.   Fixed-price.
    C.   Cost-reimbursable.
    D.   Time and materials.

31.   Your team has identified a component that they need for a project. There is some concern that they have never constructed a component like this one, but there are similar components available from sellers. Which of the following procurement activities would be MOST appropriate to perform?

    A.   Solicitation.
    B.   Make-or-buy analysis.
    C.   Benefit/cost analysis.
    D.   Source selection.

32.   The activity list serves as an input to:

    A.   Create WBS.
    B.   Activity Definition.
    C.   Activity Duration Estimating.
    D.   Resource Planning.

33.   The person or group that formally accepts the project's product is:

    A.   The quality team.
    B.   The customer.
    C.   The project team.
    D.   Senior management.

34.   The schedule activity list:

    A.   Serves as an extension of the work breakdown structure.
    B.   Is synonymous with the work breakdown structure.
    C.   Is used to create the project scope statement.
    D.   Is included in the project charter.

35. Float refers to:

    A. A method for decreasing risk on a project.
    B. How long an activity can be delayed without affecting the critical path.
    C. A time lapse between a project communication and the response that follows.
    D. The difference between the budgeted cost and actual cost.

36. If a project scope requires goods or services that must be obtained outside the project organization, what management process will be used in obtaining them?

    A. Project contract management.
    B. Project solicitation management.
    C. Project procurement management.
    D. Project source management.

37. What is the most important function the project manager serves?

    A. Staffing.
    B. Motivating.
    C. Team building.
    D. Communicating.

38. All of the following are needed for creating the project budget except:

    A. Activity cost estimates.
    B. Work breakdown structure.
    C. Cost management plan.
    D. Deliverables.

39. Your company's CIO has requested a meeting with you and two other project managers for a status update on your various projects. What is the BEST document you can bring with you to this meeting:

    A. The milestone chart for this project.
    B. The network diagram for this project.
    C. Copies of the most recent status reports from the team members.
    D. The project charter.

40. Resources are estimated against which project entity:

    A. The work packages.
    B. The schedule activities.
    C. The elements of scope.
    D. The level set by the project office.

41. Analogous estimating uses:

    A. Estimates of individual activities rolled up into a project total.
    B. Actual costs from a previous project as a basis for estimates.
    C. Computerized estimating tools.
    D. Parametric modeling techniques.

42. What does the standard deviation tell about a data set?

    A. How diverse the population is.
    B. The mean of the population as it relates to the median.
    C. The specification limits of the population.
    D. The range of data points within the population.

43. Quality management theory is characterized by which of the following statements:

    A. Inspection is the most important element for ensuring quality.
    B. Planning for quality must be emphasized.
    C. Contingency planning is a critical element of quality assurance.
    D. Quality planning quantifies efforts to exceed customer expectations.

44. Which of the following is NOT emphasized in project quality management?

    A. Customer satisfaction.
    B. Team responsibility.
    C. Phases within processes.
    D. Prevention over inspection.

45. Scatter diagrams, flowcharts, run diagrams, control charts, and inspection are all techniques of what quality process?

    A. Quality Planning.
    B. Perform Quality Control.
    C. Perform Quality Execution.
    D. Perform Quality Definition.

46. Which of the following is NOT an input to quality planning?

    A. Enterprise environmental factors.
    B. Organizational process assets.
    C. Quality baseline.
    D. Project management plan.

47. The procurement management plan provides:

    A. Templates for contracts to be used.
    B. A formal description of how risks will be balanced within contracts.
    C. A description of procurement options.
    D. The types of contracts to be used for items being procured.

48. Ultimately, responsibility for quality management lies with the:

    A. Project team.
    B. Quality team.
    C. Project manager.
    D. Functional manager.

49. All of the following are tools used in Perform Quality Control EXCEPT:

    A. Benchmarking.
    B. Pareto charts.
    C. Histograms.
    D. Statistical sampling.

50. Control charts are:

    A. Used in product review.
    B. Used to chart a project's expected value.
    C. Used to determine if a process is in control.
    D. Used to define a statistical sample.

51. Which of the following statements regarding stakeholders is TRUE?

    A. They have some measurable financial interest in the project.
    B. Their needs should be either qualified or quantified.
    C. Key stakeholders participate in the creation of the stakeholder management plan.
    D. They may either be positively or negatively affected by the outcome of the project.

52.   A probability and impact matrix is useful for:

    A.   Risk Identification.
    B.   Qualitative Risk Analysis.
    C.   Risk Response Planning.
    D.   Risk Monitoring and Control.

53.   A risk register is created during:

    A.   Risk Management Planning.
    B.   Risk Monitoring and Control.
    C.   Risk Assessment.
    D.   Risk Identification.

54.   A workaround is:

    A.   A technique for conflict management.
    B.   An adjustment to the project budget.
    C.   A response to an unplanned risk event.
    D.   A non-critical path on the network diagram.

55.   You are managing a team developing a software product. You have contracted out a portion of the development. Midway through the project you learn that the contracting company is entering Chapter 11. A manager from the subcontracting company assures you that the state of the company will not affect your project. What should you do FIRST?

    A.   Perform additional risk response planning to control the risk this situation poses.
    B.   Stop all pending and future payments to the subcontractor until the threat is fully assessed.
    C.   Contact your legal department to research your options.
    D.   Meet with senior management to apprise them of the situation.

56.   In a functional organization:

    A.   Power primarily lies with the project manager.
    B.   Power primarily lies with the functional manager.
    C.   Power is blended between functional and project managers.
    D.   Power primarily lies with the project office.

57. The process of identifying, documenting, and assigning roles, responsibilities, and reporting relationships for a project is called:

    A.   Project Interfacing.
    B.   Organizational Breakdown.
    C.   Staff Management Planning.
    D.   Human Resource Planning.

58. A Responsibility Assignment Matrix (RAM) does NOT indicate:

    A.   Who does what on the project.
    B.   Job roles for team members.
    C.   Job roles and responsibilities for groups.
    D.   Project reporting relationships.

59. Which of the following is NOT a constructive team role?

    A.   Withdrawer.
    B.   Information seeker.
    C.   Clarifier.
    D.   Gate keeper.

60. If a project team is experiencing conflict over a technical decision that is negatively affecting project performance, the BEST source of power the project manager could exert to bring about cooperation would be:

    A.   Legitimate.
    B.   Penalty.
    C.   Referent.
    D.   Expert.

61. Which of the following types of conflict resolution provides only a temporary solution to the problem?

    A.   Withdrawal.
    B.   Compromising.
    C.   Forcing.
    D.   Problem-solving.

62. The communications management plan:

    A.   Should include the performance reports.
    B.   Should always be highly detailed.
    C.   Should include the project's major milestones.
    D.   Should detail what methods should be used to gather and store information.

63. When communication links are undefined or broken:

    A.   The communications management plan should be rewritten.
    B.   Conflict will increase.
    C.   The project manager's power will decrease.
    D.   Project work will stop.

64. A project manager is having difficulty getting resources from a functional manager. Which of the following would be the MOST appropriate to help resolve this problem?

    A.   Senior management.
    B.   The customer.
    C.   Key stakeholders.
    D.   The sponsor.

65. Communicating via email is considered:

    A.   Formal written communication.
    B.   Informal written communication.
    C.   Formal electronic communication.
    D.   Informal non-verbal communication.

66. You have a team member who is habitually late to meetings with the customer. The customer has expressed dissatisfaction with the situation and has asked you to resolve it. Your BEST course of action is:

    A.   Issue a formal written reprimand to the team member
    B.   Meet with the team member to discuss the problem and ask for solutions.
    C.   Meet with the team member and the customer to promote further understanding.
    D.   Email the team member to bring the situation to his attention.

67. You are midway through managing a project with a sponsor-approved budget of $850,000. Using earned value management, you have determined that the project will run $125,000 under budget. You have also determined that if the project is delivered that far under budget you will not make your bonus since you are compensated for the hours you bill. What is your BEST course of action?

    A. Add extra features to the project scope that take advantage of the available budget, and increase customer satisfaction.
    B. Meet with the project sponsor to inform him of your findings.
    C. Maintain current project activities, and bill for the original amount.
    D. Ask the sponsor to approve additional features, given the available budget.

68. The most important factor in project integration is:

    A. A clearly defined scope.
    B. Timely corrective action.
    C. Team buy-in on the project plan.
    D. Effective communication.

69. You are a project manager for a software development firm. You are in the final stages of negotiation with a third party vendor whose product your company is considering implementing. You discover by chance that one of your employees has scheduled a product demonstration with herself, the vendor, and your boss, but you have not been notified about the meeting. What do you do?

    A. Show up at the meeting unannounced and discuss the situation with the employee later in private.
    B. Report this employee's actions to your boss using the company's formal reporting procedure.
    C. Discuss the employee's actions with her before the meeting.
    D. Report the employee's actions to her functional manager.

70.   Your team has encountered recent unanticipated problems. After extensive earned value analysis you determine that the project has a schedule performance index of .54 and a cost performance index of 1.3. Additionally your customer has just requested a significant change. What should you do?

        A.   Alert management about the schedule delays.
        B.   Alert management about the cost overruns.
        C.   Alert management about the scope change.
        D.   Reject the requested change.

71.   You are in the middle of bidding on a large and complex project that will produce a great deal of revenue for your company should you win the bid. The buyer has specified several conditions that accelerate some of the key dates and milestones. You have done extensive planning with your team and have determined that there is no way that your organization can perform the required scope of work under these new deadlines. Your boss, however, is not convinced that you are right and is also concerned that if you don't agree to the new dates you will lose the contract. What should you do?

        A.   Appeal to the buyer for additional time to estimate.
        B.   Ask your boss to make the commitment on behalf of the team.
        C.   Adhere to the estimates your team has made.
        D.   Agree to the dates the customer has requested.

72.   Analogous estimating is also called:

        A.   Vendor bid analysis.
        B.   Bottom-up estimating.
        C.   Scalable model estimating.
        D.   Top-down estimating.

73. You are beginning construction of a bridge in another country when you discover that this country requires that one of its licensed engineers sign off on the plans before you break ground. Your senior engineer on the project is licensed in your own country and is probably more qualified than anyone to sign off on this, and their engineer is not available to review the plans for another three weeks. The customer has stressed that this project must not be delayed. What do you do?

    A. Have your engineer sign off on the plans, forward them to the other engineer and begin construction.
    B. Have your engineer sign off on the plans since he is licensed in your country and begin construction.
    C. Wait to begin construction until the country's engineer signs off on the plans.
    D. Forward the plans to the country's engineer for his signature and start construction.

74. Decomposition is a technique used in:

    A. Activity Definition
    B. Activity Duration Estimating
    C. Activity Sequencing
    D. Schedule Development

75. A fixed-price contract offers the seller:

    A. A higher risk than the buyer.
    B. A risk level equal to that of the buyer.
    C. A lower risk than the buyer.
    D. Reimbursement of actual costs.

76. The individual on a project with limited authority who handles some communication and ensures that tasks are completed on time is:

    A. The project manager.
    B. The project leader.
    C. The project coordinator.
    D. The sponsor.

77. At what point in project planning would you decide to change the project scope in order to avoid certain high-risk activities?

    A.   Risk Identification.
    B.   Risk Qualification.
    C.   Risk Monitoring.
    D.   Risk Response Planning.

78. Which of the following techniques is used in Scope Planning?

    A.   Project selection methods.
    B.   WBS templates.
    C.   Expert judgment.
    D.   Inspection.

79. Which of the following statements is NOT TRUE of integration management?

    A.   Integration is primarily concerned with making sure various elements of the project are coordinated.
    B.   Integration is a discrete process.
    C.   The project management information system is used to support all aspects of the project.
    D.   The project manager must make tradeoffs between competing project objectives.

80. A project is all of the following EXCEPT:

    A.   Progressively elaborated.
    B.   Has never been done by this company before.
    C.   Interrelated activities.
    D.   Strategic to the company.

81. Your manager has asked to review the quality management plan with you to ensure that it is being followed appropriately. In which process is your boss involved?

    A.   Perform Quality Control.
    B.   Perform Quality Management.
    C.   Quality Planning.
    D.   Perform Quality Assurance.

82. Variance analysis is a tool used to:

    A. Measure variance between actual work and the baseline.
    B. Measure variance between planned value and schedule variance.
    C. Measure variance between earned value and actual cost.
    D. Measure variance between earned value and cost variance.

83. In a strong matrix organization:

    A. More power is given to the functional manager.
    B. More power is given to the project manager.
    C. More power is given to the project expeditor.
    D. More power is given to the project coordinator.

84. Team performance assessments are made during which process?

    A. Human Resource Planning.
    B. Acquire Project Team.
    C. Develop Project Team.
    D. Manage Project Team.

85. The Project Scope Statement is typically:

    A. A definitive list of all the work and only the work to be done on the project.
    B. Issued by senior management.
    C. Progressively elaborated.
    D. Defined before the functional specifications.

86. During Direct and Manage Project Team, your project team should be:

    A. Focused on making sure earned value is equal to planned value.
    B. Communicating work results to the stakeholders.
    C. Ensuring that all project changes are reflected in the project plan.
    D. Executing the work packages.

87. The system that supports all aspects of the project management processes from initiating through closing is:

    A. Information technology.
    B. The information distribution system.
    C. The project management information system.
    D. The work authorization system.

88.   In a typical project, most of the resources are utilized and expended during:

    A.   Initiation processes.
    B.   Planning processes.
    C.   Executing processes.
    D.   Monitoring and controlling processes.

89.   A project manager is taking the product of his project to his customer for verification that it meets the scope. The customer and the project manager are working together to carefully compare the product to the project's scope to ensure that the work was done to specification. The tool that the customer and the project manager are using is:

    A.   Inspection.
    B.   Perform Quality Assurance.
    C.   Perform Quality Control.
    D.   User acceptance testing.

90.   Which of the following is NOT a project quality management process?

    A.   Perform Quality Assurance.
    B.   Quality Planning.
    C.   Quality Improvement.
    D.   Perform Quality Control.

91.   Schedule constraints would likely include all of the following EXCEPT:

    A.   Imposed dates.
    B.   Key events.
    C.   Major milestones.
    D.   Leads and lags.

92.   Which of the following choices fits the definition for benchmarking?

    A.   Comparing planned results to actual results.
    B.   Comparing actual or planned results to those of other projects.
    C.   Statistical sampling of results and comparing them to the plan.
    D.   Comparing planned value with earned value.

93. The activity list should include:

    A.   The schedule activities on the project that are on the critical path.
    B.   A subset of all schedule activities.
    C.   All of the schedule activities defined on the project.
    D.   A superset of the schedule activities for this and related projects.

94. Close Project should be performed:

    A.   At the end of each phase or the end of the project.
    B.   Before formal acceptance of the project's product.
    C.   As a safeguard against risk.
    D.   By someone other than the project manager.

95. Release criteria for team members is defined as part of:

    A.   The organizational management plan.
    B.   The human resources management plan.
    C.   The staffing management plan.
    D.   The work authorization system.

96. Which of the following is NOT an input into Activity Definition?

    A.   The work breakdown structure.
    B.   Organizational process assets.
    C.   Project scope statement.
    D.   The activity list.

97. A project to lay 10 miles of a petroleum pipeline was scheduled to be completed today, exactly 20 weeks from the start of the project. You receive a report that the project has an overall schedule performance index of 0.8. Based on this information, when would you expect the project to be completed?

    A.   2 weeks early.
    B.   In 2 more weeks.
    C.   In 5 more weeks.
    D.   In 10 more weeks.

98. The term "slack" is also known as:

    A. Lag.
    B. Lead.
    C. Float.
    D. Free float.

99. Which of the following BEST describes the project plan?

    A. A formal, approved document used to guide project execution, control, and closure.
    B. The aggregate of all work performed during planning.
    C. The work breakdown structure, schedule management plan, budget, cost management plan, and quality management plan.
    D. The document that outlines all of the work and only the work that must be performed on a project.

100. Which of the following is NOT a primary goal of integrated change control?

    A. Influencing factors that cause change.
    B. Determining that a change has occurred.
    C. Managing change as it occurs.
    D. Denying change whenever possible.

101. "The features and attributes that characterize a product" describes which of the following?

    A. The product scope.
    B. The project scope.
    C. The work breakdown structure.
    D. The critical success factors.

102. You have assumed responsibility for a project that has completed planning and is executing the work packages of the project. In one of your first status meetings, a member of the project team begins to question the validity of the duration estimates for a series of related tasks assigned to her. What action should you take FIRST?

    A. Remind the team member that planning has been completed and ask her to do her best to adhere to the estimates.
    B. Temporarily suspend execution and ask the team member for updated estimates.
    C. Review the supporting detail for the estimates contained in the project plan to understand how the estimates were originally derived.
    D. Ask another team member with expertise in this area to perform a peer review on the estimates to validate or invalidate the concern.

103. Approved budget increases should be:

    A. Added to the schedule management plan.
    B. Added to the project's cost baseline.
    C. Added to the project's reserve fund and used only if needed.
    D. Added to the lessons learned.

104. An organization where the project manager is in charge of the projects and has primary responsibility for the resources is:

    A. Functional.
    B. Projectized.
    C. Matrix.
    D. Hierarchical.

105. Leads and lags are evaluated and adjusted in which process?

    A. Performance Reporting.
    B. Cost Estimating.
    C. Schedule Control.
    D. Schedule Development.

106.   You have received a report showing that your overall schedule performance index is 1.5. How should you interpret this information?

    A.   You are earning value into your project at 1.5 times the rate you had planned.
    B.   You are spending $1.50 for every dollar you planned to spend at this point in the schedule.
    C.   You are earning $1.50 of value back into your project for every $1.00 you spend.
    D.   You are earning $0.67 of value back into your project for every $1.00 you planned to earn.

107.   The project organization chart should include which of the following:

    A.   The performing organization's organizational structure.
    B.   A representation of all identified stakeholders.
    C.   The reporting structure for the project.
    D.   The organizational structure for all entities related to the project.

108.   Cost estimating should be performed:

    A.   Before the work breakdown structure is created and before the budget is developed.
    B.   Before the work breakdown structure is created and after the budget is developed.
    C.   After the work breakdown structure is created and before the budget is developed.
    D.   After the work breakdown structure is created and after the budget is developed.

109.   A list of the risks that could affect the project is developed as part of which process?

    A.   Risk Management Planning.
    B.   Risk Identification.
    C.   Risk Response Planning.
    D.   Risk Monitoring and Control.

110. Which process focuses on producing a list of the activities needed to produce the deliverables and sub-deliverables described in the work breakdown structure?

    A. Activity Definition.
    B. Activity Sequencing.
    C. Activity List.
    D. Activity Duration Estimating.

111. Whose job is it to resolve competing objectives and goals between parties on the project?

    A. The stakeholders.
    B. The project manager.
    C. Senior management.
    D. The sponsor.

112. As project manager, you have made the decision to outsource a part of your project to an outside organization with whom you have never previously worked. You are ready to begin negotiating the contract. What should be your goal in the contract negotiations?

    A. Having a lawyer or the legal department review each clause in the proposed contract prior to sharing it with any outside entity.
    B. Negotiating the best possible price for your customer or organization.
    C. Arriving at mutually agreeable terms for the contract between your organization and the subcontracting organization.
    D. Shifting as much of the project risk to the subcontracting organization as possible.

113. Which of the following is NOT an output of Cost Control?

    A. Recommended corrective action.
    B. Forecasted completion.
    C. Required changes.
    D. Project budget.

114. If the schedule variance = $0.00, what must also be true?

    A. Earned value must be equal to planned value.
    B. The cost performance index must be equal to 1.
    C. The schedule performance index must be greater than 1.
    D. The estimate at complete must be equal to budgeted at complete.

115. Schedule activities are a further decomposition of which of the following:

    A.   The statement of scope.
    B.   The work packages.
    C.   The project network diagram.
    D.   The functional specification.

116. Which statement is TRUE regarding the staffing management plan?

    A.   It is used as an input into Human Resource Planning.
    B.   It is a component of the project plan.
    C.   It should name every human and material resource who will be working on the project.
    D.   It should contain an organization chart for the performing organization.

117. Which of the following statements is TRUE regarding risk management?

    A.   Negative risks should be quantified, while positive risks should be qualified.
    B.   Identified risks should be added to the risk register.
    C.   All known risks should be listed in the risk management plan.
    D.   The risks that cannot be mitigated must be avoided.

118. You have a friend in another organization who has shared with you that he is having difficulty understanding the value of doing a scope statement. Your friend's boss is not familiar with formal project management processes and does not want to waste time on the project performing unnecessary activities. What is your MOST appropriate response?

    A.   Do not get involved since this is not within your organization.
    B.   Pay a visit to your friend's project office and educate them on the value of a scope statement.
    C.   Mentor your friend on the value of project management processes.
    D.   Encourage your friend to change organizations.

119. You are managing a project to construct 25 miles of highway at an estimated cost of $1.2 million per mile. You have projected that you should be able to complete the project in 5 weeks. What is your planned value for the end of the 3rd week of the project?

    A. $12,000,000
    B. $18,000,000
    C. $24,000,000
    D. $30,000,000

120. Which term below describes the amount of time a schedule activity may be delayed before it affects the early start date of any subsequent schedule activity?

    A. Float.
    B. Slack.
    C. Free float.
    D. Lead.

121. When are the resource requirements estimated?

    A. As soon as the scope has been adequately defined.
    B. After the schedule has been defined, but before the budget has been created.
    C. After the work packages have been defined, but before the activities have been defined.
    D. After the activities have been defined and before the schedule has been developed.

122. You have an unfavorable project status to report to your customer at a weekly meeting; however, you are reasonably certain that you can correct the situation by next week's meeting. The customer will not be pleased to hear the current status and based on past history, will likely overreact. How should you handle this situation?

    A. Report the current status to the customer.
    B. Report your anticipated project status for next week to the customer.
    C. Omit the information from your meeting and cover it next week when the news improves.
    D. Ask you project office for guidance.

123. What type of process is Select Sellers?

    A.   Planning.
    B.   Executing.
    C.   Monitoring and controlling.
    D.   Closing.

124. Who is responsible for providing funding for the project?

    A.   The qualified financial institution.
    B.   Senior management.
    C.   The sponsor.
    D.   The project manager.

125. The project has been successfully completed when:

    A.   All of the work has been completed to specification within time
          and budget.
    B.   The customer is happy.
    C.   The sponsor signs off on the project.
    D.   Earned value equals planned value.

126. What is the PRIMARY objective of the project manager?

    A.   To follow PMI's processes.
    B.   To deliver maximum value for the organization.
    C.   To deliver the agreed upon scope of the project within the time
          and budget.
    D.   To delight the customer.

127. Which of the following would NOT be an organizational process asset?

    A.   Project plan templates.
    B.   Methodology guides.
    C.   Previous activity lists from projects.
    D.   Strong communication skills.

128. Defective deliverables are repaired as part of which process?

    A.   Direct and Manage Project Execution.
    B.   Perform Quality Assurance.
    C.   Monitor and Control Project Work.
    D.   Integrated Change Control.

129. What is indicated by an activity's late finish date?

    A. The latest the activity can finish without delaying a subsequent activity.
    B. The latest the activity can finish without delaying the project.
    C. The latest probable date that the activity will finish.
    D. The worst-case or pessimistic estimate for an activity.

130. Which of the following is FALSE regarding the contract change control system?

    A. It is primarily used during the Contract Administration process.
    B. It is part of the integrated change control system.
    C. It should be defined in the contract.
    D. It should include contract dispute resolution procedures.

131. If there are multiple critical paths on the project, which of the following must also be true?

    A. Only one path will ultimately emerge as the true critical path.
    B. The schedule risk will be higher with multiple critical paths than with one.
    C. The schedule should be crashed in order to resolve the conflict.
    D. The schedule should be fast-tracked in order to resolve the conflict.

132. Which projected payback period below is the MOST desirable?

    A. 24 months.
    B. 52 weeks.
    C. 3 years.
    D. 1000 days.

133. Which of the following would be an output of Activity Sequencing?

    A. Mandatory dependencies.
    B. An activity on arrow diagram.
    C. Discretionary dependencies.
    D. External dependencies.

134. While executing the project plan, you discover that a component was missed during planning. The project schedule is not in danger, but the component is not absolutely critical for go-live. What should you do?

    A. Treat the component as a new project.
    B. Reject the component as it would introduce unacceptable risk.
    C. Appeal to the project sponsor for guidance.
    D. Return to planning processes for the new component.

135. The goal of duration compression is to:

    A. Reduce time by reducing risk on the project.
    B. Reduce cost on the project.
    C. Reduce the scope by eliminating non-critical functionality from the project.
    D. Reduce the schedule without changing the scope.

136. You are managing two projects for two different customers. While meeting with one customer, you discover a sensitive piece of information that could help your other customer, saving them a significant percentage of their project budget. What should you do?

    A. Act in accordance with any legal documents you have signed.
    B. Disclose your conflict of interest and keep the information confidential.
    C. Share the information with the other customer if it increases project value.
    D. Excuse yourself from both projects if possible.

137. What is the difference between a standard and a regulation?

    A. A standard is issued by ANSI, and a regulation is issued by the government.
    B. A standard is an input into quality planning, while a regulation is an input into initiation.
    C. A standard usually should be followed, and a regulation must be followed.
    D. There is no appreciable difference between a standard and a regulation.

138. Evaluation criteria are used to:

    A. Select a qualified seller.
    B. Measure conformance to quality.
    C. Determine if a project should be undertaken.
    D. Evaluate performance on the project.

139. Richard is a project manager who is looking at the risks on his project and developing options to enhance the opportunities and reduce the threats to the project's objectives. Which process is Richard performing?

    A. Risk Management Planning.
    B. Risk Identification.
    C. Qualitative Risk Analysis.
    D. Risk Response Planning.

140. If you are soliciting bids for a project, which of the following would be an appropriate output from this process?

    A. Proposals from potential sellers.
    B. Change requests.
    C. Contracts.
    D. Qualified seller lists.

141. The work results of the project:

    A. Are always products.
    B. Are products, services, or results.
    C. Are only considered work results if quality standards have been met.
    D. Are an output of the work authorization system.

142. The quality policy is important in quality management because:

    A. It defines the performing organization's formal position on quality.
    B. It helps benchmark the project against other similar projects.
    C. It provides specific quality standards that may be used to measure the output of the project.
    D. It details the constraints and assumptions the project must take in to consideration.

143.	During Cost Control, performance reviews are PRIMARILY used to:

	A.	Discuss the project and give the team a chance to voice any concerns.
	B.	Evaluate new budget change requests to determine if they would have an adverse effects on the project's performance.
	C.	Review the status of cost information against the plan.
	D.	Meet with the customer to evaluate and enhance satisfaction.

144.	In which of the following organizations is the project manager MOST likely to be part-time?

	A.	Weak matrix
	B.	Strong matrix
	C.	Functional
	D.	Projectized

145.	Which output would be used to show project roles and responsibilities?

	A.	A resource histogram.
	B.	An organization chart.
	C.	A RACI chart.
	D.	A staffing management plan.

146.	Kim is managing a multi-million dollar construction project so that is scheduled to take nearly two years to complete. During one of the planning processes, she discovers a significant threat to her project's budget and schedule due to the fact that she is planning to build during the hurricane season in a high-risk area. After carefully evaluating her options, she decides to build earlier in the season when there is less of a risk of severe hurricane damage. This is an example of:

	A.	Risk avoidance.
	B.	Risk transference.
	C.	Risk acceptance.
	D.	Risk mitigation.

147. You are managing the development of a software product to be created under procurement. The team will span three countries and five time zones, and because of the size of the project, you are very concerned about cost. Which of the following types of contract would BEST help keep cost down?

    A. Time and materials.
    B. Cost plus fixed fee.
    C. Cost plus incentive fee.
    D. Variable conditions.

148. A project is scheduled to last for 6 months and cost $300,000. At the end of the 1st month, the project is 20% complete. What is the Earned Value?

    A. $50,010.
    B. $60,000.
    C. $100,020.
    D. $120,000.

149. Which of the following roles typically has the LEAST power?

    A. Project coordinator.
    B. Project expeditor.
    C. Project manager.
    D. Project director.

150. Configuration management is:

    A. A technique used in Develop Project Management Plan.
    B. Used to ensure that the product scope is complete and correct.
    C. Formally defined in initiation.
    D. A procedure to identify and document the functional and physical characteristics of an item or system.

Final Exam Answers

1.   A. Pareto charts are column charts that rank defects based on the number of occurrences from highest to lowest. Because this tool is based on frequency, it prioritizes the most common causes. 'B' is used to determine whether or not a process is in control. 'C' is used to measure the difference between what was planned and what was done, and 'D' is a type of estimate used in cost management.

2.   C. Because this is being done under contract, you will need to use more formal, written communication. Many people incorrectly guess 'D' on this one, but official channels of communication could just as easily decrease since you are using another company and will probably have a single point of contact as opposed to your own team of many people doing the work. 'B' is not correct, since performance reports should be detailed regardless of who is doing the work.

3.   C. The charter is the document that officially creates the project, names the project manager, and gives him authority on the project.

4.   B. The Delphi technique is a way to solicit expert opinion by hiding the identities of group members from each other. This prevents the group from forming a single opinion or from letting one person dominate the group.

5.   B. The work authorization system (WAS) is a system used during project integration management to ensure that work gets done at the right time and in the right sequence.

6.   D. Typically you should assess, investigate, understand, and evaluate before acting. There may be exceptions to this rule, but in general you probably want to select the answer that lets you get all of the information. If there is a series of answers and you are asked what to do FIRST (as in this example), selecting the answer that allows you to be fully informed is usually best. 'A' is incorrect because halting work would probably send risks skyrocketing. 'B' is a good thing to do, but not until you have fully evaluated the risk. 'C' is something you may or may not choose to do, but you should not take action until you have fully assessed the risk.

7.   A. This is frequently missed because people do not fully understand the role of the team in planning. The team should help estimate and should support those estimates. If possible, the person who will be doing the work should have a say in the estimate. 'B' is incorrect because the project manager cannot possibly estimate all of the activities on the project, nor should he even try. 'C' and 'D' are incorrect since management and the customer are probably not aware of all of the low-level details needed, and their estimates would not be accurate.

8.   C. The stakeholders do not have to approve the project plan. They may be very interested in the final product, but the actual plan cannot undergo approval by all stakeholders. Some stakeholders may never approve of the plan since they may be against the project! 'A' is incorrect because the project plan must be a formal. 'B' is incorrect because the communications management plan will specify to whom you should communicate the plan. 'D' is incorrect since the purpose of the project plan is to guide execution and control.

9.   C. Your best source of help would be the information you can use from past projects. 'A' is incorrect since education may or may not be applicable to this project, and although it is good, education is principally theoretical, while historical information contains practical, hard data. 'B' is incorrect, since much practical experience only reinforces bad practices. 'D' is incorrect since functional managers have expertise in domains but not necessarily in the management of projects.

10.   B. The majority of a project's budget is expended in the execution of the work packages. You may have guessed 'A' due to the number of processes that occur as part of planning, but most projects do not involve as many people or resources in planning as they do in execution. Choice 'D' is incorrect because, while a project manager spends 90% of his time communicating, that does not take most of the team's time or the project budget.

11.   B. This is a very important definition. Corrective action is making adjustments to avoid future variances. 'A' is more in line with the definition of rework. 'C' is incorrect since there may or may not be a change control board, and their job would be to approve or reject change requests that have been forwarded by the project manager. 'D' is incorrect because corrective action does not come out of execution, but out of various control processes.

12.   C. This is the only one where both parts of the answer fit the definition. 'A' is incorrect since performance reports do not come out of the execution process. 'B' is incorrect since corrective action typically comes out of monitoring and controlling processes. 'D' is incorrect because performance reports do not come out of the Direct and Manage Project Execution process.

13.   D. This type of question often appears on the PMP. It is easier than it first appears. Did you think the question was asking for the estimate at completion (EAC)? It is the originally budgeted amount, or budgeted at completion (BAC) that the question wants. That is calculated simply by taking 6 stories and multiplying it by $150,000/story. This yields the total project amount, which is $900,000.

14.   B. This is an important point. The project manager is the one responsible for integration. 'A' is incorrect because the team should be doing the work. 'C' is incorrect since senior management is not involved in integration management. 'D' is incorrect since the sponsor pays for the project but is not directly involved in integration.

15.   A. You should not add the deliverable. The reason is that this represents "gold plating," or adding functionality over and above the scope. It is not a good idea since this introduces risk and a host of other potential problems on the project. 'B' is incorrect because you do not know how it will affect risk, quality, or other factors. 'C' is incorrect, because you are ahead of schedule with an SPI of 1.5. 'D' is incorrect because it is the project manager's job – not the role of senior management – to deal with this kind of change request.

16.   D. The scope management plan is the document that specifies how changes to the scope will be managed.

17.   C. Any of the words "evaluate," "investigate," "understand," or "assess" should automatically put that answer at the top of your list to evaluate. 'D' is incorrect because the customer has hired you to evaluate and approve or reject change.

18.   D. This question was very hard, but there was a way to reason out the answer. When initiating a project, you are essentially performing two processes: Develop Project Charter and Develop Preliminary Scope Statement. During those processes, it makes sense that you might use project selection methods, your methodology, and expert judgment, but choice 'D', earned value analysis, would probably not be useful until (much) later when the work was being performed.

19.   A. The project manager is officially named and assigned in the project charter, which is one of the outputs of Develop Project Charter, an initiating process.

20.   B. The project charter is a document, and that document should include the business need behind the project. This is a general description of why the project was undertaken.

21.   B. The scope statement is an output of scope planning. The next step is the Scope Definition process, and the output of that is the work breakdown structure (WBS).

22.   A. Hopefully your instincts kicked in here and said "this won't happen until later." If so, then you were right. Accepted deliverables are an output of Scope Verification. During Scope Planning, you are still trying to determine what the scope will include.

23.   D. The project manager's job during integration is to solve problems and make decisions. It is not the team's job to do this! Their job should be to execute the work packages. The project manager should be fixing the problems that come up and keeping the team focused on the work.

24.   A. Work package descriptions are contained in the WBS dictionary.

25.   B. Scope Verification is where the customer and sponsor verify that the deliverables match what was in the scope.

26.   D. The statement of work (SOW) describes the pieces of the project that are to be performed by an outside vendor. It often starts off general and is revised as the project progresses. 'A' is incorrect because the SOW does not meet the strict qualifications of a contract. 'B' is incorrect because it is too broad – the SOW is only about the pieces that will be outsourced. 'C' is incorrect because an SOW is not needed for all projects – only those that will be procuring parts.

27.   C. This meets the definition of a cost-reimbursable contract. 'A' is a made-up term. 'B' is incorrect since the price is not fixed. 'D' is also incorrect. If you selected this one, you should review the difference between the time and materials and cost-reimbursable contracts.

28.   C. Documenting the relationship between the product and the business takes place before Scope Definition. A justification of the business need is included in the project charter. 'A', 'B', and 'D' all fall under the definition of Scope Definition.

29.   B. The procurement management plan includes performance reporting specifications. If one of the choices had been "the communications management plan", that might have been a better selection, but given the choices provided, 'B' was the best one.

30.   A. Cost-revisable is not a valid choice (and from the sound of the name, it does sound particularly safe to either party)! Choices 'B', 'C', and 'D' are all valid contract types.

31.   B. In this case, make-or-buy analysis is the most appropriate. It is where you decide whether your organization should create the product or whether you should go through procurement. Choice 'A' would be an activity that was performed later in the process. Choice 'C' is a tool for measuring whether a project is worth pursuing and is performed in initiation. Choice 'D' is also an activity performed after the decision has been made to go through procurement.

32.   C. With activities, the important order is define – order – estimate. The activity list is an input in Activity Duration Estimating.

33.   B. Many people may formally accept the product, but in this list, the customer is the only one that fits the definition.

34.   A. The activity list is a decomposition of the WBS. It takes the work packages and breaks them down into activities that can be sequenced, estimated, and assigned.

35.   B. Float is how long an activity may be delayed without delaying the project. Choice 'B' is the only one that fits this definition.

36.   C. Procurement management is used when you go outside of the project for components of the project.

37.   D. Communication is the most important activity because the project manager spends an estimated 90% of his time communicating.

38.   D. The project's deliverables would not be produced before the budget had been created.

39.   A. Milestone charts are useful for communicating high-level status on a project. This represents the best of the 4 choices. 'B' would be far too much detail for an executive status meeting. 'C' would not be a bad thing to bring, but it would not be the best document for showing status. 'D' would not provide the status that the CIO seeks.

40.   B. Resource requirements should be developed against the schedule activities. That is why they are called "activity resources requirements."

41.   B. Analogous estimates, also called top-down estimates, use previous project costs as a guideline for estimating.

42.   A. The standard deviation measures how diverse the population is. It does this by averaging all of the data points to find the mean, then calculating the average of how far each individual point is from that mean. For a very diverse population, you will have a high standard deviation. For a highly similar population, your standard deviation will be low.

43.   B. This is the best answer. Modern quality management stresses planning and prevention over inspection. This is based on the theory that it costs less to prevent a problem than it does to fix one. 'A' is incorrect, since prevention is stressed over inspection. 'C' is incorrect since contingency planning is part of risk management – not quality management. 'D' is incorrect since Quality Planning seeks to satisfy the quality standards. It is not focused on exceeding customer expectations.

44.   C. Phases within processes is a made-up term and is not stressed in quality management. Many people mistakenly select 'A' for this; however, quality management does stress that the customer's specifications should be taken into account (the implication being that if the customer's specifications are satisfied, the customer should be satisfied with the product). 'B' is incorrect because Deming's TQM philosophy stresses that the entire team has a responsibility toward quality. 'D' is incorrect because prevention over inspection is a big thrust of quality management, stressing that it costs less to prevent a problem than it does to fix one.

45.   B. Perform Quality Control is the process that uses these five tools.

46.   C. Organizational process assets, the project scope statement, enterprise environmental factors, and the project management plan are all used as inputs into Quality Planning, but the quality baseline is an output.

47.   D. Contract type selection is a tool used in procurement planning. The type(s) of contract(s) used are included in the procurement management plan.

48.   C. The project manager is ultimately responsible for the quality of the product. If you guessed 'A', you were on track because Deming said that the entire team is responsible, but the word "ultimately" is the key here. The person ultimately responsible is the PM. 'B' is incorrect because the quality team is not a team identified by PMI. 'D' is incorrect because functional managers may be very involved in the quality management process, but they are not ultimately responsible.

49.   A. This one is tricky because all of these tools are used in quality management! 'B', 'C', and 'D' are all used in Perform Quality Control, but 'A' is used in Quality Planning and Perform Quality Assurance. Benchmarking is used to establish quality standards based on the quality attributes of other projects, and it is not used in Perform Quality Control.

50.   C. The purpose of a control chart is to statistically determine if a process is in control.

51.   D. Stakeholders may want the project to succeed or fail! They may benefit or lose if the project succeeds. This is contrary to the way the word is used in many circles, and it is hard for many people to think of a stakeholder as potentially being hostile to the project.

52.   B. A probability impact matrix is a tool of Qualitative Risk Analysis, and it is used to rank risks qualitatively, that is, based on their characteristics.

53.   D. A risk register is created during Risk Identification, and it is updated in the subsequent risk processes (Qualitative Risk Analysis, Quantitative Risk Analysis, Risk Response Planning, and Risk Monitoring and Control).

54.   C. When an anticipated risk event occurs, the plan for addressing that is followed; however, some risks cannot be anticipated. In that case, a workaround is needed.

55.   A. The first thing you should do is to plan for the new risks this situation presents. Remember that you should look for a proactive approach to almost everything. 'B' is incorrect because you cannot simply decide to withhold payment if you are in a contractual relationship. 'C' is incorrect because even though that may be something you would do, it is not the FIRST thing you should do. 'D' is also not the FIRST thing you should do, because this problem should be dealt with by the project manager. Running off to apprise senior management of the situation would not be the first thing a project manager does. It would be far better to do that after the project manager had assessed the situation and planned thoroughly for it.

56.   B. In a functional organization, most of the power rests with the functional manager. 'A' is incorrect since that describes a projectized organization. 'C' is incorrect because that describes a matrix organization. 'D' is incorrect since there is no explicit model in which power rests with the project office.

57.   D. Human Resource Planning is the process of understanding and identifying the reporting relationships on a project. An output of this process is the project's organizational chart.

58.   D. The responsibility assignment matrix (RAM) does not include reporting relationships. Those are included in the project's organizational chart. 'A' is incorrect because the RAM does show who is responsible for what on the project. 'B' is incorrect because it shows roles on the project for the various team members. 'C' is incorrect because the RAM can be for either individuals or for groups (e.g. engineering or information technology).

59.   A. The withdrawer is someone who does not participate in the meeting and therefore is not a constructive role. 'B' is incorrect because someone who is trying to gather more, good information is contributing in a positive way. 'C' is incorrect because a person who clarifies communication is adding to the meeting as well. 'D' is tricky, but it is incorrect. In project management terminology, a gate keeper is someone who helps others participate and draws people out. Gate keepers would help withdrawers become active participants.

60.   D. In this case, the conflict is of a technical nature, so the best way the project manager could solve the problem is by using his or her technical expertise. 'A' is incorrect because legitimate power might stop the fight, but it wouldn't solve the problem. 'B' is incorrect because it also might stop the fight, but would not solve the problem. 'C' would probably be the least effective approach to solving this particular problem, since referent power is relying on personality or someone else's authority.

61.   C. Forcing does do away with the conflict… but only temporarily. It is when the manager says "This is my project, and you will do things my way. Period, end of discussion." The root of the problem is not addressed by this approach, thus the solution is only temporary.

62.   D. Did you guess 'A' or 'B' on this one? The communication plan does not include the performance reports, and it may be either formal or informal, highly detailed or general, depending on the project and the organization. 'C' is incorrect, because it does not include the project's major milestones. 'D' is the right answer in this case because it details how you are going to gather and store information on the project.

63.   B. One of the main reasons conflict arises on a project is over communication, and one of the results of a project's communication lines being broken is that conflict increases.

64.   A. It is the role of senior management to resolve organizational conflicts and to prioritize projects, and either of those may be at the root of this problem. 'B' is incorrect since this is a matter internal to the organization, and the customer should be buffered from it. 'C' is incorrect since the stakeholders cannot always bring influence to bear inside the organization. 'D' is incorrect since the sponsor functions much like a customer internal to the organization. The sponsor does not prioritize projects and would not be the best person to go to in order to sort out an organizational conflict.

65.   B. E-mail is informal written communication. Formal written communication involves such things as changes to the project plan, contract changes, and official communication sent through channels such as certified mail. As e-mail evolves in its usage and protocol, test takers should be aware that although they may use e-mail in a formal manner, it is not considered to be formal communication.

66.   B. Again, as yourself "what is the choice that solves the problem?" In this case, 'B' is the best choice that solves the problem. Before you do anything else, you would want to meet with the person directly and discuss the problem. 'A' may be appropriate at some point but would not be considered best in this case. 'C' is not a good choice, since it is your job to resolve the problem and not the customer's job. 'D' is incorrect since it is too passive a choice and does not really deal with the problem.

67.   B. This question is not only difficult, but there is a lot of information here to distract you. In this case, you should go to the sponsor and let him know, since he has approved the budget. If the project stands to deviate significantly (over or under), then the person paying for it should know as soon as possible. 'A' is incorrect because you are supposed to conform to the scope – not increase it! 'C' is also incorrect. You are working for the sponsor here, and it would not be wise to bill them more than the project costs. 'D' is incorrect, since you do not want to gold plate the scope by adding more than was originally planned.

68.   D. Communication is important at all points in the project, but it is critical during integration. When performing integration management, the project manager's job is primarily to communicate.

69.   C. Focus on direct, polite confrontation over practically any other method of conflict resolution. In this case, you are the one who needs to resolve the conflict, so you should take the initiative. Discussing the employee's actions with her before the meeting should actually produce a resolution to the problem. 'A' appears direct at first, but it is not really a direct way to deal with the problem. 'B' is simply making the problem someone else's problem – in this case, your boss's. 'D' is incorrect for the same reason 'B' is. This is a problem that you, the project manager, should solve.

70.   A. With an SPI this far below 1, you have a significant schedule delay, and you should report this to management. 'B' is incorrect because you are doing quite well on cost, and there is no overrun. 'C' is incorrect since it is your job to deal with scope change – not management's. 'D' is incorrect because you cannot simply reject changes on the project. They must be evaluated thoroughly and fairly and sent through the scope change control system.

71.   C. The team should be involved in the estimating process, and once they have bought into those estimates, you should resist pressure to automatically slash them. 'A' is incorrect since additional estimating is not what is needed here. 'B' is incorrect since this is just delaying the inevitable and perhaps making matters much worse. 'D' is incorrect since the dates need to come from your estimates and schedule development and not from the client.

72.   D. Another name for analogous estimating is top-down estimating, because it looks at projects as a lump sum and not broken down into pieces (which is known as bottom-up estimating).

73.   C. This is a no-win situation, but you must obey laws in the country where you are performing the work, and 'C' is the only option that fully complies with the law. Refer to the PMI code of conduct and you will see that you cannot bend or break laws just to get the project done on time.

74.   A. Activity Definition uses the technique of decomposition to produce the activity list.

75.   A. In a fixed price contact, the seller is the one who bears the risk. If the cost runs high, the seller must deliver at the original cost. The buyer's costs are set (fixed), thus offering a measure of security. 'B' is incorrect since the seller has higher risk. 'C' is incorrect since the seller's risk is higher than the buyer's. 'D' is incorrect since cost reimbursable is another form of contract separate from this.

76.   C. A project coordinator is someone who is weaker than a project manager but may have some limited decision-making power. 'A' is incorrect since a project manager does not have "limited authority" on a project. 'B' is a made up term, and 'D' refers to the sponsor whose role on the project is to pay for the project, receive the product at the end, and give the project good visibility in the organization.

77.   D. Risk Response Planning would be the point at which you determine an appropriate response to the risks that have been identified, qualified, and quantified. Only after the risks are fully understood and analyzed would you make a change to the scope.

78.   C. Scope Planning is all about one thing: creating the scope management plan, and the tool of expert judgment is used to help create it.

79.   B. Integration (in addition to most of the other processes) is not discrete. In other words, it isn't performed in a vacuum, but instead it is performed with all of the other processes in mind. This is even more pertinent for integration than any of the other knowledge areas. Also keep in mind that the word "integrated" has nearly the opposite meaning of the word "discrete." 'A' is incorrect because that is exactly what integration does. 'C' is also a purpose of integration, because the PMIS is the tool that the project manager uses to know what is going on with the project. 'D' is incorrect because that is also a definition of integration. The project manager is supposed to keep people focused on the work while he solves problems.

80.   D. Definitions are very important, and this definition question is missed by many people. Understand that projects may or may not be strategic to the company. Although everyone wants their project to be exciting and strategic, more mundane projects also must be undertaken. 'A', 'B', and 'C' are all part of the core definition of a project.

81.   D. In this case, your manager is auditing the process, and audits are used in Perform Quality Assurance. Audits are performed primarily to make sure that the process is being followed. 'A' is incorrect because quality control is inspecting specific examples and is not focused on the overall process. 'B' is incorrect because quality management is too broad a term to fit the definition of this process. 'C' is incorrect because quality planning is the process where the quality management plan is created.

82.   A. Variance analysis looks at the difference between what was planned and what was executed. Choice 'A' is the one that correctly identifies this.

83.   B. In a matrix organization, power is shared between the project managers and functional managers. In a strong matrix, the project manager is more powerful, while in a weak matrix, the functional manager has more power. In no circumstances would 'D' be correct, as the project coordinator is, by definition, weaker than a project manager.

84.   C. Team performance assessment is a tool of the Develop Project Team process. When using this tool, the project manager evaluates the team's performance with the goal of understanding strengths and weaknesses.

85.   C. The project scope statement typically starts off general and becomes more specific as the project progresses. Progressive elaboration is a term that describes the way in which the details of the scope are discovered over time. 'A' is incorrect since it is more descriptive of the WBS than the project scope statement. 'B' is incorrect since the project scope statement is created by the project team and not by senior management. 'D' is incorrect because the project scope statement is a functional specification.

86.   D. In Manage Project Team, the team is executing the work packages and creating the product of the project. Your job as project manager is to keep them focused on this. 'A' is incorrect because that may be your focus, but it is not the team's focus. 'B' is incorrect, because that is the project manager's job and not the team's focus. 'C' incorrect for the same reason. It is the job of the project manager and not the team.

87.   C. The project management information system (PMIS) is the one described in the question. 'A' is not a good choice because you don't have to have information technology from beginning to end in order to successfully deliver many projects. 'B' is a made up term. 'D' is not a good choice because the work authorization system (WAS) is used to make sure that the work is performed at the right time and in the right sequence.

88.   C. On typical projects, most of the resources (both human resources and material resources) are expended during executing processes. Many people incorrectly choose 'B' because there are so many planning processes, but on the average, project planning takes less effort and resource than execution.

89.   A. Inspection is a tool of Scope Verification, which is the process being described in the question. In inspection, the product of the project is compared with the documented scope.

90.   C. "Quality Improvement" is something you may strive for, but it is not a process.

91. D. Schedule constraints would not contain leads and lags for activities. 'A', 'B', and 'C' would all make sense to include as schedule constraints.

92. B. Benchmarking is a tool of quality management for both the Quality Planning and Perform Quality Assurance processes. It takes the results of previous projects and uses them to help set standards for other projects. 'A' and 'C' are incorrect because they would be more closely aligned with Perform Quality Control. 'D' is largely unrelated to quality.

93. C. The activity list should include every schedule activity defined on the project. These schedule activities are then used to create the project network diagram.

94. A. The Close Project process should be performed at the end of each phase or at the end of the project. It is the process where the project is formally accepted and the project records are created. It is important to understand that Close Project may happen several times throughout the project.

95. C. The release criteria for team members is defined in the staffing management plan.

96. D. The activity list is the output of the Activity Definition process. 'A', 'B', and 'C' are all inputs into Activity Definition.

97. C. There are many ways to mathematically solve this problem, but perhaps the simplest is to divide the schedule performance index against the length of the project. 20 weeks ÷ 0.8 = 25 weeks. Therefore, we would expect the project to be 5 weeks late. 'A' should have been eliminated because with a schedule performance index less than 1, there is no way the project should be finished early.

98. C. The term slack is synonymous with float.

99. A. The project plan is a formal document. It is created during planning, and is used to guide the execution processes, monitoring and control, and closure. 'B' is incorrect because that would be closer to the definition for the product. 'C' is close to correct, although it is an incomplete list of what makes up the project plan and the question specifically asks for the BEST description. 'D' is incorrect because this is closer to the definition of the work breakdown structure than it is to the project plan.

100.   D. As part of integrated change control, the project manager will need to know when change has occurred, manage the changes, and influence the factors that cause change, but the project manager should not take on the attitude of denying change whenever possible. Some change is inevitable, and all change requests should be evaluated and not automatically rejected.

101.   A. There is a difference between the product scope and the project scope. The scope of the project may be much larger than the scope of the product! This question defines the product scope. 'B' would have a much broader definition than this. 'C' is the work that needs to be done to complete the project, but it does not deal with the attributes of a product. 'D' is a phrase often used in project management, but it is unrelated to this definition.

102.   C. The supporting detail should be included with the estimates, and that supporting detail is included for situations just like this one. It will help you and the team member understand how the estimates were derived in the first place. 'A' is incorrect since the team member may well have a valid point. 'B' is incorrect because there is no reason to either stop work on the project or to send the team member scrambling for new estimates. 'D' is not a bad choice, but it isn't the FIRST thing you would do. As a starting point, go back and check the facts first. Then if it would be helpful to get another expert involved, you may elect to do that.

103.   B. The term "baseline" causes grief for many test takers. Memorize that the baseline (whether it is the scope baseline, schedule baseline, cost baseline, or quality baseline) includes the original plan plus all approved changes. Once the budget change was approved, it should be added to the cost baseline.

104.   B. Although it is unusual in the real world, a projectized organizational structure gives the project manager near total control of the project and the resources. 'A' is a structure where the functional manager is in charge of projects and resources. 'C' is a structure where the project manager runs the projects and the functional manager manages the people, and 'D' is not a real term for organizational structures.

105.   D. Leads and lags are adjusted as part of the Schedule Development process.

106. A. Just as important as understanding a formula is being able to interpret it. That is what this question is calling on you to do, and it can be quite hard. The schedule performance index (SPI) = EV ÷ PV. Studying the formula, you can see that it compares how much value you actually earned (EV) and divides that by how much you planned to earn (PV). In this case, you have earned value at 1.5 times the rate you had planned.

107. C. The project organization chart, an output from the Human Resource Planning process, shows the reporting structure for the project.

108. C. Most of the planning processes have a logical order to them, and this question relies on an understanding of that. The work breakdown structure has to be created before cost estimates are performed, and the cost estimates have to be created before the budget. This should make sense when you stop to consider it.

109. B. The list of risks, contained in the risk register, is an output of the Risk Identification process.

110. A. Activity Definition is the process where the work breakdown structure is further decomposed into individual activities.

111 B. A good rule is that if in doubt, select the "project manager." For this question, that would be correct. It is the project manager's job to resolve competing stakeholder requests and goals.

112. C. Your goal is to create a win-win situation in the negotiations. A win-lose agreement will usually not let you win in the long term.

113. D. The project budget, also known as the cost baseline, is an output of Cost Budgeting. 'A', 'B', and 'C' are outputs of the Cost Control process.

114. A. The way to approach this question is to remember how to calculate the schedule variance. It is EV-PV. If the schedule variance = 0, then EV must be equal to PV.

115. B. Schedule activities are a further decomposition of the work breakdown structure, and work packages exist at the lowest levels of the work breakdown structure.

116. B. This one is easier than it first appears. All "management plans," including the staffing management plan, become part of the project plan. 'A' is incorrect because it is an output of Human Resource Planning. 'C' is incorrect because it describes the approach to staffing and not every detail. 'D' is incorrect because the organization chart for the performing organization would not be a typical component of the staffing management plan.

117. B. All of the identified risks should be added to the risk register. 'C' is incorrect since the risk management plan only contains the plan for how risk will be approached. It does not get down to the specifics of listing risks.

118. C. You have a responsibility to help mentor others in the field of project management. 'A' would be inappropriate, because your responsibility extends to the profession – not just to your organization. 'B' is incorrect because the best place to start is with your friend. 'D' is incorrect because a job change would represent withdrawal and would not solve the problem in any way.

119. B. Planned value is the value of the work you planned to do at a given point in time. The first step is always to calculate your budgeted at completion. It is 25 miles * 1,200,000 / mile = $30,000,000. Now you want to calculate the planned value for 3 weeks of the 5 week project. Simply multiple the budgeted at completion by 3 and divide by 5. This yields $18,000,000. The interpretation of this is that you planned to earn $18,000,000 worth of value back into your project after 3 weeks of work.

120. C. Read this one carefully. It is the definition of free float. 'A' and 'B' were synonyms, which should have thrown up a red flag for you. Those terms tell you how long a task may be delayed before it changes the finish date of the project.

121. D. Knowing the order in which these steps are performed is important and shows that you understand what is really taking place within the process. In this case, resources are estimated after you have defined the activities, but before you have created the schedule. This is the only answer that works, since the resources are based on activities, and you must have the resource requirements before you can create the schedule.

122. A. Even when news is unpopular or unpleasant, you must deliver accurate statuses. 'B' and 'C' attempt to cover up or hide the news. Choice 'D' is unnecessary since you should report the current and accurate status to the customer.

123. B. Select Sellers is an executing process of procurement, and yes, it is important that you know this type of information for the exam. In this process, the buyer evaluates the responses from the potential sellers and chooses a seller to perform the work.

124. C. Know the roles of each person or group on the project. It is the sponsor who provides funding for the project.

125. A. Most importantly, the project should satisfy the scope, schedule, and budget. These are the principal factors of success. 'B' is important in many organizations, but you cannot control happiness as a project manager. The best you can do is to satisfy the scope of work. 'C' may be good to have, but it does not make the project successful. 'D' is also good in that you did what you planned to do when you planned to do it, but it is only an ingredient of project success.

126. C. Your primary objective is to satisfy the scope of work on the project within the agreed-upon cost and schedule. 'A' is the means to your end goal of a successful project, but it is only the way you go about it. 'B' is a great goal, but there are other parties here that need to be considered – not just the performing organization. 'D' is good, but you should focus on doing so by delivering what you promised on time and on budget.

127. D. Organizational process assets are anything you can reuse, such as a document, a previous project deliverable, or a methodology. Strong communication skills was not a good fit for this question.

128. A. It stands to reason that problems are fixed in the same process where deliverables are produced. In this case the process is Direct and Manage Project Execution.

129. B. An activity's late finish date is the latest an activity can finish without delaying the project. If it exceeds the late finish date, the critical path will change, ultimately resulting in the finish date slipping. Choice 'A' is close to the definition of free float.

130.   C. The contract change control system is defined in the procurement management plan and not in the contract itself.

131.   B. The critical path represents (among other things) the highest risk to the project's schedule. If there are multiple critical paths, then the risk of finishing the project late will be higher, since the critical path has no margin for error.

132.   B. With a payback period, the shorter the time the better. The hardest thing about this problem is to reduce all of the times to a common denominator so you can see which one is the shortest! B is one year, and that is the shortest period of time of the choices.

133.   B. A project network diagram (like activity on arrow) is an output of activity sequencing. The other 3 types of dependencies fall under the tool of dependency determination in Activity Sequencing.

134.   D. The processes are not set in stone so that once you have finished planning you can never return. Remember that projects are progressively elaborated, and that often times you will need to revisit processes again and again. There is no reason not to return to planning in the example given here.

135.   D. The goal of duration compression is to accelerate the due date without shortening the scope of the project.

136.   B. Conflicts of interest should be disclosed and avoided. 'A' is not a good choice, because you are not only bound to act legally, but also ethically! 'C' is not correct because you would not be keeping information confidential. 'D' would not be a rational choice. Resigning from both projects would cause more problems and solve nothing.

137.   C. A standard usually should be followed, while a regulation has to be followed.

138.   A. The evaluation criteria are created in the Plan Contracting process. In the Select Sellers process the evaluation criteria are used to select a qualified seller after responses have been received.

139.   D. Richard is performing Risk Response Planning. After the risks have been identified, qualified, and quantified, they should be responded to. Risk Response Planning looks at how to make the opportunities more likely and better and the threats less likely and less severe. Remember that a risk is an uncertainty that could be good or bad.

140.   A. In order to answer this question, you must first be able to identify in which process you solicit bids. It is the Request Seller Proposals process, and the output of Request Seller Proposals are the proposals from your potential sellers.

141.   B. The work results of the project may be products, services, or results. 'A' is incorrect because work results could be a product, a service, or a result. 'C' is incorrect because the work results don't have to meet quality to be considered work! 'D' is incorrect because the output of the work authorization system is not the work itself, but that a resource is authorized to do the work.

142.   A. Some companies rest their reputation on the high quality of their product. Others do not. The quality policy defines how important quality is on this project from the performing organization's perspective.

143.   C. Performance reviews review the current status against the plan.

144.   C. In a functional organization, the project manager has little formal power and may even be part-time! It is the functional manager who is more powerful in this structure.

145.   C. A RACI chart is a type of responsibility assignment matrix created during Human Resource Planning. It is a chart that can show roles and responsibilities on the project. 'A' is incorrect because it shows resource usage levels across the project. 'B' is incorrect because it shows reporting relationships but not specific responsibilities. 'D' is incorrect because this general document tells how you are going to approach staffing the project.

146.   D. Risk mitigation is when you try to make the risk less severe or less likely. By accelerating the construction, Kim is mitigating the likelihood of a hurricane damaging her project.

147.   C. The answer "fixed price" would have been the best here, but it was not in the list of choices! Of the ones listed, cost plus incentive fee would provide the seller with an incentive to keep their costs down. 'A' provides no incentive at all for the seller to keep costs down. 'B' would not provide the same incentive since the seller gets a fixed fee regardless of the project costs. 'D' is not a real contract type.

148.   B. Earned value is what you have actually done at a point in time. In this case the budgeted at completion for the project is $300,000, and you have completed 20% of that. All of the other facts in the problem are irrelevant. The answer is $300,000 * 20% = $60,000.

149.   B. The project expeditor is the weakest role here. This person is typically a staff assistant to an executive who is managing the project. 'C' is the most powerful, and 'A' would be next. 'D' is not a term identified within PMI's processes.

150.   D. This is a definition of configuration management. 'A' is incorrect because it is part of the Integrated Change Control process and not Develop Project Management Plan. 'B' is incorrect because that is more descriptive of inspection – a tool of scope verification. 'C' is incorrect because this is performed after initiation.

Index

A

B

Index

Index

M

N

O

Index

Index

Punishment (form of power) 240
PV   *See* Planned Value; *See* Present Value

Q

Qualifications (for the PMP Exam) 4–6
Qualified Sellers List 311, 314
Qualitative Risk Analysis 275, 277, 281, 281–283, 283, 287, 295, 297, 299, 350, 369
Quality Assurance 97, 202, 203, 204, 227, 228, 348
Quality Audits 214, 223
Quality Baseline 211, 222
Quality baseline 203, 231, 349
Quality Checklists 211, 216
Quality Control 59, 89, 202, 203, 227, 228, 349, 379, 384   *See also* Perform Quality Control
Quality Control Measurements 203, 213, 221, 261
Quality Management 33, 201–218
Quality Management Plan 25, 203, 211, 212, 214, 215, 223, 231, 255
Quality Metrics 211, 213, 215
Quality Planning 227, 349
Quantitative Risk Analysis 275, 277, 283–286, 287, 294, 297, 299, 332
Quantitative Risk Analysis and Modeling Techniques 284

R

RACI charts 233, 294
RAM   *See* Responsibility Assignment Matrix
RBS   *See* Resource Breakdown Structure; *See also* Risk Breakdown Structure
Recognition and Rewards 242
Recommended Corrective Action 27, 58, 61, 91, 95, 143, 177, 203, 214, 222, 246, 263, 292, 298, 320, 363
Recommended Defect Repair 59, 61, 222
Recommended Preventive Action 61, 222, 246, 292
Records Management System 319, 322
Regulation 12
Rejected Change Requests 57, 62
Replanning 94
Requested Changes 28, 56, 58, 61, 75, 83, 88, 91, 95, 113, 120, 124, 140, 142, 143, 167, 173, 177, 203, 214, 222, 246, 259, 263, 292, 308, 316, 320
Request Seller Responses 311–312, 323, 325
Reserve 194, 195
Reserve Analysis 129, 166, 171, 292
Reserve Time 149   *See also* Contingency
Resolved Issues 266
Resource Availability 122, 238, 239, 316
Resource Breakdown Structure 124
Resource Calendar 124, 127, 131, 170
Resource Histogram 235
Resource Leveling 135
Return on Investment 46, 189, 192
Risk 66, 70, 99, 134, 146, 148, 149, 153, 157, 160, 273–292
  residual 299
Risk-related Contractual Agreements 289
Risk (contract) 307
Risk Analysis   *See* Qualitative Risk Analysis, Quantitative Risk Analysis

Index

Scope Statement 75, 77, 78, 80, 81, 82, 83, 84, 85, 88, 90, 92, 94, 95, 97, 101, 102, 110, 115, 126, 130, 169, 257, 275, 277, 281, 283, 305
Scope Verification 75, 89–92, 97, 100, 102, 103
Screening System 314
Selected Sellers 315, 318
Select Sellers 313, 314, 315, 316, 318, 323, 325, 328, 329, 366, 390
Seller 303, 307, 311, 312, 313, 315
Seller Rating Systems 315
Senior Management 14, 47
Sensitivity Analysis 284, 295
Share (risk) 288
Simulation 149
Six Sigma Quality 206, 225, 228
Slack 149, 155 *See also* Float
Smoothing 247
Sources of Conflict 245
Source Selection 366, 390
SOW *See* Statement of Work
Special Causes 207
SPI *See* Schedule Performance Index
Sponsor 15, 97, 98, 102, 152, 156, 247, 251, 265, 271, 366, 374, 375, 381, 382, 383
Staffing Management Plan 235, 237, 238, 239, 244, 247, 251, 364, 370, 389
Stakeholders 15, 20, 92, 268, 379
Stakeholder Analysis 82
Standards 78
  definition 13
  in quality 225
Standard Deviation 128, 205–206
Standard Forms 309
Statement of Work 43, 48, 308, 345, 376
Statistical Independence 204, 227
Statistical Sampling 221
Status Meetings 292 *See also* Meetings
Status Review Meetings 262
Summary Nodes 119
Sunk costs 186
SV *See* Schedule Variance
SWOT Analysis 278
System ii, 218
  definition 13

T

Team 17, 37, 39, 41, 67, 71, 87, 96, 102, 150, 152, 195, 202, 229, 248, 265, 269, 270, 334
Team-Building Activities 241
Team Development 37, 248
  Team roles 248
Team Performance Assessment 242, 244
Technical Performance Measurement 291
Templates 78, 85, 87, 111, 117, 356
Terms (project management) 8–12, 32–35, 146–150, 334
Theories of Motivation 242
Threats and Opportunities 289

Use the key inside the back cover flap to access:

http://insite.velociteach.com

CAPM Exam content, additional questions, and study aids